The Rumour

The Rumour
A Cultural History

Hans-Joachim Neubauer

Translated by Christian Braun

"an association in which the free development of each
is the condition of the free development of all"

FREE ASSOCIATION BOOKS / LONDON / NEW YORK

Published in 1999 by
FREE ASSOCIATION BOOKS
57 Warren Street
London W1P 5PA

Translation © 1999 Christian Braun

Originally published as *FAMA: Eine Geschichte
des Gerüchts* © 1998 Berlin Verlag, Berlin

A CIP catalogue record for this book is available
from the British Library.

ISBN 1 85343 472 8 hbk

Designed and produced for the publisher by
Chase Production Services, Chadlington OX7 3LN
Printed in the EU by TJ International, Padstow

Contents

Preface

To write a book like this one takes a lot of time. It had the particular fortune of finding in Eberhard Lämmert a mentor who always encouraged me with his critical attentiveness. He was also the advocate whose friendly recommendations first brought about the material basis for *The Rumour*: the German Academic Exchange Service enabled my extensive research at the Maison des Sciences de l'Homme in Paris; this was facilitated by the hospitality of Maurice Aymard, the director of the Maison am Boulevard Raspail, and his staff, as well as by the staff of the Academic Exchange Service in Paris. They all saw to it that my time in Paris will always be remembered by me as one of the most pleasant and stimulating. In the first months of this year a research grant awarded by the Deutsche Forschungsgemeinschaft gave me the opportunity to devote myself wholly to the completion of the manuscript.

The first thoughts on the theme of "rumour control" came to me in 1996 at a conference at the Berlin Centre Marc Bloch; Jörg Dieter Kogel from Radio Bremen invited me to script a broadcast about "Science and Rumour". Out of both these pieces of work emerged a chapter of this book.

Without guides I would never have found my way around the "Kingdom of Hearsay". It would be impossible for me to name here all those who in the course of the last few years supplied me with tips about books and other sources. Many friends, relatives and colleagues helped me with their questions and comments, some by putting me in contact with people who could help me in my research, some with other forms of support. To this list belong in the first instance the staff at Berlin Verlag; with their understanding for a difficult project they gave my book a home from the very beginning. Christiane Schmidt, my editor, shaped and fostered *The Rumour* for many months with an insightful eye and great understanding. Otherwise I would particularly like to mention Aurore Blanc, Pierre Bourdis, Dominique Bourel, Rolf Wilhelm Brednich, Christophe D. Brumme, Steffen Dietzsch, Ralph Dutli, Kerstin Ebeling, Arlette Farge, Gennaro Ghirardelli, Frank Gotta, Stephen Greenblatt, Harald Günzel, Andreas Hartmann, Helwig Hassenpflug, Antonis Hilbers, Alexander Košenina, André Kostolany, Margarete Kraft, Frank Meilchen, Peter Meisenberg, Wolfgang Mendler, Anne Micallef and Christoph

Ziermann, Dieter Müller, my parents Marie-Theres and Hanns Neubauer, my brothers Thomas and Dominik, Elisabetta Niccolini, Maurice Olender, Krysztof Pomian, Ulrich Raulff, Henning Ritter, Uwe Schmitt, Christoph Strieder and Denis Thourd. To have taken up all their ideas would have greatly overtaxed my abilities. Had I not been able to speak again and again with David Bernet, Michael Schmidt and Christiane Seiler the better pages of *The Rumour* would never have been written. For their help I most heartily thank them and all the people and institutions mentioned here.

Much time that I spent writing would have belonged to my daughter Charlotte. This book – although no substitute – belongs to her.

Berlin, June 1998

Acknowledgements

Permission to reproduce illustrations is acknowledged as follows:
p. 9 Paul Klee, *Fama* (1939), 502 (AA2), oil on canvas, © DACS 1999.
p. 28 A. Paul Weber, The Rumour (1969), © DACS 1999.
p. 29 A. Paul Weber, The Rumour II (1960 or 1968), © DACS 1999.
p. 173 Jean-Luc Cornec, TribuT (1989), © DACS 1999.

Introduction

When at the beginning of 1998 word began to circulate that the president of the United States had been having an affair with an intern, the hour of rumour had arrived. A flood of gossip, conjecture and insinuation broke out, which the White House sought to stem with protests and denials. What was about to line the pockets of lawyers was not only an actual scandal but also a further chapter in the long cultural history of the rumour. Forever rumours have been casting their spell over individuals; forever individuals have been asking whether it is true what "people" are saying. Whether they travel from the periphery to the centre or the other way round, rumours provoke panic and pogroms, fear of war or ecstatic triumphalism, that is to say, they make history. This book attempts to show how history, on its part, answers the voice of rumour.

On the following pages I present some images and technologies that have been designed under different historical and cultural conditions in association with rumours. For rumours, like people, are not "simply there", rather they are complicated entities and explain the history from which they arise and upon which they exert an influence. Like their siblings "news" and "gossip", they appear in all possible media: in the spoken word, in the newspaper, radio, television, Internet. What is more, whether they are true or false counts for little. What is important is that they are up to date and that they do not hide their status as rumours. Their proper and primary medium is hearsay. Formulations such as "they say", "people are saying" or "there's a rumour going round" are the keys with which rumours gain entry to ears and hearts.

Leaving aside the isolated and often very exciting advances made by the few researchers into the cultural history of the rumour, it is on the whole an almost completely unexplored, untrodden area. Many peculiar

1

and enigmatic trails thread through the "Kingdom of Hearsay". Whoever follows them is liable to stray, for none of the epochs that he or she visits allows itself to be researched exhaustively. Yet no passe-partout theory of the rumour can forge a path through the whole. For even if it is the case, as it probably is, that rumours can crop up in any age and in just about any place, still there is no possibility of finding a universal explanation for them all. This book is merely *one* cultural history of the rumour among imaginable others. "Each history is a choice" said Lucien Febvre,[1] and whoever looks for the meaning of rumours has to come to a decision as to what questions to ask. This book gives space to a few of them.

Because of these factors some readers might notice that there is no chapter on the Soviet Union and its history; others may be surprised that instead of Cagliostro, Aretine or other virtuosi of rumour, they meet such figures as the slave Clemens, the rumour theoretician Francis Bacon, and Matt Drudge, the man in the Internet. The choices made are to be put down to the, as old Stechlin once called it, "panopticon education" of the author. It is also connected, however, with the structure of the book. Concrete examples are used to flesh out for the first time various dimensions of an aspect of history which has until now not been considered systematically. And individual examples are therefore not presented as facts, as articles of knowledge, rather as means of gaining new insight into the known or unknown. As is always the case in the study of history, only the questions and never the answers can be transported to different places and times.

A cultural history of hearsay and rumour must include wider historical contexts in its analysis of individual examples. For as events, as relationships "between a specific event and a given symbolic system",[2] rumours first gain their significance in terms of their association with the references that enframe them. They so often evade capture that, on the whole, they constitute an invisible literature, one that is forever changing shape.[3] *The Rumour* looks at the ways in which different epochs and cultures have represented these phenomena, and discusses the social conventions with which rumours have been banished, combated or produced. For this reason what follows deals not so much with the oft proclaimed "rhetoricity of history", but instead attempts to make a contribution to the history of speech and gossip.

Rumours are artefacts. As fleeting, collective events they exist only in the moment of their communication. They are oral, transient and untamed, and always stand in the mode of up-to-dateness. Yet they can survive only in that with which they contrast so sharply, in texts, in written reports or other, most varied forms of material testimony. A poetics and cultural history of the rumour has for this reason no choice but to be forever wrapped up in a contradiction: the historical investigation of the rumour can only ever produce precisely what a rumour is not. Herein lies the special relationship of the language of rumours to the language with which they may be interpreted and described.

Rumours are paradoxical. They are of public character and yet at the same time represent public character. Whoever passes on a rumour is dealing explicitly in both news and medium, in both the message and the messenger. It is upon this issue of paradox that I base my own concept of the rumour: in the first instance I understand a rumour to be what it is generally thought of as being, that is to say, as a convention that changes through history, and one that can signify extremely diverse phenomena. Yet a rumour is also an up-to-date piece of information that circulates in a group in the medium of hearsay or some other, related form of communication; what everyone says is not necessarily a rumour. Rather a rumour is that about which it is said that everyone is saying it. Rumours are quotations with a loophole. It can never be determined who is being quoted; and nobody knows who it was who originally set it in motion.

This parallel conception of the rumour enables a "solid" historical description: as social chatter and at the same time as its reflection in texts and images. Rumours are reflected in treatises in the fields of psychology and the social sciences, in anecdotes, biographies, dramas, epics, stories, films, turns of phrase, research diaries, questionnaires, poems, history books, iconologies, Internet graphics, war memoirs, pamphlets, police reports, propaganda directives, novels, statistics, statutes, dictionaries, newspaper articles and innumerable other media. Everyone can be touched by rumours, be it as their subject, or as their recipient or propagator, here and now, but also in the past and in other parts of the world. Whoever wishes to find his or her way around this profusion requires not just works of reference but also a fair bit of luck.

How difficult and problematical it can be to define the concept of the rumour can be seen in several common misunderstandings. To begin with, rumours are not necessarily false, although they can, of course, be divided up along the lines of true and false. Also, rumours are not a mature form of gossip. Gossip is definable in terms of both form and content; it is founded on the finely balanced relationship and often apparent proximity of gossiper and gossipee, whose roles, in principle, could be swapped. It is the "social form of discreet indiscretion".[4] Gossip can take the form of rumour, but does not necessarily constitute it.

Equally, rumours are not lies; in fact they are stirred up when knowledge and conditions combine. As a rule, however, the motivations of those involved play a subordinate role, for hearsay has no individual subject.[5] Whoever hears a rumour and passes it on joins the linear sequence of "people" who constitute the "they", the agents of collective speech.

Rumours often indicate a prejudice, and the victims of rumours are often scapegoats. Yet, unlike rumour, prejudice is not a social occurrence, rather an essentially passive component of a society's cognitive system. So while rumours may indeed express or even intensify a latent prejudice, rumours can never be identified exhaustively with prejudices since topicality is an essential component of them.

Rumours are also not a medium, as is often claimed.[6] Unlike modern forms of mass media, rumour is founded originally upon the simultaneous presence of at least two participants. It can, however, serve the mass media. Rumours broadcast the success of a story and are at the same time factor and sign of this success. In the structure of initial locution and dependent relay of indirect speech, it refers to what "people" are saying; it is mediated, dependent talk, the citation of a citation. For this reason denials are not given an easy ride; the main clause of a rumour – "people are saying" – is not something that they can refute, and the substance of the rumour – "that president Clinton had an affair with an intern" – is immune to the denials because the logic of the whole sentence is not touched by them. a rumour can be apprehended only with difficulty; it is a hot potato on which everyone warms their hands before quickly passing it on. Taken precisely, every rumour is about a rumour; it is essentially a rhetorical figure, a form of assertion.

This touches upon the uncanniness of the rumour: a rumour is entirely self-contained, and yet always refers back to its previous transmission, to the rumour from which it originated. Like laughter about a third person, talk of the apparent plans, shortcomings or atrocious deeds of this other person brings about social tension. In this way those who are party to a rumour are similar to those who laugh over an absent person.[7] Even in a rumour one is not alone; that is its ambivalent promise. It is always connected with the fears, hopes and expectations of people. These need to be separated out. How and why this takes place can best be seen in fiction:

"Apart from this, it was also said that they abducted children, hung them up in the forest, slit them open with knives, and collected their blood in flasks."

"Why?"

"So that they could sell it to blood banks and make a fortune out of it."

"Oh, what nonsense!"

"What do you mean, nonsense! You've heard it yourself, that children are abducted, hung up in the forest and slit open with knives, and that their blood is collected in flasks."[8]

And so it goes on, and will continue to go on as long as people are still talking to one another. The everyday existence of a rumour is often inconspicuous. It is usually first heard in an aside to the story to which it is connected; unnoticed it emerges from a question or conjecture. Against the "you've heard it yourself" there is no argument.

A further word about my predecessors: the loosely chronological structure of this book is not intended to imply that the history of the rumour runs in a straight line from an "origin" through to a fixed point.[9] What is important is not the linearity of the book's structure but the parallelism of the historically distant manifestations of the rumour presented here. I use paradigmatic examples to hint at larger contexts and horizons. The very choice of this "material" already belongs to my interpretation.[10] Only when a cultural history manages to strike a balance of examples and frames of reference, of foreground and background, can it successfully tell its stories and become history proper. Only then will it avoid that historical presentation of "original" finds that once again is in vogue in this genre.[11] Not everything that happened in the past is necessarily history.

Myth, rumour, war, stigma, control, turns of phrase: the buzzwords in the title of the following chapter hint at my attempt at presenting paradigmatic points of reference in order to demonstrate "certain characteristic features"[12] of rumours and to examine their historical resonances. Whenever it helps my interpretation, I also come to discuss theoretical questions and problems connected with these points of reference; those interested in pursuing these points further can find tips in the endnotes.[13] The textual models I have constructed with which to present these points of reference remind me of cobbled-together toy ships. You take them down to the water, see whether they float, and then watch them drift up or down "the river of time". In doing so, as Fernand Braudel suggested forty years ago, the moment of shipwreck is always the most significant.[14] Since the historical validity of my models is limited, they are also designed in each case to highlight other aspects of the rumour.

To begin with I attempt to show the relationship of the "divine voice" to Greek myth and to early written histories. Already back then, as is not only demonstrated with my first example, which concerns an Athenian hairdresser, it was a problem of evidence. Much later the rumour appeared to the Romans as dreadful Fama. The second chapter attempts to demonstrate how this deity was associated with and ultimately transformed into a rhetorical strategy to achieve mastery of the multitude of ancient Rome's political registers. Later Fama developed into the icon of fame. Through the Middle Ages and beyond, hearsay, that technology of seditious, anonymous talk, is encountered in other guises. The First World War exemplified the extent to which rumours still exert control over modernity. While killing and telecommunications were perfected, European soldiers and historians suddenly found themselves transplanted back to the fearful age of mythical folklore. Anti-Semitic pogroms bear witness to the centuries-old imaginative power of the rumour; in the fifth chapter, which pays particular attention to specifically literary findings, I ask whether the fictions spread by rumours must always imply social stigma. Beginning with American "rumor clinics", mechanisms have been in development since the 1940s that relate to the social control of informal speech. They reflect the need, detectable right up to the present day, to defend the dwindling social centre from the increasing growth of the periphery. At the end of the book I present some techniques and models used by social scientists for decades in their attempts to get to grips with the rumour. It appears to them as an admittedly irrational yet still calculable quantity on the periphery of society. Here it also turns out to be the case that the long cultural history of the rumour is above all a history of errors.

With an eye on all these attempts by ordinary people, powerful politicians and great artists of the trade to banish rumours with complex cultural technologies, I attempt to reveal not only the social aspects of artistic and literary works but also the aesthetic aspects of social practices. But even by doing this only a few of the peculiarities that one comes across when on the trail of the rumour can be highlighted to any great degree. Yet when viewed purely in its cultural contexts, the rumour can be described in terms of what it has been and, in the age of the Internet, will certainly remain: an often fatal poetry and constant companion to history.

1
"Divine Voice", Myth and History

A Martyr of Rumour – "even Talk is in some ways divine" –
The Trace of the Voice – Signal Post – Wetter than Water

Whoever says what people are saying is risking life and limb. This was
the painful experience of a Greek barber in October, BC 413. In his
shop in Piraeus, the port of the metropolis of Athens, he is trimming the
hair and beard of an unfamiliar customer. He has no idea that in the
next few minutes world history will overtake his life, giving him the
tragic lead role in a morality play about historical criticism of sources.
For what the stranger brought with him from far away will change the
life of the hairdresser. It is a succinct, yet terrifying, piece of news: it has
crossed the Mediterranean, has leapt from port to port. In a port it has
also reached its destination as now the foreign traveller tells his hairdresser that the Athenian fleet has been defeated and annihilated in
the great port of Syracuse. Demosthenes and Nicias, the Athenian
strategoi and commanders in chief in Sicily, have been murdered, the
Greek army has been completely wiped out. The messenger himself, a
slave, escaped with his master. Later, in his *History of the Peloponnesian
War*, Thucydides will confirm all this and report on 7000 captured
Greeks in the Sicilian quarries.

A Martyr of Rumour

Yet the barber as yet cannot know this much. What he has heard is
enough, and he quickly makes his way to Athens, four miles away, to tell
the people and authorities the news that so concerns them. "The barber
left his shop and hurried at full speed to the city, lest another might
win the glory of imparting the news to the city, and he come second",[15]
Plutarch reported much later, in his account of the story. The stunned

Athenians assembled to get to the bottom of it; in the end for the bearer of the message it boils down to his being the practitioner of a trade not renowned for its trustworthiness. "It is not strange that barbers are a talkative clan" reasons the chronicler, "for the greatest chatterboxes stream in and sit in their chairs, so that they are themselves infected with the habit". This is a view with which the Athenians of the year 413 would appear to have been in agreement.

"So the barber was brought forward and questioned" reports Plutarch further, "yet he did not even know the name of his informant, but referred the origin to a nameless and unknown person. The assembly was enraged and cried out 'Torture the cursèd fellow! Put him on the rack! He has fabricated and concocted this tale! Who else heard it? Who believed it?'"[16] What are lies, what is fiction? The search for historical truth is set in motion with the crude methods, customary in those days, of criticism of sources; "*martyros*" is the Greek word for whoever was there and can remember, for the witness: "The wheel was brought and the man was stretched upon it", until other sources confirmed the news, until the rumour turned into certainty, namely until eyewitnesses and messengers appeared, "men who had escaped from the slaughter itself. All, therefore, dispersed, each to his private mourning, leaving the wretched fellow bound on the wheel", writes the chronicler about ingratitude and care of sources in Athens.[17]

Strictly speaking, rumours need not be of historical importance. They appear too fleetingly to those who experience them. Their medium, hearsay, is no more than a fleeting phenomenon on the fringes of society. Nevertheless, already through Greek antiquity there is a strong trace of the rumour. Biographies, epics, songs, plays and other documents record the strong impression made by this fundamentally oral phenomenon also in those times. If one follows this trace of the rumour you will stumble upon a complex ensemble of historical practices connected with the ambivalences of the oral. Discussion of the rumour in antiquity will often centre on the theme of war and also on strategies connected with myth – and on the question of its relationship with history. In a society built extensively upon oral communication, such questions naturally throw up dangers. As can be seen, particularly for naïve messengers.

Plutarch tells his story the same way twice: once as a horrifying example in his treatise on talkativeness, that is to say, with unmistakably didactic intentions; a second time in his biography of the general Nicias,

Paul Klee, *Fama* (1939), 502 (AA2)

that is to say, in an historical context. Seen from the present it is not clear whether Plutarch reports a "real" historical reality with his barber or whether in the report about the past he takes up a myth or on his part invents one. In each case there is a moment of mediation between the event of the narrative and its recording a half millennium later. It is at least thinkable that Plutarch, as a good historian, invents a minor character to formulate more clearly his story of the downfall of Nicias.

The little hairdresser just fits too well into the web of the story. This figure allows a stretto of abstract processes, such as that of the communication of a piece of news. Plutarch counteracts the main action of the text by means of a socially more fundamental secondary stage and, in addition, narrates the event synecdochically by having the barber vicariously endure what the Athenians suffer: the pain of bad news. And what the anthropology of the end of the second millennium presents as a discovery, namely that "what we call our data are really our own constructions of other people's constructions of what they and their compatriots are up to",[18] was obvious to Plutarch. Whether "historical" or "mythical" reality, the story of the fate of the hairdresser from Piraeus reveals some details about the genesis and dissemination of rumours in antiquity. They characterise the social milieu in which rumours arise and spread, and they indicate the social status of informal talk as well as the character of rumorous messages.

The rumour of the destruction of the fleet first appears at the periphery of the metropolis of Athens. Like shoemaker's shops and particularly the ateliers of perfumers,[19] hairdressing salons were considered in antiquity as they are today – as places in which gossip and other types of news are exchanged. Men, women, slaves – in such establishments everyone could take part in idle talk. For where the public and the private collide, the *logopoios*, the inventor and story-teller, finds an ideal stage for his entrance.[20] For this is where he is close to strangers, and it is in precisely this often homely proximity, where distant paths cross, that one is invited to exchange stories. The martyr of rumour would have been spared much had he considered this and had spread "his" story only among his customers. The micromilieu of the beard-trimmer is situated within a characteristic milieu. Ports are places of reshipment of goods and people just as much as of news. Not only those who have returned from a journey have got a story to tell, but also those who see a ship land, who watch the unloading of the cargo and chat with foreign sailors can place stories into the world, be they authentic, probable or invented. Every ship is a message.

While, as one can imagine, the news told by the unknown slave spreads through Piraeus, the message leaves the port behind and heads along the long walls into the city. Thus it chooses the path taken shortly after the beginning of the Peloponnesian War by the alleged plague epidemic. Throngs of refugees at that time sought refuge between the long walls in the face of the attacks of the Spartans. The corresponding hygienic conditions saw to it that, starting in the port, the "epidemico-historical centaur",[21] consisting of pox, typhoid and fleck-typhus, spread at terrific speed: between the long walls, but then also in the town. A third of the inhabitants of Attica, among them Pericles, fell victim to the epidemic. Rumours, it can be seen, spread like a contagious disease, and what the Athenians do to the hairdresser, as finally, all worked up, he reaches the city, reminds one of the measures instituted in the face of an epidemic: one isolates those taken ill to reduce the risk of infection for the healthy. Only subsequently does one begin the treatment. In contrast with the medicine of Greek antiquity, the politicians of the time had a thorough knowledge of immunology and of the risk of infection – at least when it came to rumours.

As an opponent of the Epicureans, Plutarch disapproves of idle talk. For this reason he also expands upon the story of the barber and discusses it at great length, and describes with relish other cases in which gossips and rumour-mongers have had to suffer severe punishments. Of course, not everyone who spreads unconfirmed news must end up like the beard-trimmer from Piraeus, and many also avoid the just consequences of their talkativeness. Some pay for idle talk with their lives. The tyrant Dionysius had, as Plutarch explains, his hairdresser hammered to a cross, not because he knew too much, but because he said too much. However, the backdrop of Plutarch's criticism of rumour and gossip intimates the special status of informal talk. The inhabitants of Athens at least had a refined sense for the nuances of the *diabole*, of defamation and denigration, of slander and gossip.

Sophisticated orators understand the usefulness of citing rumours in court as witness against their adversary, and this is something that in the year 345, almost seventy years after the day of the barber, the Athenian financial politician Timarchos, another victim of unconfirmed rumours, learnt. His antagonist, the orator Aeschines, casts an aspersion of commercial prostitution on him. In the prudish society of Athens, this sophisticatedly instrumentalised scandal threatens to break the neck of the encumbered politician. To corroborate its charge, the accusation does not, however, come up with a real person, rather with an invisible witness. Aeschines now merely needs to allude to hearsay to crush his opponent politically. For *pheme*, "a goddess speaking in words",[22] is something that nobody dares contradict. And this is why it fits all too well into the calculations of political rhetoric.

As much as this voice may also inspire respect, the reputations of those who spread it are always, nevertheless, questionable. Long before Plutarch, Theophrastus, another declared opponent of tittle-tattle, describes how the rumour-smith holds his iron in the fire. With his sketch out of the "Characters" this pupil of Aristotle stresses the ethical aspect of gossip and rumour:

> The rumour-monger is the sort who, when he meets his friend, immediately relaxes his expression and asks with a laugh, 'Where have you been? Do you have anything to tell me? How's it going?'... he has ways of vouching for his stories that no one can refute. He relates, as he claims these people told him, that Polyperchon and the king were victorious in battle, and Cassander has been taken prisoner. And if you say to him 'Do *you* believe it?' he will say he does, because it's the talk

of the city, and the discussion is intensifying; all the people are in unison since they tell the same story about the battle; it was a huge bloodbath... And as he tells his story, he somehow believes he is persuasively indignant when he says, 'Miserable Cassander! Poor fellow! You see what Fortune can do? Well, he had power once' and 'You must keep it to yourself.' But he has run up to everyone in town with the news.[23]

Characteristic are the three levels in the work of the rumour-smith: he acquires the news; he speaks to the receiver of the message personally and seemingly exclusively, thereby profiting from the social dynamics of the secret; and he is a master of the art of citation, of indirect speech, in that instead of alluding to facts, he alludes to people, to the "all" who say "the same thing". These first critical instructions for use of the rumour, this listing of the relevant customs, composed after his time, are something that the poor barber could not know. Otherwise he would have been able to take it as a warning about the possible consequences of allowing himself to serve as the messenger of the divine voice. For the art of indirect speech is only of use as long as the person who is passing on the information manages to have himself forgotten in the face of the news.

The news itself remains. What two thousand four hundred years ago worked its way from the peripheral melting pot of Piraeus right into the centre of Athenian community, the agora, this terrifying news about the sinking of the Greek fleet, is a classic rumour: important and at the same time unconfirmed. For a piece of news can only become a rumour when it is of interest to many people; it will circulate as a rumour for as long as it is neither confirmed nor disproved by publicly recognised authorities. When the real eyewitnesses finally enter the agora, the rumour mutates again into news: "All, therefore, dispersed, each to his private mourning."[24]

Whoever takes part in a rumour is dealing with information, the truth of which is merely guaranteed, not confirmed, even if he wrangles like the congregation of the Athenians: "Who else heard it? Who believed it?" The question about the witness is a basic practice in connection with what is told wildly. Either one carries it further, or one tries, like the Athenians, to define more precisely the "one nameless, unknown person".

The painful interpretative procedure that Plutarch's barber must suffer demonstrates a differing awareness of roles, a juxtaposition of two different conceptions of the same thing. What is fateful is that they reach into one another: if *pheme* is immortal and a goddess, it must extend its protection to the barber. It is not that he acts so naïvely (as his later chronicler, with his exclusively psychological understanding of the situation, would have us believe) when he carries the message confidently and proudly to the expected glory into the city and to the authorities, rather he is moving entirely on mythologically secure terrain. Perhaps he believes that the terrible message is intended also to confirm the mythological order.[25] It will surprise him all the more that mighty Athens will understand the horrifying news as the wholly illicit attack

Charlotte Seiler (8 years old), *The Rumour* (1998)

of an idle gossip on the fragile order of their society in a state of war. With reasonable justice and not without violence, the community protects itself against the wildly told *pheme* which has come to them in the form of the moron of myth. It brings him back down to historical reality. That it hurts, must however be the case, and afterwards there is, correspondingly, no talk of an apology.

The hairdresser rushed to the city for the biggest day of his life; it will be his worst: for he is received, entirely understandably, as a political orator who must be held accountable for his words. The foolish piece of news becomes his undoing in that he seeks to transfer it out of the context of gossip into that of politically relevant oration, and, what is more, he wishes to do this quicker than would hearsay itself. "He was set free late in the day when it was already nearly evening",[26] one learns about his agonies. Up until then this man of sorrows of rumour had been stretched out on the executioner's wheel, beneath the autumn sun of Athens, with occasion to think about the way of the world and, in particular, about the power of rumour.

Perhaps while doing this his gaze fell upon the altar of *pheme*,[27] which had at that time already embellished the agora for fifty years, and had before his eyes a reminder that a message is always handled differently from the person who transmits it. The tortured man will certainly have missed the irony of this. And whatever he may have thought about on this long afternoon, all his thoughts will have fallen under the umbrella of the triad of war, myth and rumour. As for the pitiable barber himself (or his fiction), one need not shed too many tears; even under torture the most important part of his body, his tongue, remained unharmed. For hardly had this martyr of *pheme* and dilettante of myth been set free, than "he asked the executioner if he had also heard 'how the general, Nicias, had died'".[28]

"even Talk is in some ways divine"

War and rumour belong together; this is hardly a discovery of Plutarch. Already long before he sketched out the anecdote about the barber, the Homeric beginnings of war reporting show that the Greeks before, at the time of, and after their battles – and above all in their pauses – were aware of rumours, and viewed them as a power bound up with the gods: as messengers of the immortal and a divine voice.

Already the second song of the *Iliad* shows hearsay, the messenger of Zeus, in action. The Greek armies lie before Troy. Nine years of siege have exhausted the warriors. They sense that the gods have not always been on their side in their struggle against Priam's perfectly fortified city. But without divine favour no battle can be won, no walls can be razed. Then Agamemnon "lord of men" has his well-known dream, sent by Zeus, of near victory. Awoken, the commander-in-chief of the army before Troy consults with the other leaders; hope burgeons, suddenly the signs point to victory. The soldiers also get wind of the good news:

> From the camp
> the troops were turning out now ...
> Like bees innumerable from ships and huts
> down the deep foreshore streamed those regiments
> toward the assembly ground – and Rumour blazed
> among them like a crier sent from Zeus.[29]

As swiftly as the forces of nature, the messenger of the god, *ossa*, summons the first thing of literature. With quick success: "streamed those regiments". The same voice will much later, at the end of the *Odyssey*, after the carnage of the suitors, spread the news of the bloody victory of Odysseus. Also here, in Ithaca, it collects together people who beforehand were scattered. While Odysseus and his loyal companions have their victory feast inside, word breezes about outside: "Rumour as herald was streaming hotfoot through the city, crying the news of the suitors' hideous death and doom."[30] On the one hand therefore *ossa aggelos* is the voice of Zeus, that is to say, his functionary, while on the other hand it is an independent force. Its news goes beyond the particular. It manages to achieve what the leaders standing before Troy are no longer able to: It unites an army divided and scattered along the coast. Whoever manages that must be in league with the gods.

   The Athenian cult of *pheme* also has its origins in war. It honours one of the "greatest gods"[31] and probably goes back to the year BC 465. At that time the Athenian general Cimon was laying siege to the fleet and army of the Persians at the river Eurymedon in Asia Minor, which today flows through Turkey and is called Köprü-Su. Apparently, the news of this double victory reached Athens on the same day as the battle.[32] Whether a hairdresser had anything to do with this telecommunications masterstroke is not documented. Whatever the case, an alter was dedicated to the swift medium. When Pausanius, late in the second century AD, travelled through Greece and visited Athens it seems he could still find the place of worship of *pheme*; at least he could still identify what remained of it. It stood not far from the altar of, among other things, "Shamefastness",[33] *Aidos*, a proximity that indicated to the well-known traveller Greek piousness.

How this divine voice is to be invoked, which offerings or even sacrifices it receives, all this is not known; its contours have become

Jacopo de Barbari, *Victory and Renown* (c. 1500)

blurred, it has become mute. All that remains is a sense of the respect in which its was held. Nevertheless, even at this historical distance, one can still imagine what *pheme* spoke of when not just spreading news of victory or defeat. However, only seldom is what it says and why it says it so clearly described as in a famous passage in Hesiod's *Works and Days*:

> Never make water in the mouths of rivers which flow to the sea, nor yet in springs; but be careful to avoid this. And do not ease yourself in them: it is not well to do this.

The poet advises his brother and contemporaries with truths which transcend time. Still, it is not for reasons of hygiene alone that he warns of the power of *pheme*, continuing:

> ... and avoid the talk of men. For Talk is mischievous, light, and easily raised, but hard to bear and difficult to be rid of. Talk never wholly dies away when many people voice her: even Talk is in some ways divine.[34]

Talk is itself divine, and not only the voice of the crowd. The opaque word *"theos"*, which Hugh Evelyn-White here loosely translates as "divine", need not necessarily refer to a person, but can indicate a more abstract force. Yet it is very true that Hesiod here places *pheme* "as a new God among the many already in his theogony".[35] Whoever encounters it knows that they are dealing with something not of human fabrication, even if it is people over whom the power of gossip sets in and whom it subjects to rigorous social control with the always sharp weapon of rumour and gossip.[36] This *pheme* is more than a medium; it has immortal power and exercises it freely.

The Trace of the Voice

Whoever today looks for the trail of this divinity and its myth is directed to the literary echo of its fleeting voices. Not all of these are recognisable; some have become blurred in the course of the centuries, and some of what the Greeks wrote about the "divine voice" and hearsay one only knows about in turn through hearsay, for many texts, mainly from late antiquity,[37] have vanished like their subject. Nevertheless, at least the outline of a mythical picture of rumour and hearsay can be sketched from what remains.

With individual cases it is often difficult to differentiate the rumour from phenomena like renown, reputation and news about a person. It is almost incomprehensible to us how the Greeks could so accurately differentiate between meanings and their individual nuances while also being able to let them merge with one another. Depending on author, time and context, *ossa, baxis, phatis* and *pheme* stress different aspects of the empire of hearsay, be it a hardly audible murmur, be it a message that flies from one place to another, be it a person's reputation, or the renown that lasts through the ages. The only thing common to all of them is that they are difficult to grasp, fleeting like another, similarly "liquid" medium that many Greeks hang on to just as carefully as they do their gossip until they give it out: money.[38]

To this must be added the special, contradictory and ambiguous logic of "mythical" thinking, that forever removes it from logic's dissecting needles. It does not necessarily refer to something else, rather stands alone. Myth is "a mode of signification, a form"[39] and it says "what simply could not be said in any other way".[40] It tends to speak paradoxically, ambiguously and enigmatically, at least when one gauges it with the measure of Logos. That these mists should then disperse as soon as the fleeting voice of *pheme* is heard can hardly be expected. Quite the opposite, this double obscurity belongs to the antique image of phenomena such as rumour and hearsay.

Most of the antique traces of the rumour which have been passed down to us are to be found in contexts in which fundamental problems of myth, war and history are discussed. In a wider sense then, they deal with the question of how descriptions of events allow themselves to be disseminated and transmitted, in space as well as in time. With this the "divine voice" appears repeatedly as a figuration of the autopoetic effect of rumour and hearsay; they speak as if of their own accord.

It is not at all easy to locate the "divine voice" between myth and medium. This can be seen in Sophocles' tragedy about Ajax, the prince of Salamis: the most important and powerful leader in the Greek camp in front of Troy after Achilles has decided to kill himself; he has already rammed his sword into the ground with the blade pointing upwards. Soon it will bore into the Ajax's chest. He turns one last time to Zeus in order to declare his last will. He prays to the father of the gods for a comparatively modest favour: "Send a messenger to bring the evil news to Teucer, so that he may be the first to handle me when I have fallen upon this sword, then newly bloodstained."[41]

Then the hero takes leave of this world and falls onto his sword. As the tragedy has it, so too does the myth narrate. There is a whisper of rumour. Finally Teucer hears the news. Shaken he enters the scene: "O dearest Ajax, O brother who gave me comfort, have you in truth fared as the rumour said?" A rumour, hearsay, informs him of the death of his brother: "Yes, a swift-moving rumour, as though the work of some god, went through all the Achaeans, that you were dead and gone." The *aggelos*, the divine message for which Ajax asked, has here taken the form of *baxis*, of gossip, that is as quick as if "the work of some god". The change from *phatis* to *baxis* demonstrates the mythical power of the gods; *pheme* determines the medium, the form of its appearance.

The rumour belongs to two spheres at the same time, that of the gods and that of humans. Zeus sets it in motion, humans communicate it. And in the end it proves to be apt. Teucer's hope that *baxis* has erred and misled him does not prove to be the case. Only as long as a rumour can be neither confirmed nor disproved can hope remain. Rumours belong to informal talk, as do fear, terror and also ambivalence, which has more claim to hearsay than any other emotion.

It is difficult to interpret the divine voice correctly. It is the "Sweet-speaking message of Zeus".[42] As such it is addressed by the chorus in Sophocles' Oedipus Rex: "Tell me, child of golden Hope, immortal oracle". What is meant is the prophesy with which Creon returns from Delphi and the whole drama is set in motion. Also, as a prophecy *phama* (Doric for *pheme*) has at its disposal the attributes of *pheme* as a rumour: like the goddess Athena, addressed in the following verse, it is immortal. Only with difficulty can mortals fathom its essence. For the daughter of Elpis, hope personified, can ally herself just as well with entirely different forces, for example with *diabole*, slander and denigration. Then it is thought of as *kakon*, as evil, precisely because it mixes the true and the false undifferentiatedly.

Theatre-goers in the time of Sophocles would have recognised the phrase "immortal voice" as a play on the divine *pheme* in Hesiod. At the same time it may have reminded them of the personified news that Pindar extols in the fourth Isthmian ode, a lyric poem in praise of "Melissos of Thebes, Winner, Pancratium":

[Poseidon] by granting this marvellous hymn to the clan
is rousing from its bed their ancient fame
for glorious deeds, for it had fallen
    asleep; but now it is awake and its body shines
like the Morning Star, splendid to behold among the
    other stars.[43]

If the news of the pancratiast's victory is spread among the sport-loving people, then the slumber of renown will also come to an end: Melissos' lineage will be lauded and known by all. The actual victory of the athlete establishes the time-transcending renown of his lineage. With this vivid image of *phama*, at first slumbering, then rising from its reclining position, Pindar forms a connection between rumour and renown, the spatial and the temporal sides of news, thereby forming a new concept. Its purpose resembles that of love poetry. A poem should spread through both world and time like *phama*. In doing so it travels along similar paths to those later travelled by the rumour at the time of the barber of Piraeus: "I am not a sculptor, so as to fashion stationary / statues that stand on their same base. / Rather, on board every ship / And in every boat, sweet song, / go forth … and spread the news …"[44] The message spreads even further in time: "But the ancient / splendor sleeps; and mortals forget / what does not attain poetic wisdom's choice pinnacle / yoked to glorious streams of verses", which indicate a vehicle for spreading *phama* through not only the present but also history. If the horizons of effectiveness of poem and rumour fuse, the resultant

Anne Louis Girodet, *The Rumour informs Jarbas* (date unknown)

literature radiates both in the present and, as *phama*, also beyond, into the future, as moulded speech, as song.

A child of hope and of confusion, the rumour, as the divine voice, has at its disposal elementary power. It appears where there are issues of victory and defeat, of death and deliverance, and it is precisely its complex ambivalence that makes its proximity to the gods plausible. Pindar's *phama* is more than just the expression and outlet of divine power; it knows sleep and wakefulness, and its body shines like the stars. When in the year BC 23, that is to say, about five hundred years after Pindar's birth, Publius Virgilius Maro enchants Emperor Augustus and his family with his reading from the *Aenead*, the Romans will also remember that Fama is a strange entity, one that knows its own mind.

But even when we find in Pindar something that resembles Roman Fama, the Greek concept of *pheme* is not identical with its younger, anthropomorphic successor.[45] Without exception, *pheme* appears as the figuration of an incorporeal voice, as a mythical metaphor for ambivalence. What it says, when the gods so wish, is confirmed or disproved. The period of tension between the moment in which the divine voice is first heard and that in which it proves to be true or false can be of different lengths. In Athens it lasts a painful afternoon; in Sophocles it is equal to the length of a drama.

Signal Post

Pheme is dependent upon human voices to bear it; in Athens slaves and barbers speak of the destruction of the fleet, and Teucer receives the information about the death of his brother by means of the "public voice", by means of what people are saying. The duality of divine power and human medium is what makes the rumour of antiquity so mysterious. Nobody knows where they stand with this voice of hearsay; it refers to other, absent narrators, to people who are not there. In the background of conversations in which this voice speaks there is a chain of anonymous speakers begun somewhere indeterminate and leading nowhere in particular. This series, this virtual network of further speakers, gives rumours their strange authority. It is so because everyone is saying it, and everyone is saying it because it is so. *Pheme* is the cultural convention for the attempt to represent this powerful ambivalence as an ambivalent power. All those who hear and pass on help weave the social fabric of the rumour, but only because of this can it engulf everyone and create a meaningful pattern, following a divine directive like the chatter that informs Teucer of Ajax's death.

Rumours' immense speed and their power over society have a supernatural feel. When Agamemnon left for Troy he promised Clytemnestra that he would, on the day of the sacking of the city, send a signal to her by beacon. At home, after an absence of ten years, no one has forgotten the promise; Aeschylus' tragedy about Agamemnon's end presents to the audience the watchman who has the task of sending the signal as soon as it appears. At the beginning of the play this lookout lies on the ground, bemoaning his arduous lot, "from this high roof / On Atreus' palace"[46] and waits for "the beacon-flare", for the news, *baxis*, of the sacking of Troy. Already in the introduction of this part of the Oresteia, the tragedy reveals itself as a drama about the power of symbols and the dilemma of their meaning. When the unified symbol of the "beacon-telegraph" at last appears, the play of interpretations and conjectures is set in motion.

> Since the beacon's news was heard
> Rumour flies through every street.
> Ought we to believe a word?
> Is it some inspired deceit?[47]

Thus speculates the chorus about the news of the arrival of Agamemnon, of the commander-in-chief of the Achaean forces. Borne by the telecommunications network of antiquity, the rumour hurries, similar to his dream before Troy, ahead of Agamemnon. But everything remains unsure, that is before a forerunner personally confirms what people are saying. For rumours are all "hasty-headed", fired as they are by "women's voices". Above all, however, it travels as swiftly as hope, as fear. Here we can see Greek antiquity's affixing wings to *pheme*, a means of expressing its speed metaphorically. The Chorus asks Clytemnestra, "What messenger / Could fly so fast from Troy to here". This attribution of the ability to fly, of wings, will stay with the rumour until into late antiquity and well beyond; it is a message which is all wings and which blows on the wind.

When Agamemnon has at last arrived to swap the role of general for that of king, the experienced leader demonstrates his respect for hearsay, for the *phatis demokratou*: "A nation's voice, enforced with anger, / Strikes deadly as a public curse."[48] He would like to avoid the magnificent reception that the false Clytemnestra wishes to prepare for him.

With this he appears to have in his mind Hesiod's warning about *pheme*; he dreads envy, malevolence and spiteful talk. As a clever king, Agamemnon knows that he cannot rule without their favour. In just a few verses Aeschylus demonstrates the entire social dimension of this voice. It spreads news in the town and forms the social area of resonance for the great event in the royal house. *Pheme, phatis* and *baxis* see to it that events of the world of the palace reach the collective consciousness; at the same time the divine voice of rumour exacts social control over the ruler.

Fama malum (16th Century)

The cultural concept *pheme* stands in closest proximity to myth. For *pheme*, when it speaks as the voice of myth, is always simultaneously both up-to-date news and its medium: In Plato's *Laws* it whispers the fundamental cultural norms. As "public opinion" it expresses not only what people are saying but also the unwritten rules, the taboos of society, even the incest taboo. "Thus much at least you are quite right at saying", concedes Plato's Megillos to the Athenian Stranger in his opinion about *pheme*, "that public opinion has a surprising influence, when there is no attempt by anyone ever to breathe a word that contradicts the law".[49] This *pheme* enlarges the scope of the writer in his task of transmitting collective knowledge in "pleasurable and memorable form",[50] to the dimensions of the orally transmitted and shared messages of the Hesiodic divinity.

Staggered according to the ages of the singers, three choruses make known the laws. They enrich the collective imagination "in their songs, their tales, and their discourses"[51] with knowledge about the correct customs, norms and mores. Those who are, however, too old to sing, those above the age of sixty, "shall handle the same moral themes [*theia phemes*] in stories and by oracular speech", Plato writes about the oral transmission of norms. Since the old men can no longer take it upon themselves to be the mouths of public song, they play the part of mythologer of *pheme*; the "divine voice" speaks through them when they tell their stories about the just life or, with a "brief sentence",[52] compare what is right and what is wrong. In them, the organs of the divine, the community comes into its own.

Thus is *pheme*, as far as can be determined from the *Laws*, more than just an anonymous and unsure voice. Like an acoustic "antipode of letters"[53] it serves as an oral umbilical cord to the primordial origins of myths. It expresses "what didactic presentation, detailed discussion, the furnishing of compelling evidence are not capable of expressing",[54] and passes from generation to generation, from mouth to mouth. In competition with the rational, with the *logos* and the written tradition, *pheme* creates and maintains something like a collective consciousness. With its countless sentences, words and sounds it spreads facelessly through "hearing and repetition channels throughout the whole social body". Thus arises an ever renewed and self-renewing system of repetitions, simultaneously both socially complex and historically deeply structured.

With the chorus of the old men and its play of repetition and variation, Plato erects for the "divine voice" over a hundred years after the construction of the Athenian altar a second, much more lasting monument. "Constantly there are a thousand and one stories in circulation",[55] attempts Marcel Detienne to interpret this monument. "Where there are no experts at the art of memory – mnemotechnicians of one kind or another – each version obliterates or covers over the earlier, for their only substance consists of the voice of an interpreter and in the echo they trigger among their audience." The proximity of the Platonic *pheme* to both rumour and myth can be seen in the fact that the same voice expresses them. This voice points beyond its speakers; it needs no first draft, no primordial text. The rumour varies and repeats itself, continues and mutates; its narratives hurry from mouth to mouth. Unidentical with itself, forever in a flux from *ossa* to *baxis* to *phatis* to *pheme*, it is itself "in some ways divine", perhaps no more, but certainly no less than a voice that blows about in the domain of its transmission.

Wetter than Water

Rumour evades the clutches of traditional history. The voice of *pheme* stands at a distance to the universe of writing. It can arise in all possible places and emerge from any quarter – at the sea-shore, on the banks of rivers, in harbours, barber's shops and above all in towns. Whoever is at home everywhere has no home. *Pheme* is as tied to one place as is the wind, but even this cannot be said with certainty. For sometimes its voice can be heard completely in enclosed darkness, in the hidden interior of houses, in that district dedicated to the tutelary gods. It therefore also has chthonic aspects.[56]

Since Thucydides, history has concentrated principally on written texts. "And it may well be that the absence of the fabulous from my narrative will seem less pleasing to the ear", the historian suggests, and continues, "but whoever shall wish to have a clear view both of the events which have happened and of those which will some day, in all human probability, happen again in the same or a similar way – for these to adjudge my history profitable will be enough for me. And, indeed, it has been composed, not as a prize-essay to be heard for the moment, but as a possession for all time."[57] This cannot be said of the divine voice. Apart from those who would seal it off in a cult, nobody has permanent possession of it. To guard against this, the historian has at first to test "any and every piece of testimony". "So averse to taking pains are most men in the search for the truth, and so prone are they to turn what lies ready to hand", he complains – a dig at Herodotus, who liked using this turn of phrase. "But as to the facts of the occurrences of the war, I have thought it my duty to give them, not as ascertained from any chance informant nor as seemed to me probable, but only after investigating with the greatest possible accuracy each detail, in the case both of the events in which I myself participated and of those regarding which I got my information from others." Only he who understands how to interpret it can use *pheme* as a source for history.

For right behind the realm of the established begins the realm of *pheme*. One cannot look into it in terms of every last detail; whoever does not disprove it only confirms it. History rallies against exactly this. The task of the historian consists precisely in maintaining this distance of history from the fabulous, in differentiating between facts and mistakes. "And the endeavour to ascertain these facts was a laborious task", Thucydides writes about his handiwork, "because those who were eye-witnesses of the several events did not give the same reports about the same things, but reports varying according to their championship of one side or the other, or according to their recollection".[58] The project of the *History of the Peloponnesian War* is an attempt to take the realm of wild stories, of ever repeating myths and vagabond rumours, the uncertain ocean of myth, and give it a secure foundation: the continent of history.

Looked at in this way, history arose as the other of myth and *pheme*. The problem of the barber, who, if he really existed, perhaps once even trimmed the beard of his contemporary Thucydides before or after his twenty-year banishment, lies in the fact that he – like the rest of us – and like historians too – is at least up to his ankles in the sludge of hearsay. As long as it is still damp from the present, the realm of history is not secure. Only once the mists of rumour have lifted can history begin its never-ending work, for the rumour is not only swifter than the wind, but, in a sense, also wetter than water, whatever one may take this to mean.

Thucydides stresses the difficulties he had with the witnesses of what happened when he tried to isolate the heart of the facts from the diverging stories. Does this questioning of the sources also extend to rumours? Like myth, *pheme* leaves behind historical traces, in epic poems, odes, plays and other texts, in the architecture of an age, in the repulsive text of the scars of a tortured barber. Its trace is the history that has just come into being. Historians have difficulty reading and grasping this event; *pheme* requires, more than other witnesses, interpretation before it can become a textual figuration of the oral. Nobody was there, nobody is the author of the things, if they really occurred, of which *pheme* speaks. And always as soon as it is apprehended it has already just about faded away. "Who else heard it? Who believed it?"

2
Fama, a Model

The Last Aristocrat – Eyes, Ears, Mouths, Feathers –
Arrest Warrant – The House of Fama – Material in Red Pasteboard

A lindworm, formed from countless heads and faces, is flying through a city canyon. From countless windows more and more forms descend upon it, becoming a part of its enormous body, melting into a single, huge chimera. "The Rumour", A. Paul Weber's lithograph, is considered by many to be *the* representation of the phenomenon in the visual arts. The writer Arno Schmidt, who regarded Weber as "the greatest of our new graphic artists", even labelled "The Rumour" "the best allegory since Leonardo".[59] Obviously he was very impressed.

There are numerous versions of the picture, all of which are very similar. The first drafts date back to 1943, and we can therefore assume that Weber was making a critical statement about the rumour in the Third Reich. But which rumour does the picture represent? The informal talk personified in the drawing is certainly not made up of kind words. Too ugly are its expressions and body. Its pointy ears, the glasses, the huge mouth from which the tongue is extruding, its long nose, all this gives the figure an acrid, caustic, snooping quality. While Weber was drafting out this picture, rumours were playing an important role in Germany, then at war. For this reason National Socialist propaganda specialists were going to great lengths to "immunise" people against rumours.[60] It was thought that uncontrolled talk both at home and on the front were demoralising the armed forces. It actually was the case that rumours could express something of a subversive potential, and modern sociologists go so far as to view their "areas of circulation" as "centres of resistance to manipulation by the media".[61] Was Weber, who had

27

caricatured Hitler as early as 1932 and had been held in custody by the Gestapo in 1937, attempting to portray this aspect of the rumour?

"Weber carries around with him a stack of new drawings in metre format", a friend of the artist notes in his diary a good four years after the end of the war; one drawing in particular grabs his attention. It shows "a flying, monstrous mythological creature wreathing before an enormous tenement block, out of the windows of which loom countless human faces, distorted in glee at the sight of scandal"; he gives the title of the drawing as "Defamation".[62] And it was probably this aspect of the phenomenon that Weber originally had in mind not only in this, his most famous political caricature, but also in other works: the aspect of defamation and, more precisely, of denunciation.

This interpretation is supported by another lithograph which goes back to Weber's first sketch. Here the rumour sits, somewhat like a snake with arms and legs, on the lookout upon the ridge of a roof, ready to pounce. But in contradistinction to that final version of the theme, the monster on the roof lacks the decisive element. For the secret of the rumour is a paradox of the masses, simultaneously "many" and "one", the sum of its parts and more. The famous version of the drawing on the other hand shows the relative unity of the conveyed news and at the

A. Paul Weber, *The Rumour* (1969)

same time the multiplicity of its bearers. In a rumour many different people say the same thing. And because of this they become a crowd, the individual parts of which are not simultaneously present. Indeed, it is precisely on the spatial non-presence of others that hearsay, the medium of rumour, is based. It always cites those who are not there at that moment. In the rumour the absent crowd speaks; its members only become visible in allegory.

Just as Weber's picture points back to its own preliminary drafts (as well as to other models), the concept portrayed graphically by him, the notion that rumours constitute a unity, has its own history, its own sequence of historical documents. And in Paris it even has a signature: whoever sits in the inner sanctuary of the old *Bibliothèque Nationale de France* in the Rue Richelieu, beneath the old dome at a long table that was reserved for the users of rare editions, can hold hearsay in his hands. It is a four-paged pamphlet from the French Revolution, stored in red pasteboard and composed by an *advocat patriote*, an educated man with patriotic sentiments. With the typical rhetoric of his time, the author declares himself a supporter of the Revolution, who "feels passionately for his fatherland and wants to see it content, even if it should cost him his last drop of blood".[63] Whether he, like so many, had to pay this price, nobody can know. Perhaps he got off more cheaply.

A. Paul Weber, *The Rumour II* (1960 or 1968)

The Last Aristocrat

Probably immediately before the proclamation of the Republic on 21
September 1792 (the *Royaume Français* was still in existence) the patriot
and representative of the Enlightenment turns to his *chers compatriotes*
and *citoyens* to warn them of the "only and last aristocrat": the rumour.
For, along with the insurgents, hearsay seized the streets and squares of
the capital, turning them into its theatre, its medium.[64] At the same
time it can be seen that the revolution is fuelled by media: placards
hang on the walls and announce news; "people's books",[65] newspapers
and other publications appear in huge print runs; criers announce
decrees and proclamations. An important voice of the Revolution is that
of the peddlers: "Early in the morning one hears the news being shouted
out. And the people, deceived in their thousands by these unreliable
announcements, nevertheless listen to them. The cafés and drinking
dens are alive with the words of the rumour-mongers."[66] They are the
messengers of the *révolte des français*, of the new age. In the capital they
sell caricatures, etched or engraved in copper, while their colleagues in
the countryside mainly proffer wood-engravings. Since they also offer for
sale the texts of the songs and street-ballads of the time, this popular
iconography simultaneously speaks as an "écriture parlée", as a spoken
text; anyway, this is how contemporary observers describe the semi-oral
culture of peddlers and its reception.[67]

Alongside the usual authors of pamphlets and "newspapers", there
now suddenly appear new producers of this sort of literature, such as the
Sociétés Patriotiques, then from 1790 the *Sociétés des Amis de la Constitu-
tion*, the clubs and societies that are springing up all over France.
Together with self-proclaimed public enlighteners of the same stamp as
the author of this pamphlet, they effect a boom of this "little literature".
It consists of court records, speeches, poems, slogans and songs – the
Marseillaise also belongs to it. Pamphlets adopt not without irony the
religious style of catechism in order to explain the new political forms,
institutions and symbols to the simple people in Paris and the provinces.

With these pamphlets and brochures the revolution also reaches
people who can neither read nor write. "The first thing that stands out
when we look at the throng of people surging all about are the many,
tightly packed groups to be spotted in front of the doors of houses in
which there are either civil guardrooms or in which bakers live, or in
front of those houses, the walls of which are plastered with notices",

writes the journalist and publisher Johann Heinrich Campe on 9 August 1789 in his second letter from Paris. He goes on to note:

> In front of each house plastered with the same bulletins, printed on large sheets in large type, one sees an ever-changing assembly of colourful people, a mixture of porters and fine gentlemen, of fishwives and sophisticated ladies, of soldiers and priests, in tightly-packed but always peaceful and almost familiar groups, all with raised heads, devouring the contents of the bulletins with ravenous expressions, sometimes quietly, sometimes out loud, forming judgements about them and debating among themselves.[68]

In this way the revolution seizes on the conversation of the streets. Campe proceeds to describe how brochures and pamphlets are a factor in this conversation. He mentions another "just as colourful and mixed group, formed around a table leaned up against a wall, under a small shade, upon which the fly-sheets and pamphlets of the day are offered up for sale, which at this time are broadcast throughout the streets of the city by many hundreds of colporteurs, not just their titles, but also often the main substance of their texts"; thus it comes to an explosion of the "partaking of everyone in everything" in the medium of spoken text.

"*On me l'a dit*, someone told me this", is the heading given by its author to the pamphlet that is stored at the *Bibliothèque Nationale*. Perhaps they were shouted out in the streets with slogans like "Attention! Rumour!" The style and rhetoric of the text make one think of a sermon – a verbal admonition to the "dear fellow citizens" to be careful and to learn from most recent history. The author inculpates rumour as if it is a criminal, "against which one should proceed with the full weight of the law". He reminds his listeners and audience of two excesses of raging violence. On the one hand he plays on the carnage at the Champ de Mars on 17 July 1791, when La Fayette for the first time let the guard fire on the people, whereby, depending on historian, between "about fifteen" and "over fifty" revolutionary Parisians were killed.[69] He also appears to speak of the September Massacres, holding rumour responsible for the blood "in one of the houses of the gentleman" and which later flows through the whole town.[70] In both cases, according to the author, rumour and hearsay alone sparked off the violence; for this reason, he suggests, the *on me l'a dit* is the bitterest enemy of the revolution.

What he asserts with polemic brevity other witnesses also confirm: the new public life in revolutionary Paris fosters both the emergence and dissemination of rumours. "The unrest was discussed by the people on the basis of true and false rumours", the witness of the times Konrad Engelbert Oelsner reports from Paris.[71] Johann Heinrich Campe describes how the Paris mob gathers and the flow of words begins:

> Two or three men stand engrossed in conversation; the sound of their voices grows louder, their gesticulations become more lively; immediately they attract the attention and curiosity of passers-by; they join company with them – whether they know them or not – in order to take part in their conversation; there forms a group, and in just a few minutes it swells to many hundreds of heads. Only those near the middle can hear what is being said and add their own comments. Among the others the question circulates: que dit-on? (what are they saying?) like wildfire, without anyone to whom it is directed's being able to answer it.[72]

One clearly sees the difference in information between centre and periphery. The urge to exchange news is so great that this conversation forms new centres:

> Again and again there arise in the swelling circles many centres to many smaller groups which form within the main one and in which often something entirely different is discussed from that which first gave rise to this flocking together. Thus one often sees the same groups the whole day long at one and the same place, as if rooted to the spot, despite the fact that the individuals of which they comprise hardly remain the same for half an hour, and despite the fact that the subjects discussed in the different parts of these groups often differ enormously.[73]

People come and go, conversation remains, organising itself, an autopoetic social entity. Chatter, rumour and hearsay can be counted among the fleeting "constellations of the real", appearing spontaneously against the backdrop of political and social distortions and then fading away. This happens outside established institutions and organisations and in an historical "side room"[74] of the great events about which they speak or in which they play a part. Collective talk in the groups which spring up as if of their own accord is the expression and engine of the new situation.

But the ferment of revolution is also their enemy. Konrad Engelbert Oelsner experienced the September Massacres from closest proximity, and what he reports from Paris in 1792 is confirmed by the two hundred-year younger findings of historical research: that namely a "monologue or polylogue on all street corners" first shows violence its goal and that this carnage is often the "result of an epidemic of fear".[75]

"*Que dit-on*, what they saying?" asks the mob. When gossip binds together its public, its mongers and agents as easily as on the squares of Paris, the first step towards outrage, towards riot and excess is quickly taken. And while discussing the "swelling circles" of frantic discourse with "many centres to many smaller groups", the author of the pamphlet bound in red draws a picture of the *on me l'a dit*. He elevates rumour to the level of author, auteur, of "the cause of many, if not all our ills". And just as wildly as his invisible opponent, this alarm-raiser reaches for all possible metaphors and heavy tropes: like an "ingenious and supple snake" rumour is simultaneously "everywhere and nowhere"; it is "a monster with a hundred heads, with a hundred voices" and it resembles the slithering viper that lifts its arrogant head to spray its poison. Here rumour is the all-threatening accessory, and like "a true Proteus" adopts "every form it so desires".

Enemy of the revolution, monster, criminal: rumour, this Proteus, hides its intentions like the arsonist his face.[76] Seductively it ensnares those who listen to it as the serpent did Adam and Eve: "It seems to please us to hear everything that comes from him. This is how one nurses a viper in one's bosom." The rhetoric of hearsay creeps in where one speaks and listens, permeates the writer's feather, takes hold of every house, be it in the town or in the country. "It gives the purest intentions a malevolent and mean interpretation." Rumour, anonymous and in disguise, is the arbitrary author and interpreter of the social. Only radical scepticism helps counter its insinuations: "Take profit from what people tell you, but do not pass on this talk too blindly. Above all: doubt", admonishes the preacher in cases of hearsay, recommending laughter to his readers and listeners as the best weapon against it. As long as one is laughing one does not believe, not even the whispers of a Proteus.

The author of the pamphlet could count on willing listeners. The revolutionary French, his implicit readers and listeners, had every reason to understand rumours as being dangerous; for them it was difficult, if not completely "impossible to separate rumours and insurrections from one another".[77] The "Great Terror" of 1789 with its violent disturbances which spread throughout almost the whole country had enabled them

Doubting Thomas (from the Bible of St Teresa of Avila)

to get a sense of how rumours can make history in times when the powers of the state are weakened. The result is anarchy.

But earlier rumours had also already given form to indefinite fears. In these cases they do not always necessarily appear as false, on the contrary. The older Parisian readers and listeners of the revolution could well remember the riots of 1749 and 1750, which still floated in the collective consciousness of the "unstable world of the small unqualified trades".[78] Back then the rumour had circulated that King Louis XV was having children abducted and killed in order to be able to bathe in their blood; it was said he wanted in this way to cure his leprosy, this "illness of the soul". The disturbances that came about because of this were outwardly quelled by the execution of a porter, a petty criminal and a coal deliverer on 3 August 1750. What, however, remained despite or because of this state rumour-censorship was the suspicion, the rumour as factor and unabating echo of contemporary history. This at least symbolically fitting knowledge of the rumour about the unpopular king could not eradicate the most severe punishments. "*Que dit-on*, what are people saying?" was therefore the question about up-to-date news and at the same time also the question about truth.

The rumour, writes Jean Delumeau in his book about fear in the West, is "equally acknowledgement and elucidation of a general fear and, further, the first stage in the process of abreaction, which will temporarily free the mob of its fear. It is the identification of a threat and the clarification of a situation that has become unbearable."[79] All this belongs to the historical resonances of the *on me l'a dit*. The warning of this pamphlet therefore comes at a moment at which one can count on finding a sensitive audience for this theme. Of all this the preacher against hearsay is conscious. With his sophisticated rhetoric he also offers solutions. The *on me l'a dit*, the "Someone told me this", sees its receivers in the chain of what the "someone" is saying. Such a "someone" is an anonymous, transpersonal author-figuration, for finally it speaks, expresses itself and has the impersonal power of the neutral. In the calculations of literary campaigners against the rumour, a new figure appears on the scene: the critical citizen who steps out of the line of anonymously peddled talk in order to escape from the "trap" of hearsay.

Paragon and archetype of this figure is the most famous specialist in the criticism of hearsay, Doubting Thomas. The disciple with his finger in the wound is held to be the Christian archetype of the sceptic. With the Thomas episode John the Evangelist ends his description of the Resurrection: "Jesus said to him, 'Have you believed because you have seen me? Blessed are those who have not seen and yet believe.'"[80] For this reason, because he does not want to believe just what he has heard, Thomas plays a questionable role in popular Catholic belief and tradition. As a symbol of spiritual darkness, the longest night of the year is dedicated to him, that of 21 December. In the Austrian Alpine foreland it has for a long time been a custom that on this day nobody may switch on the radio, a modern medium of hearsay. But the alarm-raiser about the anonymous voice wishes to see precisely such artists of scepticism in the "swelling circles with many hundreds of heads" on the streets of Paris: "The Apostle Thomas was right when he doubted." And he certainly put his finger into the wound of Proteus.

This pamphlet, with its more worldly concerns, rehabilitates this "twin" Thomas as the counter-figure of that Proteus, rumour: "The *somebody told me* already existed in his day, but it had no success with the disciple Thomas, who carefully remained unconvinced."

The reference to Thomas in fact leads into an epoch for which hearsay plays a decisive role, not only in politics but also in literature. Like our modern image of the rumour, the "Proteus" of these revolutionary times in many ways also follows the examples of Roman antiquity. For back then rumour arises as a mythical or allegorical figure, as an active being that can run, jump, fly, hear, whisper, lie and betray. "Fama" is the name of the divinity of rumour. Its history is that of a literary motif and at the same time that of an exemplary model.

Like every historical phenomenon, an allegory like this can also be understood "only within the framework of the investigation of its time"[81] as being that which it is: mirror and echo of historical mentalities. At the same time it is located in texts which do not just wish to be understood as examples of the history of the rumour, but also individually.[82] More important than the only approximately determinable moment of origin of the figure of Fama is the fact that it appears with increasing frequency in the early Roman Empire and thereby develops relatively constant formal characteristics.

Eyes, Ears, Mouths, Feathers

Everything begins with an African love: the gods have their hands in play as the North African princess encounters the young refugee Aeneas, the man whom Europe and Asia expelled. In the seventh year of his flight from destroyed Troy, storms cast the mythical founder of Rome onto the Phoenician coast. There this "grandson of Venus"[83] comes across Dido, who is building her royal city in Carthage. At the first meal the two nobles have together, Cupid, at the behest of his mother, places longing and desire in the hearts of his half-brother Aeneas and his hostess. Cupid sits on the lap of Dido, the young widow's heart "afire with love, wholly infatuated". She shows the handsome widower from Asia Minor her developing town, caresses his son and flirts, love having taken hold of her, with the Trojan hero.

A great hunt, organised by Dido, wearing "a Phoenician habit, piped with bright-coloured braid: / … her hair bound up with a golden clasp," drives the love story forward. She leads the man she loves and her international guests into the "trackless haunt of the game", into the mountains. This time Juno undertakes to keep Aeneas from his Italic destiny. She employs the proven meteorological weapon as the hunters are driven forward into the mountains: "At this stage a murmur, a growling began to be heard / In the sky: soon followed a deluge of rain and hail together. / … Torrents roared down from the mountain-tops", and Dido and Aeneas take cover in a cave, with passion, even love, welling inside them. Yet, as is well known, in the cave there is to be no happy ending, rather great tragedy. As they make love they are overtaken not only by the play of their natural drives, but also by the forces of nature itself:

Primordial Earth and presiding Juno
Gave the signal. The firmament flickered with fire, a witness
Of wedding. Somewhere above, the Nymphs cried out in pleasure.
That day was doom's first birthday and that first day was the cause of
Evils: Dido recked nothing for appearance or reputation:
The love she brooded on now was a secret love no longer;
Marriage she called it, drawing the word to veil her sin.[84]

So the love finds no favour in the eyes of myth and of the poet, who now has the task of separating the lovers. For as long as the love lasts, the empire will not be founded. Virgil must set the father of Rome on the right path and bring him to Italy, without at the same time discrediting his feelings for Dido. Otherwise Rome would have an erotomaniac hothead as its founding father.

The author therefore is faced with the problem of mediating plausibly between the relative privacy of this love affair and the mythological publicity of his hero. Virgil decides on a telecommunications intervention in the lovers' happiness standing in the way of the great national-mythological project. In the moment of clandestine love, a monster enters the beautiful valleys and heights of this North African Arcadia. It is Fama, a beast with neither peer nor pity, the goddess of rumour.

But who is Fama? In Latin the word has a host of meanings, such as fame, public opinion, reputation, idle talk and rumour. A good name as much as a bad reputation is called *fama*. The word's meaning is double-edged: for while meaning "information" in the sense of news, fama also means the image that is formed of a person on account of this information. And both Dido and Aeneas have a good fama, a good name, which precedes them – and that therefore contributes to their becoming attached to one another. Out of passionate love, but also in order to honour her fama, her good reputation, which for a princess is everything, Dido will finally go to her death.

The experience that this fama as a principle of reputation is often reconciled with love only with difficulty is a basic model in the poetic and dramatic representation of conflicts of love. "Hard it is to maintain our good name; for with Amor, my master, / Only too well I'm aware, Fama is always at odds."[85] Will Goethe, long after Virgil and with a sense of irony, write about the contradiction of rumour and love, which springs from the mythological dawn of history? Their dispute, according to the XIX Elegy, goes back to an Olympic conflict and to the alertness of Hercules:

Since that time the feud I have mentioned has raged unabated:
Hardly she's picked her man, after him chases the boy.
Him who most worships her, most efficiently, surely it catches;
And it will compromise worst those whose righteousness shines.[86]

As he does so often, Goethe alludes to his own difficulties in keeping amorous self-image and unfamiliar, social image in harmony. Yet already in antiquity, Fama is not exactly Fama: as *bona fama*, as good reputation, it becomes the certificate of virtue, as *fama mala* it stands for a bad name.

Cicero writes that renown does not depend on the recognition of the masses, that is to say on *fama popularis*, rather "Glory consists in a person's having a widespread reputation accompanied by praise."[87] Early Christianity shifts the criterion for renown entirely into the transcendent realm. With Paul, the *imitatio Christi*, the following of the Messiah, becomes the decisive feature. Not the esteem of one's fellows, but only the love of one's neighbour, *caritas*, indicates this supreme transcendent good. Thomas Aquinas will separate *vana gloria*, vain

Jean Jacques Boissard, *Fama virtutis stimulus* (1593)

renown, from this *gloria Dei* in order to differentiate the divine from the worldly principle.

As the shady side of Fama, *fama mala* is also *infamia*. In both the ecclesiastical and secular law of late antiquity, and above all of the Middle Ages, *infamia* plays an important role. For whoever loses the esteem of his fellows, whoever is spoken of "infamously", can be saved by nothing, at least according to the *Liber Augustalis* of Friedrich II, from the loss of symbolic capital of reputation and from the corresponding legal consequences.

Fama signifies therefore prestige and news about a person. It has two aspects, temporal and spatial. In terms of time it can, when it is *bona fama*, bring about renown, both during a lifetime and posthumously; as *fama mala* it can bring about the opposite. This period may be short: "After short-lived clamour Fama lies down to sleep / Forgotten is the hero just like the debauchee."[88] In contrast to this, Fama can appear spatially as spreading news, idle talk and information about a person. Already in antiquity, Fama is a concept with ethical, political and social connotations. And this mutating historical semantics forms one of the backgrounds of the cultural history of hearsay.

The fact that Fama itself can, however, be an allegory of rumour is what gives it a central role in this history. Firstly as rumour, not as renown, Virgil's allegory of Fama in the *Aenead* has the characteristic traits of a person.[89] And only as such can it accept instructions – such as the instruction to shatter the happiness of lovers. She carries out her business without as much as batting an eyelid, and with the precision of a professional:

Straight away went Fama through the great cities of Libya –
Fama, the swiftest traveller of all the ills on earth,
Thriving on movement, gathering strength as it goes; at the start
A small and cowardly thing, it soon puffs itself up,
And walking upon the ground, buries its head in the cloud-base.
The legend is that, enraged with the gods, Mother Earth produced
This creature, her last child, as a sister to Enceladus
And Coeus – a swift-footed creature, a winged angel of ruin,
A terrible, grotesque monster, each feather upon whose body –
Incredible though it sounds – has a sleepless eye beneath it,
And for every eye she has also a tongue, a voice and a pricked ear.
At night she flits midway between earth and sky, through the gloom
Screeching, and never closes her eyelids in sweet slumber:

By day she is perched like a look-out either upon a roof-top
Or some high turret; so she terrorizes whole cities,
Loud-speaker of truth, hoarder of mischievous falsehood, equally.
This creature was now regaling the people with various scandal
In great glee, announcing fact and fiction indiscriminately.
Item, Aeneas has come here, a prince of Trojan blood,
And the beauteous Dido deigns to have her name linked with his;
The couple are spending the winter in debauchery, the whole long
Winter, forgetting their kingdoms, rapt in a trance of lust.
Such gossip did vile Fama pepper on every mouth.[90]

Virgil's is not just any goddess; and she does not just happen to appear, or indeed do so without purpose. When she appears she informs Iarbas, the king Dido despises, about the love affair: "Not long before she came to the ears of King Iarbas, / Whispering inflammatory words and heaping up his resentment." He plots revenge; however it is not with a human hand that the happiness will be brought to an end.

Only a god wields enough power over historical events to lead Aeneas to his destiny. Iarbas turns to Zeus, seeing, heated as he is, in his Trojan rival Aeneas a second Paris at work. This is of course an exaggeration, for there has been no pledge of fidelity between Dido and her unsuccessful admirer, yet nevertheless it has an effect. Iarbas prays "and Jove / Omnipotent, hearing him, bent down his gaze upon Dido's / City and on those lovers lost to her higher fame", and sends his messenger Mercury to remind Aeneas of his final goal: if he is to found Rome he must depart. Aeneas follows his destiny, with the well-known consequences, the tragic death of Dido for love. With this success Virgil ends the mission of Fama. She is the message and the medium, an instrument of divine fate. She destroys the African love by spreading publicly the carelessly kept secret of it.

Arrest Warrant

A strange being meddles in Dido and Aeneas's affairs of the heart, just as there are many strange creatures in the Aenead. Merely by means of hints about her genealogy, Virgil gives Fama a mythological programme. She is the daughter of Terra, of Mother Earth, at the mention of whose name a Roman touches the ground. And as the youngest sister of the Titans murdered by the gods, she is at the same time a blood-relative of the Furies, the Nymphs and also of Venus, the Roman Aphrodite. Such an, in part, so disreputable web of relations indicates the chthonic descent of the divinity: the Titans – of which there can be counted about one hundred and fifty – already stand in Greek myth for the dark and chaotic primordial world. The gods triumphed over these uncouth, tree-trunk throwing beings with their ugly, scaly feet. Enceladus, one of

Fama (London 1658)

the unkempt brothers of Fama, perished when Athena, so it was said, threw Mount Etna or even the whole of Sicily on his head. Another member of the tribe was killed by a bolt of lightning from Zeus. Another had his eyes shot out by Apollo and Hercules. Roman Fama, though, spawn of wrath and vengefulness, survived her despised clan. She appears where she wants and says whatever she wants to – or what fate determines.

Beautiful she is not. Virgil paints her as a "monstrum horrendum", something that does not exactly recommend this being as a symbol of renown. He plays with allusions to Homer's portrait of the sister and companion of homicidal Ares, the goddess of discord: "frail at first, but growing, till she rears / her head through heaven as she walks the earth. / Once more she sowed ferocity, traversing / the ranks of men, redoubling groans and cries."[91] Fama too reaches right up to the clouds. She runs quickly and has wings; her body is covered with feathers, ears, tongues, speaking mouths, pointed ears. In the ugly disharmony of this at first small, then large, form, Virgil transforms the paradox of the rumour into an allegory: it is just a single piece of news or allegation, but many mouths pass it on to many ears. The individual bearers of the rumour are inconspicuous, and it spreads discreetly: from person to person, from mouth to ear.

Yet what arises from this, the rumour itself, is a monster. Just as any crowd is more than the sum of its individual members, so too is the power of Fama greater than the collective power of all the people that bear it and pass it on. With her size, power, speed and unified form she embodies the often vile message of the rumour; with her heterogeneous attributes she represents its medium, hearsay. This paradox is what makes her so mysterious.

A. Paul Weber's drawing shows the rumour as a figure made up of many different people. Its body loses itself in formlessness. The allegory of Proteus in the pamphlet from the revolution proceeds in a similar way. The water god Proteus is a being without a clear form; he can change shape as can the element to which he belongs. As an allegory he embodies the uncanniness of the rumour. He has external contours, yet whoever tries to grasp him is grabbing at the formless. And in this way another figure is attributed to the paradox, here in the embodiment of formlessness. This is not the first instance of Virgil's using such a device. Fama unfurls her poetic power not as a mere "symbol",[92] rather as a figure; were she not a person she could not be an allegory.

Fama plies the classic trade of betrayal: she observes, is vigilant, eschews sleep. Truthfulness and accuracy are of no interest to her, and her lust, her joy in telling, constitutes her evil nature. This is no longer the voice of a god, no longer just an organ that executes a function, as she was for the Greeks, rather she is wilful action and the intended evil of a personal force.[93] She finds her tools in the eyes, ears and mouths of people. As a piece of news she travels faster than the wind. She transmits her information in subordinate clauses, as reported speech, a mixture of invention and truth.

Rome is a project of the gods, and this is why it is a divine, mythological figure of such immoderation, a figure which has to appear in order to bring about the reversal in the Dido drama. This is something that no human could do. Today the divinely inspired assiduity with which Aeneas so easily abandons his beloved may be astounding. But in the first instance this is not a matter of psychology, rather of the *fatum* of the founder of Rome, which towers above everything else. Virgil personally read out Books II, IV and VI of his epic to Augustus in the year 23 BC, four years before his death, and with them the tragedy of Dido. Not only in this court will it have been noticed that the dual figure of Fama, despite always wishing to perform evil, sometimes also brings about good; without Fama, no Rome.

Rumours play a big role in the capital at the time of Virgil, and also in the decades after his death. In a way entirely different from Western cities of modernity or Paris of the eighteenth century, Rome of antiquity is a place of gossip, of hearsay, of rumour. In Rome, Fama permeates the entire public realm, for she speaks the language of the political both on a day-to-day basis and in times of war and election. The organisation of the political is dependent upon hearsay. To an extent this is due to the oral nature of communication. Along with this, however, topography and politics in Rome interact in an entirely peculiar way. Without Fama there would have been no political openness in the capital, and whoever was interested not only sought out information about "decrees of the senate", but also had to know all "gossip, rumours"[94] if he wanted to get an overview of political events. And to this end an institution that first appeared at the time of Augustus could be helpful, the *cursus publici*, the public relays by means of which the leaders of government optimised their supply of important news and other things.[95]

That Rome is also the capital of Fama is to do with the social geography of the *urbs*. The forum – along with the comitium, a segregated square in front of the curia – forms Rome's political centre, for that is where the speaker's stands, the *rostra*, are traditionally located. From there speakers direct what they have to say to the senate and above all to the people of Rome. Here in 51 BC it was announced that Cicero had died while on a journey to Sicily. Starting out at the forum, the rumour had soon taken hold of the whole city and remained in circulation for a long time before it was finally refuted. When, eight years later, it really was the case that the orator had been murdered, his head was displayed on a rostrum to dispel any doubts.[96] Historians conjecture that the *rostra* were surrounded by people who "specialised in trading information and generating rumour"[97] – half-professional political scandalmongers, forerunners of modern-day journalists. Orally they counteract the procedure introduced by Caesar in 59 BC whereby important political affairs and resolutions must be put in writing so that they can be checked and uncontrolled gossip guarded against. It is apparent that a large proportion of Roman citizens had at least a minimal ability to read.[98] Nevertheless, sensational or less important rumours could still emanate from the forum.

Hieronymus Greff (?), *Fama* (from Sebastian Brant's Virgil translation of 1502)

In the time of the republic, at least, the patron–client relationship – still stable in those days – carries and maintains the public communication of the capital. It sows rumours like that of the death of Cicero on fertile soil. Election campaigns and the day-to-day notification of public questions run through the same social channels. In Rome, like everywhere else, reliable knowledge of the exact facts seeps out gradually from the centre to the periphery. While the elite, as "insiders", know almost exactly what is going on and exchange this information with their *amici*, they choose to pass on this knowledge to their clientele in measured quantities. In this way they generate concentric circles of information supply, of insight, and with this a three-tiered clientele system of morning *salutatio*: "There were those whom the patron saw individually, those he saw in small groups, and those he addressed as a group"[99] letting them know what they are to know.

The clients, for their part, are located at the centre of their own, variously sized circles of knowledge and gossip. Furthermore, the members of each tier of the clientele system naturally communicate both with their own social class and also beyond it to members of neighbouring strata of society. This increases the diffusion of information and interpretations of events. Since the administrative reforms of 64 BC, a second structure overlies this in itself already complex public system of potential informing mouths and listening ears. For the population of Rome is now divided into different *vici*, which are in turn split into the *collegia* with their *decuriae*. This organisation "united the urban plebs at a local level".[100] Now the state elite can optimise their control over the information to which the base of society has access. And now they can dictate much more precisely what the little people know and do not know.

Let know and know what the people know: the *princeps* and later *pater patriae* Augustus once again modernises the administrative structure of the state. He divides the *urbs* into fourteen regions. Thus arise new social structures which further complicate the network of channels of communication. Within this complex structure of social areas of resonance, important political questions produce their echoes. For this reason informants, the *delatores*, collect what people are saying, write it down and transmit it to the centre. Controlled transparency – that is the system of public communication in Rome. The elite must know that what is decided above arrives below, and at the same time the periphery is to remain transparent for the centre. This is a goal that can only be achieved with difficulty, for the further one travels out from the centre towards the periphery, into the depths of the *vici*, the more uncertain is the knowledge that is to be encountered, and the more important (and unclear) is the resonance of each piece of information. The further one travels down the social hierarchy, the more numerous are those who only hear and say what others have heard and said. The information they lack they make up for with speculation, questions, interpolations and harmonisation with what they already know. Thus arise echo chambers of hearsay; in them rumours can spring up and spread throughout Rome. And in turn there is reason to control this gossip by means of a network of informants, so that the potentially subversive knowledge of the little people does not lead to uncontrollable disturbances.

The House of Fama

Rumours are swift, as if they had wings, and seem to set themselves in motion. This is the impression one receives, at least, from Ovid's *Metamorphoses*. With his description of Fama, the young contemporary of Virgil responds to the latter's dreadful vision. As Augustus stands at the pinnacle of his power, Ovid sketches an uncanny counterworld to the one structured with the rationality of Augustine rule and administration: the House of Fama. If one reads the passage as a counterpart to the Virgilian lines cited above, one will recognise a complex picture of the dangers of the rumour for the order in a capital that is continuously growing and becoming ever more anonymous:

> At the world's centre lies a place between
> The lands and seas and regions of the sky,
> The limits of the threefold universe,
> Whence all things everywhere, however far,
> Are scanned and watched, and every voice and word
> Reaches its listening ears. Here Fama dwells,
> Her chosen home set on the highest peak,
> Constructed with a thousand apertures
> And countless entrances and never a door.
> It's open night and day and built throughout
> Of echoing bronze; it all reverberates,
> Repeating voices, doubling what it hears.
> Inside, no peace, no silence anywhere,
> And yet no noise, but muted murmurings
> Like waves one hears of some far-distant sea,

Or like a last late rumbling thunder-roll,
When Jupiter has made the rain-clouds crash.
Crowds throng its halls, a lightweight populace
That comes and goes, and rumours everywhere,
Thousands, false mixed with true, roam to and fro,
And words flit by and phrases all confused.
Some pour their tattle into idle ears,
Some pass on what they've gathered, and as each
Gossip adds something new the story grows.
Here is Credulity, here reckless Error,
Groundless Delight, Whispers of unknown source,
Sudden Sedition, overwhelming Fears.
All that goes on in heaven or sea or land
Fama observes and scours the whole wide world.[101]

Fama herself appears only briefly. Ovid gives her no face, no form. She is the principle of anonymity personified. She has sought out a privileged location for her house. From this centre of the world she has an overview, in a way similar to Homer's "sun-god, who sees all things and hears all things",[102] of worldly events. She is powerful, as if she were the only divinity; before her all are equal, for nothing – not even in the world of the gods – escapes her attention. She is the eye of the world. Ovid does not show us any more of the divinity Fama; she remains an unclear, shadowy figure at the edge of the picture. At other places in the *Metamorphoses*, however, she resembles precisely Virgil's harm-bearing monster, described as a being "who talks and loves to tangle true / With false, and from near nothing flourishes / On her own lies".[103] But despite the odd parallel, Ovid surrounds Fama with a completely different web of relations than does Virgil. Only envy, hunger and sleep, all forces that themselves appear personified in other parts of the *Metamorphoses*, are as powerful. They too sweep like gods over humans, full of wilfulness and with unearthly violence.[104]

With Ovid, Fama does not hear and speak personally. He turns his attention more completely to the description of her house. It becomes a description of anonymous chatter, of the "they say", and of the forces that this "they" sets into play and utilises. The position of the house alone demonstrates the violence and magnitude of the rumour; optically and acoustically it recognises no distance. Thus it stands above everything and everywhere. Its architecture is difficult to describe; it comes across as a gigantic musical instrument, a resonance space of amorphous form.

The building material of the house serves only to intensify the sound and echo; the rest is transparency. In this public acoustics transformed into architecture there is no peace, no silence. Murmurings, *murmura*, a rumbling like that of thunder or waves. In the house of Fama the talk appears in the materiality of the sound of its voices. Meanings mix with one another, new meanings arise. This is not a human place, rather a place of anonymous chatter. Here names carry only negative characteristics personified, the composers of scandal and whispers of uncertain origin: madness, futile happiness, fear and gullibility.

They complete the metamorphosis of the voice, of murmuring, into the rumour. "With regard to rumour and common report, one party will call them the verdict of public opinion and the testimony of the world at large; the other will describe them as vague talk based on no sure authority, to which malignity has given birth and credulity increase",[105] writes Quintilian in his *Institutio Oratoria*. Correspondingly ambivalent can be the rhetorical entry of Fama in the early Roman Empire. In a society in which republican institutions of control like the senate have

Hendrik Goltzius, *Miserliness is the Root of all Evil* (16ᵗʰ Century)

lost power and influence over public pronouncements about political events, at a time when public esteem counts as a political factor of the highest order, hearsay can very quickly decide between slavery or freedom, between life and death. Whoever is attributed too much respect by *rumor* or *fama*, whoever's *reputatio* is too good, runs the risk of appearing to offer too much competition in the struggle for power. In Rome even good repute can have deadly consequences.

In the voice of rumour, public opinion appears as a political factor – in war, when there has been a rout,[106] and always at the death of a powerful figure. Mouths and ears are also not asleep when the man to whom Virgil personally read out his portrait of Fama dies. Immediately after the death of Caesar Augustus, rumours spring up about the manner of his demise. Soon it is said that his wife Livia poisoned him in order, by means of a swift coup, to clear a path to power for Tiberius. The murder of Agrippa Posthumus further sets the beginnings of the rule of Tiberius "in twilight".[107] And for the Romans, the background to such a turnabout of power and of generations is harder to fathom than it is for historians. Fama begins where the motives of power become opaque.

Tacitus describes just how persistently Tiberius' regime is dogged by rumours and how his opponents make use of them, among them the slave Clemens: going into hiding until his hair and beard have grown, "for in age and general appearance he was not unlike his master",[108] he passes himself off as his master Agrippa Posthumus after the latter has been murdered, and has it spread in Etruria, "at first, in whispered dialogues, as is the way with forbidden news", then "in a rumour which ran wherever there were fools with open ears, or malcontents with the usual taste for revolution" that the person believed to be dead is actually still alive. "He himself took to visiting the provincial towns in the dusk of the day. He was never to be seen in the open, and never over-long in one neighbourhood: rather, as truth acquires strength by publicity and delay, falsehood by haste and incertitudes, he either left his story behind him or arrived in advance of it." When Pseudo-Agrippa finally comes to Rome, Fama has already prepared the ground for a grand reception. The elated throng, blinded by Fama, sees this false Caesar enter the city – and pay their respects to a gifted actor and virtuoso of the rumour. Enraged Tiberius is well aware of the power of rumour. Soon he makes up his mind and, in a secret quarter of the palace, brings the roll-play of Clemens and Fama to a bloody end.

The voice of rumour dogs the rule of the Roman emperors, above all that of Nero. When in the year 64 AD Rome burns, he reduces the price of grain, gives the people the gardens of his palace as ground upon which to build, has food imported, donates to the poor and sacrifices to the gods. Yet with all this he is unable to silence the rumour that, "at the very moment when Rome was aflame, he had mounted his private stage, and, typifying the ills of the present by the calamities of the past, had sung the destruction of Troy".[109] In order to silence Fama, Nero tries to lay the blame on the sect to which doubting Thomas also belongs. As a strategy against the *rumores* and Fama he instigates the first persecution of the Christians. Yet he is unable to wipe clean his reputation. Quite the opposite, after he has taken his own life in 68 AD, Nero-doubles spring up in various regions of the Empire and contribute to the maintenance of the "twilight" of uncertainty and the rumours about him even after his death.[110] To the present day, Fama determines his image.

Rumor, fama, sermones, opinio, rumour, gossip, public opinion – this is the field, overviewed only with difficulty, in which the goddess Fama raises her head, the field upon which her house is built. The foremost chronicler of his time, Publius Cornelius Tacitus, strenuously attempts again and again to differentiate carefully between hidden facts, reliable eyewitness accounts and hearsay. As a historian of his times he stresses, with rumours in mind, the necessity for criticism of sources: "I would not venture to assert that we have any firm evidence."[111] Where there is no "auctor certus", no "definite authority",[112] the antique historian limits himself to the reporting and critical interpretation of gossip. Yet the persevering and unique care of the chronicler Tacitus in questions of informal communication allows us to see the immense historical space of resonance in which Virgil's Fama and Ovid's hearsay arise.

Both portrayals are also commentaries on the political life of their time. Virgil describes the rumour as a monster. Ovid goes a step further. Instead of the goddess, he shows us her habitation; instead of with a figure he presents us with faceless and bodiless forces. With Virgil the rumour is a figure in the world; his Fama is weighty news that shocks and unnerves people. Ovid, on the other hand, counts on the medial characteristics of the phenomenon. He makes the house Fama occupies the centre, and the world the periphery. With him the rumour is only anthropomorphic when it is in action. In this sense it is hardly similar to the gods at all. It encompasses all three worlds; it collects up and magnifies all the bad qualities of humans. The news carried by the rumour and its effects he only mentions in passing. For Ovid it is a question of the manner of its arising and the medium of its dissemination as an anonymous and omnipresent voice, hearsay. Here one asks: "Que dit-on?", here one hears the *on me l'a dit*, the voice of the absent many, of the "they" who "is not this person, not that person, not oneself and not some people and not the sum of them all".[113] As with a head with ears and mouth, in the house of Fama "hear" and "say" coincide.

Material in Red Pasteboard

Hearsay and rumour: the images of Fama in Virgil and Ovid reflect literary strategies for developing an image for anonymous, transpersonal speech. Where no author is to be found, it is replaced by the concepts of rumour and hearsay, based on Fama of antiquity. Since then the allegory of Fama has, in various forms, become a topos of cultural history. Whenever writers, engravers or painters wish to give rumour a form they can reach back to the examples of Virgil and Ovid. Above all, the incomparable effect of Virgil – and particularly the renown of the Dido episode – in the Renaissance and Baroque made the personified rumour Fama known throughout Europe.

The figure of Fama is a graphic concept of rumour presented as an ontological unity. She is "material"[114] in the reflection on rumour in literature and art. The model of Fama enables the unity of the rumour and, at the same time, the multiplicity of those who play a role in it to be thought of in a coherent image. The figure represents a cultural manner of engagement with anonymous talk. Every era and every cultural field utilises and interprets in a new way what this model has to offer.

The allegory reflects, depending on its context, different aspects of the phenomenon "rumour". It indicates specific needs; each image suggests a solution, an answer to a problem. Whether in high brow literature or in the popular reading matter of the little people in the streets of re- volutionary Paris, the allegory says about rumour and hearsay what could not be said in any other way.

Not only the educated but also the simple people knew the monster Fama from pamphlets, from books and, later, from the classroom. Books and pictures have forever adapted and modified the motifs, and even now everyday metaphors demonstrate the power of earlier images. A most clear example of this is to be found in Beaumarchais' *The Barber of Seville*, in which Bazile's description of slander, "raising its head, hissing, puffing, and swelling before your very eyes",[115] clearly alludes to Fama of antiquity.

Clearly the essence of the allegorical images of rumour is to be found in the wilfulness, the independence of mind of Fama. The allegory captures what even enlightened times fail to see other than as a problem: the autopoeis of the rumour. The rumour creates its own reality, one which mixes with "normal" reality, and not without consequence. As hearsay, it is self-referential: "people are saying"; as news it refers to a – correctly or falsely – observed reality. The night of the lovers in the mountain cave and the night of blood in Paris, both rumours arise and spread with a dynamics that appears autonomous; the first corresponds with the rumour of an external reality, the second produces this reality itself.

While most classical allegories have largely lost their sense of reference and have become merely material with which to play, Proteus and the *on me l'a dit* stand for the model "Fama" and the present-day concepts of rumour and hearsay in a form of double substitution. As already in Tacitus and the other authors of antiquity, the play of metaphors is meant to reveal the power of the rumour. No readers or listeners would ever believe that this "Fama", this "Proteus", this "last aristocrat" actually exists as a person outside the rhetorical world in which it is presented. Yet still the allegory enables the "person" rumour to be grasped as a counter-figure, as an adversary of the oral, and that means in France of the late eighteenth century, of the political subject who experiences the revolution through writing and reading. Some of the revolutionary pamphlets had print runs of over a hundred thousand.[116]

At a time when a boom in newspapers, sensational literature and other media[117] are transforming the literary market, and when the production, distribution and reception of literary (and oral) works are being revolutionised, that is to say in the historical moment of the transformation of passive subjects into active citizens, the pamphlet of the *advocat patriote* reflects the new political role of this *citoyen*. In place of chaos, violence and panic, the new age, with the citizen and patriot answerable for his actions and opinions, is bid enter. And against the Proteus of rumour, the author of irresponsible gossip which *on m'a dit*, this citizen of the state is implored to become the author of political action. Thus the struggle against the rumour is the struggle of the new author against the old. The pamphlet is its battleground.

"Writing is therefore the public communication of ideas; printed discussion; loud talk intended for everyone who wishes to hear it; con-

16th Century, no title, anonymous

versation with those who read",[118] wrote Baron von Knigge in 1793, that is to say, at the same time as the *on me l'a dit*. It describes well the style and manner of address of the pamphlet: Its readers are an audience, are *chers compatriotes* and *citoyens*, and writing and communicating in public is a form of trade.

At this time there arises in Europe – and especially in France with revolutionary haste – an understanding of the author as an individual with legal rights. In July 1790 the last printing privilege was granted according to the old law of privilege. After that "a loophole appeared where there were neither bookseller guilds nor customs nor licences nor laws, where there was neither intellectual property nor the infringement thereof, since justice and injustice were not yet differentiated, where either nobody held sway or anarchy did so."[119] On 19 July 1793 the *Assemblée Nationale* passed a law that guaranteed the exclusive right of "authors, composers, painters and engravers to sell their work or have it sold"[120] – and for the period of their lives and ten years beyond that.

Behind the coexistence of metaphors and descriptions, behind the rhetorical division of good and evil, of paradise and hell, there is evident in this modest pamphlet a historical dichotomy: the new author against the old gossip. The figure of the author is intended to replace the rumour.

In the turn away from irresponsible and unanswerable gossip there appear the characteristics of this other author. This author will operate as the representative of his class, he thinks politically and is also a legally-acknowledged figure. With the eighteenth century, and particularly with the French Revolution, begins the age in which the institution of the author becomes established. It is a *fictio iuris*, upon which copyright will be based. It stands for the unity of the literary function "author" and the political subject who thinks out and writes down his text, his message. This transformation runs through the little pamphlet with the title *On me l'a dit*. It is not a novel, not fictional literature, rather a functional literary design, a thin, unbound and therefore flimsy document to be consumed by the little people. Even if it has no emphatic author in the literary sense, it still has a composer. At the bottom of its fourth and last page is printed the name or pseudonym of a long forgotten: "R. L. A. Boussemart, Avocat patriote", the person whom we only know through his pamphlet, who in a side-room of history took a stand against hearsay, and whose disappearance was only hindered by historical accident: the system of classification of the library and the red pasteboard of the archivist.

3
Rumour and the Loophole in Hearsay

Half a Dozen Cobbler's Pegs, Two Fanfares – In the House of Fame – Dynamic Architecture – The Land of Tapestry – Rumore – Rumor's Cloak

Half a Dozen Cobbler's Pegs, Two Fanfares

"The room, on the ground floor, the only one there was, had on the far wall a large bed with no curtains, while the kneading-tub took up the wall with the window, which had one pane patched with a star of blue paper."[121] Madam Bovary has for the first time entered the wretched cottage of her small daughter's nurse, a destitute joiner's wife. The furnishings are more than modest, and every aspect of the abode reflects poverty and sadness. "In the corner, behind the door, gleaming hobnailed boots were arranged under the washing-slab, near a bottle full of oil with a feather in its mouth."[122] And Emma Bovary goes on looking around at the everyday items, registering them with cold detachment: "The most recent superfluity in this room was *Fame Blowing Her Trumpet*, a picture no doubt cut out from some perfumier's catalogue, and nailed up on the wall with half a dozen cobbler's pegs." Emma takes it all in; only then does she go to her child.

Allegories also have changes of fortune. Before Fama brought cheap scents to women in provincial French towns and adorned the living rooms of the little people, she already had a brilliant career behind her as a symbol of renown. Sine the Renaissance she has become an important allegorical figure in the artist's repertoire. She appears in print, in engravings and on pamphlets, as much in the small-format art of emblematics as in large, representative painting. And she mainly informs of victory, when not over time, then at least over vice. With this cultural background, Fama acquires the bitter aftertaste of sarcastic allusion. Fama is from now on just a shabby reference to herself. For nothing is

Hendrik Goltzius, *Fama and Historia* (1586)

further from life in Yonville than renown and importance, a fact that cannot escape Emma Bovary.

In an engraving of 1586, Hendrik Goltzius has Fama rise above or out of a history book which Historia is reading. Overgrown ruins, a skull, smashed crockery, the ears of corn in Historia's lap, yet above all the winged, hovering hour-glass symbolise time and transience as motifs of the image. With its dynamism, the half-naked body of Fama demonstrates the power of renown. Exuberantly she kicks her left leg out in front of her, while her loose clothes flare out to her sides from the motion of flight. Below, beside Historia, there stands a stag, symbolising the circular course of nature; it has thrown off a beam of its antlers. With her half crouching, half kneeling position, the allegory of history gives an impression of collectedness and calmness while she reads. Her left leg is knee-deep in a hole, and thus she seems to belong to the earth. And unlike the goddess of renown, as which Fama here appears, she has no wings.

Fama's two fanfares are the traditional symbols of good and bad reputation, of *fama buona* and *fama mala*. In many pictures the instrument of bad news appears dark, while that of good news shines brightly, a paradigmatic opposition that goes back beyond Roman antiquity. For the two fanfares that the British military trumpeter James Tapper played in a live radio transmission, broadcast world-wide in 1939, were also different in tone and colour. The one was silver, the other made of bronze, and both came from the grave of Tutankamun. It was said that they sounded shrill and somewhat tinny – even the silver one.[123]

Goltzius' Fama embodies the concept, passed down from late antiquity,[124] of the good reputation which can only be obtained through virtue. The question of who will be granted historical or even eternal renown, the *gloria Dei*, depends on this renown. According to this, Fama is a fundamental ethical principle, and that is why she can also appear in images which have a religious context. In Golzius' engraving she lifts with her right hand what appears to be the lighter of the two fanfares to her lips and blows into it. Behind her back she holds the second instrument, ready for use. Her hair is blowing about in the wind, and on her spread wings can be made out the eyes and ears which were once the undoing of Dido and Aeneas' love. Like rumour, renown also perceives what is going on.

The element of this Fama is, unlike the Fama of rumour, the air. In contrast, Historia belongs entirely to the ground, to the earth, something indicated by her attributes and posture. In her left, half-raised hand she holds a fire, out of which a phoenix rises, the symbol of permanence, of repetition and of resurrection. The inscription on the stone sarcophagus reads: "Death overtakes everything; virtue alone escapes it and remains an inextinguishable force in the world of those who continue living." This is the principle of Fama: she heralds the good reputation of the good, and she survives death.

Since the Renaissance the divinity of renown has celebrated her entrance as a shining figure, as powerful Fama triumphans. Facing the sun and with the swagger of victory over time, she can be seen in a publisher's mark made by the Nurnberg master wood-engraver Jost Amman for the publisher Sigmund Feyerabend; in this she carries a twisting fanfare, and from this hangs a banner upon which is written her most wonderful promise: "Fama inmortale, immortal fame."

This Fama is no monster, rather quite the opposite, the cult figure of history. As mediator between earthly and heavenly stature, she calls forth posthumous renown for the virtuous. And sometimes she even blows two instruments at the same time. Tobias Stimmer, for one, stands her in contrapposto upon a stone plinth; she reaches up to the sky and holds still in this position, sea and land in the background, all three parts of the world placed next to one another, with the now familiar eyes on her spread-out wings. A maxim assigns the goddess her place in the symbolic and ethical economy. She is the wages for a "brave heart". For Fama allies herself with virtue; in another picture one finds the allegory of personified, smiling virtue's strolling towards the plinth of renown. The title of this image alludes to its late antique origins: "Fama is the incentive for virtue."

In early Modernity this allegory, especially among book illustrators, became a popular symbol of good reputation. And this symbolisation of renown also reflects the social context of this art. It reminds us how people in the Renaissance – the sovereign – could and had to acquire a reputation and stature in order to enter history, the history of which renown is the measure.

Most illustrations created to accompany the Fama passage in the *Aeneas* show the monster to be more or less how Virgil described it: with wings, with eyes, ears or mouths, a symbol not only of rumour, but also of uncertain, unverifiable talk, hearsay, which was depended upon by people as much as it was feared by them. In the Renaissance, and far beyond it, Fama allegorically stands for the newspapers evolved from hand-written newsletters,[125] and above all for unsure news from far away. In 1777, for example, "Madam Fama has two trumpets, one facing forwards, the other backwards. With the latter she spreads lies, with the

Jost Amman, *Fama with a Fanfare* (date 16th Century)

former, truth."[126] In the nineteenth and twentieth centuries Fama has still been useful for ironic, intellectual or witty intimations of the power of rumour. Thus does an Austrian author send up the modern press in the form of Virgil's monster as "Miss Fama", who lives a "scandalous life": "Who gobbles up truth and lies / With equal pleasure / And what she spits out / Is a fricassee of both."[127]

If Fama, as in the Virgil illustrations, also appears sporadically after antiquity as rumour-Fama, this does nothing to alter the fact of a fundamental shift in its meaning horizon. Ever since Petrarch's "Triumphs" of allegorically transhistorical forces such as Morte, Amor, Tempo,

Eternità and Pudizia, Fama has stood in the main for reputation and renown. Where she once stood for rumour and stepped into the systematic loophole in hearsay, the loophole of the missing author, of the missing originator, of the "they" with which this witness is replaced, there has itself appeared an historical loophole. And this loophole also has a history.

In the House of Fame

"As I slepte, me mette I was / Withyn a temple ymad of glas."[128] Over six hundred years ago, in the night of 10 December 1383, a Thursday it has been determined, the poet Geoffrey Chaucer visits the Temple of Venus. He is on the lookout for love stories and similar material for his poems. Dreaming and full of wonder, he watches as the story of Aeneas plays itself out before his eyes: the destruction of Troy, the end of Creusa, the flight with father and son, the hero's love affair with Dido and her sad end, then the journey to Italy etc. "And nere hyt to long to endyte",[129] the dream chronicler remarks laconically, "Be God, I wolde hyt here write." The dream continues. Following the *Aenead* in its time-lapse effect, Chaucer leaves the sad Temple of Venus unexpectedly to find himself at the zero-point of civilisation, in a "large feld, / As fer as that I myghte see, Withouten toun, or hous, or tree." There he encounters an enormous golden eagle, which, acting on the orders of Jupiter, promises him a reward for the effort of writing poetry. It wishes to take him to the House of Fame, to where "wonder thynges" are to be perceived. This house, it quickly transpires, is built according to Ovid's plan; even in its details it reminds the reader of its model in the *Metamorphoses*.

Before poet and bird arrive there, they discuss Ovid's discovery that "every soun"[130] reaches this house. The eagle speaks about the connection between tone of voice and the dissemination of spoken words: "Thou wost wel this, that speech is soun, / Or elles no man myghte hyt here" The sound, that is to say every spoken word, travels outwards like a circle in water. Fama is therefore following a law of nature when she chooses her location "Ryght even in myddes of the weye / Betwixen hevene and erthe and see", since indeed "every speche, or noyse, or soun, / Thurgh hys multiplicacioun, / Thogh hyt were piped of a mous, / Mot nede come to Fames Hous". And the poet does not fail to take the opportunity of telling us that language is "but eyr ybroken".

Thus the poet of the late Middle Ages reads Ovid's allegory as a physical poetics of the spoken.

After a long flight in unfamiliar heights they approach the House of Fame. Here there is "grete soun",[131] for every word appears as a person, and moreover resembles the person who said it. The eagle sets Chaucer down; it continues on its way. Its final destination is a rock made of ice, "a feble fundament",[132] and in the ice can be found the traces of names. Some have almost completely wasted away, others can be deciphered without difficulty. They are the names of great rulers and generals. Renown, for this is what the mountain of Fama is all about, perishes like ice.

The castle of Fama is itself a mythical location. At the same time both strange and magnificent, it is made entirely from the green precious stone beryl. The building material and rich decoration demonstrate the power of Fama. She surrounds herself with an army of poets, singers, musicians, generals and mythical heroes. In the entrance hall of Fama, upon pillars made out of symbolic metals, stand the poets of antiquity: Virgil, Homer, Ovid, Statius etc. Chaucer follows Virgil's model exactly when describing the mistress of the house:

> But al on hye, above a dees,
> Sitte in a see imperiall,
> That mad was of a rubee all,
> Which that a carbuncle ys ycalled,
> Y saugh, perpetually ystalled,
> A femynyne creature,
> That never formed by Nature
> Nas such another thing yseye.
> For alther-first, soth for to seye,
> Me thoughte that she was so lyte
> That the lengthe of a cubite
> Was lengere than she semed be.
> But thus sone in a whyle she
> Hir tho so wonderliche streighte
> That with hir fet she erthe reighte,
> And with hir hed she touched hevene,
> Ther as shynen sterres sevene,
> And therto eke, as to my wit,
> I saugh a gretter wonder yit,
> Upon her eyen to beholde;

But certeyne y hem never tolde,
For as feele eyen hadde she
As fetheres upon foules be,
Or weren on the bestes foure
That Goddis trone gunne honoure,
As John writ in th'Apocalips.
Hir heer, that oundy was and crips,
As burned gold hyt shoon to see;
And soth to tellen, also she
Had also fele upstondyng eres
And tonges, as on bestes heres;
And on her fet woxen saugh Y
Partriches wynges redely.[133]

Tobias Stimmer, *Fama* (16th Century)

As the sister of "dame Fortune", Fama holds court, as in Ovid. At her command, Aeolus, the god of the wind, blows his trumpet with its "foul soun" or the "trumpe of golde". Fama pays out arbitrary wages for good or bad deeds. *Fama mala* appears, synaesthetically emphasised, as stinking smoke, "Blak, bloo, grenyssh, swartish red". *Fama buona* is described correspondingly "As men a pot of bawme helde / Among a basket ful of roses".

This Fama is like the sum of the two antique models – Virgil's monster in the house of Ovid. And this literary dream does indeed shed light on an important reduction in meaning. Fama now embodies only one dimension of the antique models; she now only stands for time-conquering posthumous fame, no longer for the actual rumour. This poem clearly shows this semantic shift: the hero is bored. In the palace of renown he can experience nothing. That people are vain and strive for recognition is something he knew before his dream journey. Yet precisely in this moment of surfeit of the conventional allegorical motifs connected with Fama, the dream takes a decisive turn. A secretive, unfamiliar figure addresses the traveller and asks the reason for his being there. To see something new, Chaucer answers. "But these be no such tydynges / As I mene of."[134]

Dynamic Architecture

He is in luck. The unknown person leads the disoriented poet out of the palace; they leave the castle of renown. In a nearby valley there stands a strange house. Chaucer takes the time for an exhaustive description:

And ever mo, as swyft as thought,
This queynte hous about wente,
That never mo hyt stille stente.
And therout com so gret a noyse
That, had hyt stonden upon Oyse,
Men myghte hyt han herd esely
To Rome, y trowe sikerly.
And the noyse which that I herde,
For al the world ryght so hyt ferde
As dooth the rowtynge of the ston
That from th'engyn ys leten gon.
And al thys hous of which y rede
Was mad of twigges, falwe, rede,

And grene eke, and somme weren white,
Swiche as men to these cages thwite,
Or maken of these panyers,
Or elles hottes or dossers;
That, for the swough and for the twygges,
This hous was also ful of gygges,
And also ful eke of chirkynges,
And of many other werkynges;
And eke this hous hath of entrees
As fele as of leves ben in trees
In somer, when they grene been;
And on the roof men may yet seen
A thousand holes, and wel moo,
To leten wel the soun out goo.
And be day, in every tyde,
Been al the dores opened wide,
And be nyght echon unshette; ...
And loo, thys hous, of which I write,
Syker be ye, hit nas not lyte,
For hyt was sixty myle of lengthe.
Al was the tymber of no strengthe,
Yet hit is founded to endure
While that hit lyst to Aventure,
That is the moder of tydynges,
As the see of welles and of sprynges;
And hyt was shapen lyk a cage.[135]

In this non-house live hearsay and rumour. The nomadic whirligig stretches out broadly. Its transparency is familiar from Ovid. Yet other than in antiquity, there is here in the late Middle Ages a dynamic architecture made out of organic, transient materials. Nothing is certain any more, too quickly turns this thundering spinning top. Jupiter's eagle yet again brings help. He takes the curious writer on the search for material into the vortex: "And therwithalle, me thoughte hit stente, / And nothing hyt aboute wente – / And me sette in the flor adoun."

What he is presented with is precisely what readers of Ovid would expect, the hubbub of thousands of speakers, listeners and conveyors of gossip. Among them, in particular, are travellers and people with other mobile occupations, who, as rumour-mongers, pass on news and gossip, people such as seamen, pilgrims, pardoners, hawkers, envoys, messengers and runners. "Whan oon had herd a thing, ywis, / He com forth ryght to another wight, / And gan him tellen anon-ryght / The same that to him was told." Thus does gossip change and increase, until finally it forces its way out into the open through a window or gap. "Thus saugh I fals and soth compouned / Togeder fle for oo tydynge." This transfer of information links the House of Fame with that of Fama.

The poet is silent about precisely what the true and false words look like, whether they have wings, what colour they are. He sets to work fulfilling the purpose of his visit, to collect material for his poetry, that is to say, gossip, tittle-tattle, love stories. These are traded in a recess of the hall, to which those present are drawn. It is the communicative centre of this uncentred architecture.

> And everych cried, "What thing is that?"
> And somme sayd, "I not never what."
> And whan they were alle on an hepe,
> Tho behynde begunne up lepe,
> And clamben up on other faste,
> And up the nose and yën kaste,
> And troden fast on others heles,
> And stampen, as men doon aftir eles.[136]

In the centre of all this gossip Chaucer locates the master of the House of Fame; he gets ready to describe him: "Atte laste y saugh a man". Yet he at once breaks off from this. This figure eludes his observer, he writes, the man is one "Which that y [nevene] nat ne kan". He is a shadowy being, one who makes a striking impression. "But he semed for to be / A man of gret auctorite." That is not much. But before the reader learns more about the spectre in the airy House of Fama, about the enigmatic man of high authority, the poem abruptly comes to an end. At least, none of the manuscripts upon which the modern editions of Chaucer are based offers more satisfactory conclusions to this dream-allegory of anonymity; perhaps The House of Fame was never finished? Whatever the case, the text provides evidence for the decisive change in the semantics of the allegory of Fama. Since the fourteenth century her figure has been – despite several illustrations of Fama to accompany Virgil's Dido episode – above all a symbol of renown.

The Land of Tapestry

On the part of the rumour, this shift leaves behind a systematic loophole. Chaucer's apparition is an empty shell. It has no name, nor does the house of rumour, and the unknown person who leads the poet there from the palace of Fama also remains nameless. In a similarly cryptic way Alexander Pope will, in his rendering of the *House of Fame*, introduce in this place "some power unknown".[137] Somebody speaks, yet nobody knows who. That is the fundamental principle of hearsay. Yet other allegorical figurations as a consequence take on attributes and functions of Fama. Within the literary-iconographic cosmos of the Renaissance and Baroque they symbolise aspects of the rumour and hearsay. What they have in common with the allegory of Fama is that they provide an answer for the loophole in the system of the rumour; this loophole is a result of hearsay's only ever consisting of mediated talk; the "people" cited are always absent.

Some of these figures indicate the extent of the Europe-wide dissemination of similar cultural strategies. They are doubles of Fama; they hail from various medial contexts: the following examples are from a Roman, an iconographic and a theatrical context.

The first substitution is a figure from a novel which its author presents as a *chronique* or *histoire*. It lives, like Chaucer's dream figure, in a literarily remote and therefore mythologically central realm at the Mediterranean Sea. This region, named the "Land of Tapestry",[138] is home to a colourfully allegorical and mythological range of characters: Triton with the great shell, "Glaucus, Proteus, Nereus, and countless other gods and monsters of the sea. We also saw an infinite number of fish of different kinds, dancing, flying, jumping, fighting, eating, breathing, copulating, hunting, skirmishing, laying ambushes, making truces, bargaining, swearing, and sporting." Apart from these there appear Aristotle and, "like a bailiff's bulldogs", around five hundred other philosophers. Faced with this strange population, François Rabelais, in the fifth book of their adventure, at once sends his forever hungry heroes, Gargantua and Pantagruel, on a search for something edible. While doing this they come across the embodiment of hearsay.

"While searching this land, therefore, to see if we could find any food, we heard a strident and confused noise, like that of women washing linen or the clappers of the mills at Bascale, near Toulouse. Without delay we went over to the place where it came from and saw a little old hunchback, all misshapen and monstrous. His name was Hearsay, and

Illustration for Rabelais, *Gargantua and Pantagruel*

his mouth was slit to the ears. In his throat were seven tongues, and each tongue was slit into seven parts. Nevertheless he spoke on different subjects and in different languages, with all seven at the same time."[139] Babel mixes itself up with hearsay. To this are added attributes of Fama: "He had also, spread over his head and the rest of his body, as many ears as Argus of old had eyes. But, for the rest, he was blind and his legs were paralysed." Rabelais is playing with allusions to Virgil's Fama; unlike her, though, his old man is blind and lame; what he lacks, others have:

> Around him I saw innumerable men and women listening to him attentively, and amongst the group I recognized several with very important looks, among them one who held a chart of the world and was explaining it to them succinctly, in little aphorisms. Thus they

became clerks and scholars in no time, and spoke in choice language – having good memories – about a host of tremendous matters, which a man's whole lifetime would not be enough for him to know a hundredth part of.[140]

There follows a catalogue of travel writers and historians from antiquity and early modernity: Herodotus takes pride of place in this gallery of hearsay or, better, of hearwrite, in which such authors as Thucydides and Tacitus do not appear. Instead we find Pliny and Philostratus among others from antiquity, Albertus Magnus and Pope Pius II, Marco Polo and other authors "and I do not know how many other modern historians, hiding behind a piece of tapestry and stealthily writing down the grandest stuff – and all from Hearsay."[141]

In the sixteenth century, the wondrous and the strange are an essential part of the real world. At a time in which just about everything was considered possible,[142] Rabelais delivers a polemic against some of the corner-stones of the image of the world then current among his contemporaries. The descriptions of journeys to the New World and other corners of the planet not only speak of new markets but also demonstrate how these places served as undreamed-of areas of projection for collective fantasies. Where only a little is verifiable, hearsay comes into its own, and a map draw by rumours is something even the blind can read. This era has yet to define the difference between news and rumour, for the approximate and uncertain contaminate every message from a world continuously growing while at the same time getting ever smaller.

Long after this, youthful newspaper culture is still getting to grips with the modalities of broadcasting by taking a good look at the model of the rumour. Thus some newspapers call themselves *Couriers*, "because they run from one town, indeed (as is usual with lies and confabulation,) from one house to another ... . Instead of postmen there were in olden times couriers or runners, whose written or oral little delivery thereupon was called a courier or running newspaper, a running rumour."[143] For as long as there are neither criteria nor possibilities for checking written rumour, this writing will remain the pendant of its oral sister.

The world of news in those days appears as a cosmos of autopoeis, "a world of the approximate", the "Kingdom of Hearsay".[144] This is what the old man with the seven tongues split into seven and the ears on his body stands for. With its attributes borrowed from the figure of Fama, it symbolises her fictional potency, something presented as real. The satirically intimated currency of the mythological and allegorical demonstrates the power of myth at that time. The satire serves a sceptical procedure, and the allegorical old man Hearsay shifts the horizon of the hidden somewhat further out into the universe of the approximate.

This is true not only for history, rather also in law. Polemically the "little old hunchback"[145] Hearsay stands for the dilemma between bearing witness and dishonesty in court: "Behind a piece of velvet embroidered with leaves of dupe's-mint, I saw, close to Hearsay, a great number of men from Perche and Maine, good students and fairly young", the narrator explains. "When we inquired what branch of learning they were studying, we were told that ever since their youth they had been learning to be witnesses, and that they profited so well by their instruction that when they left this place and returned to their own provinces, they lived honestly by the trade of bearing witness. For they would give sworn evidence on any subject to whoever would pay them the highest wage by the day – and all this from Hearsay." As an allegory of judicial and historical autopoeis, as a personification of Herodotus' "I record whatever is told to me as I have heard it",[146] the system of hearsay knows no bounds. It can extend in time and into real or imaginary space. The attempt to exercise any form of control over it is difficult. For everywhere it conjures up its own reality with ever new, indiscernible witnesses. The poetical image of the miscreated old man in the Land of Tapestry symbolises the aporia of hearsay, that everyone is saying it and yet nobody can confirm it.

Rumore

The man appears muscular, fit to fight. Focused and attentive, he is standing upon uneven ground; he looks as if he is waiting for something. He is identified as "Rumore", a short text that accompanies his image speaks of an armed man, an "Huomo armato".[147] He makes his entrance at the beginning of the seventeenth century in various editions of Cesare Ripa's *Iconology*, that is to say, in that great compendium in which the writers and engravers of the Renaissance and Baroque assemble antiquity's inventory of myths for the use of "speakers, poets, painters, sculptors, illustrators and other studies".[148] This extensive catalogue of myth forms the standard iconographic archive of its time. It informs of the great historical and literary dimensions of different material and motifs, and supplies the data for a cartography of the antique mythical universe. A commentary on antiquity, they construct a new, mythological horizon for the contemporary knowledge of an international public.[149]

R   V   M   O   R   E .

P p   Picrio

Cesare Ripa, *Rumore* (1669)

The figure of Rumore appears therefore in an archive of the "mémoire mythique". In this context, the ensemble of images and adjoined texts forms something like an iconographic arrest warrant. It gives hints as to the mythical and ethical implications of this figure. Rumore stands for danger. The word stands for insurrection; it means not only what is signified by the modern word "rumour", that is to say, a spreading or swift piece of news, rather at the same time the "situation that arises when the individual speakers and bearers are physically present in one place and have gathered into a crowd".[150]

This personification of seething unrest wears a short, flimsy garment under which can be seen a light cuirass. Rumore has a helmet and a beard; he is heavily-built, the strong legs look ready to propel him forward or to have him move in defence. The slight turn of his body gives the figure dynamism and direction; the half-open left hand at the right edge of the picture makes him look as if he is fully concentrated, and seems to indicate where he is to aim the arrows he is holding in his

FAMA CHIARA.
Nella Medaglia di Antinoo.

VNA

Cesare Ripa, *Fama Chiara* (1669)

raised right hand; the picture does not contain the bow to which they might belong. Nevertheless Rumore appears alert, ready to deliver or defend against a blow, standing in wait between attack and defence, prepared for anything.

His significance is first revealed when he is put into context, that is to say, when he is set against a figure from the same iconology: an image of Fama Chiara copied from a medal. Playing the part of Fama one here finds Mercury, naked, leading Pegasus, a creature which is itself a symbol of news and of speed. The figure is heading towards the left-hand border of the picture, and therefore looks, if one puts the two portraits together (something that involves skipping across the many pages of the book which separate them), as if he is heading straight for Rumore.

While Rumore radiates the tension of a warrior ready for battle, the figure of good reputation expresses relaxed movement: Pegasus rears up boisterously, his tail blowing in the wind, his wings spread, and Fama is also, as Mercury, winged at the head and the heels. In his left hand he is holding a winged herald's staff. These two images show how the Renaissance translates the different dimensions of the antique concept of the rumour. What for a time came together in Fama, the dangerous and pleasant sides of news, is here, in the iconology, split into two figures. If one places them next to each other one can see how much each concept, that of antiquity and that of the Renaissance, is determined by its cultural context. Chaucer dreams of two houses, that of renown and that of rumour; the Renaissance eliminates the virtual ambiguity of Latin Fama in favour of a clear separation of the two principles of rumour and reputation. Only from the historical distance of the Middle Ages and Renaissance is the individuality of the antique patterns of signification definable. "Rumour" is only a part of what the Romans understood by Fama. However, some of her attributes: wings, feathers, ears, eyes, mouths, her power itself, can disconnect themselves from the figure of Fama and travel over to other, related concepts. Like rumours themselves, the images of them are also of historical significance.

Rumor's Cloak

Among the semiotic systems, the theatre has always had a special significance. It is considered a "paradigmatic institution" because the signs it uses are always signs of signs. Not only are the fundamental elements of the theatre public, but also the view onto it. The publicity of the theatre is representative. What relevance this has to the rumour is demonstrated by a bit-part actor of the Elizabethan theatre, an unimportant, minor character who nevertheless inhabits his own, special referential framework. Whether on a great stage or in a small provincial theatre, whenever a messenger was required by the plot, the authors and actors of the time could rely upon an established theatrical convention, which today no longer exists, the figure of Rumor. By this the audiences of the day understood a figure whose costume, either because of its colour, or by means of needle, thread and a little colourful material, was attributed with certain characteristics. The costumers and actors of sixteenth- and seventeenth-century England styled Rumor's garments along the lines sketched out by Virgil. The Renaissance thereby did not just adopt antique knowledge simply as canonical cultural tradition. They understood – and used – it much more as a repertoire of aesthetic and philosophical models for political and social questions, at least, as far as the rumour was concerned.

For the wedding of the Earl of Somerset, King James I's favourite, and Lady Frances Howard in 1614, Thomas Campion writes a play, a singspiel and dance according to the tastes of the day. In the presence of king, queen and prince, the noble guests of the bride and groom and the male relatives of the bride appear as allegorical figures; they play music and sing various songs honouring the soon-to-be-married couple. Since "satyres, nymphes, and their like"[151] have gone out of fashion, the poets of the time have to reorient themselves, something acknowledged by the author. His play falls under the genre of masque. Décor, costume and a luxurious stage setting make up, Ben Jonson remarked polemically, the essence of this type of theatre.[152] Despite its being relatively static, not to say boring, a masque such as Thomas Campion's stands at the centre of a complex framework of symbolic references. Some of them also concern the representation of the rumour. In Campion's masque there appear all manner of allegorical figures, among them the four winds, the elements and the four continents.

The dramatic conflict, if that is the right word, of the masque develops from the contrast of these allegories with a competing force, the dark principle which disrupts the harmony of nature. This is represented by four "curst enchanters",[153] of whom it is said: "these, these alone / Turne all the world into confusion." To these belong: Credulity, whose costume and cap is painted with ears; Curiosity, who wears a coat "full of eyes" and corresponding headgear; Error, in a scaled costume decorated with snakes; and, the fourth, Rumor. He wears "a skin coate full of winged Tongues, and ouer it an antick robe; on his head a Cap like a tongue, with a large paire of wings to it".

Costumes like these indicate the specific allegorical references of their wearers. Campion and his actors could take it for granted that all would see and recognise Rumor as Rumor. These costumes were requisites of the allegories that appeared in Elizabethan theatre as characters. "The Eyed, the Eared, and the Nosed"[154] is the description of Rumor's companions in another play. Already in the decades before this piece of wedding theatre, costumers were dressing Rumor in garments decorated with tongues for his entrance onto the stages of England. With fitting gestures and movements, the actors could also do their bit to emphasise what these figures stood for. They could be sure that their audience had the same iconographic horizon as they themselves, a horizon such as no longer exists today.[155]

Campion put on his singspiel and dance right in the heart of the City of Westminster, in the Banqueting House of the Palace of Whitehall inspired by the architecture of Palladio and built by Inigo Jones. The special occasion and the noble audience, that is to say, obvious social factors, emphasised the representative character of the stage onto which Rumor made his entrance that evening. The conflict between good and evil took place on a divided stage; while the lower, front part of the stage contained a victory arch, the raised, rear part of the stage represented the "state". The scenic hierarchy represented a social order which also included nature, a lake with "ships, some cunningly painted",[156] a forest and a "beautifull garden", among other things.

In a space as scenically and socially loaded as this one, everything points to another level of meaning. But what did the powerful, the rulers of England *see* when there appeared before their eyes a man in a costume of tongues with small wings on his head?

It may be that Campion, with his figure of Rumor, was inspired by the figure of Rumour which makes its entrance in 1598/1600 at the beginning of Part Two of Shakespeare's *Henry IV*. Here it summarises the events of the first part of the drama,[157] and does so erroneously, thereby triggering some dramatic complications. Shakespeare's figure appears "painted full of tongues"[158] in front of Northumberland's castle and gives a description of itself which is representative of how the rumour was understood at that time:

Open your ears, for which you will stop
The vent of hearing when loud Rumour speaks?
I, from the orient to the drooping west,
Making the wind my post-horse, still unfold
The acts commencèd on this ball of earth.
Upon my tongues continual slanders ride,
The which in every language I pronounce,
Stuffing the ears of men with false reports.
I speak of peace while covert enmity,
Under the smile of safety, wounds the world;
And who but Rumour, who but only I,
Make fearful musters, and prepared defence,
Whiles the big year, swollen with some other grief,
Is thought with child by the stern tyrant War,
And no such matter? Rumour is a pipe
Blown by surmises, jealousies, conjectures,
And of so easy and so plain a stop

That the blunt monster with uncounted heads,
The still-discordant wavering multitude,
Can play upon it. But what need I thus
My well-known body to anatomize
Among my household? Why is Rumour here?[159]

Thus begins the induction. And there follows the intricate nature of the rumour: "The posts come tiring on / And not a man of them brings other news / Than they have learnt of me. From Rumour's tongues / They bring smooth comforts false, worse than true wrongs." The theatrical figure Rumour not only attempts to clarify events, but also brings dramatic irony into play. Thanks to Rumour, the audience knows more than do the dramatis personae. The well-known traits from antiquity can be seen once again: the tongues that stem from Virgil, the personified qualities that point back to Ovid's House of Fama, and the relationship to wind and air. Yet Shakespeare does not attempt to point his audience in the direction in which the allusions point. On the contrary: his Rumour, although an allegorical pointer to antiquity, relates concretely to the times of the play. The "blunt monster with uncounted heads" is the multitude, the crowd, in which Rumour also includes the audience in the theatre.

To this sort of "household" belongs also the fine public at Campion's singspiel for the wedding of the noble couple; while the royal family watched personified rumour, a certain man may well have stood in the background who himself was the subject of many rumours and, as Attorney-General, had entrance to the elite circles: Francis Bacon. Among the things that were said about him and continued to be said after his death was the contention that he personally composed Shakespeare's works. There is now no way of knowing whether he was actually there; the guest list no longer exists. He is not mentioned on the theatre programme and therefore appears not to have condescended to appear in Campion's play as did his compeers. But he would have enjoyed seeing Rumor on stage in his tongue costume and winged cap.

For the well-known intellectual and supremely loyal statesman had himself, five years before the entrance of Rumor in Whitehall, produced his own description of Fama. With this description he presented to an educated audience what Shakespeare, with his Rumour, had, since the turn of the century, been prescribing to the masses.

In his *Wisdom of the Ancients*, written in Latin, a contemporising reading of the mythology of antiquity, Bacon marks out the mythological horizon of Roman Fama. Until well into the nineteenth century the English word "fame" meant both renown and rumour, reputation and gossip. *The Wisdom of the Ancients* mainly discusses the possibility of achieving and securing political dominance through insight into the nature of man and society. As is often the case also in his scientific writings, Bacon proceeds by analogy, searching for the "similarities and analogies of things, both in whole things and in their parts":[160]

> By the Earth is signified the nature of the vulgar, always swollen and malignant, and still broaching new scandals against superiors, and having gotten fit opportunity, stirs up rebels, and seditious persons, that with impious courage do molest princes, and endeavour to subvert their estates, but being suppressed, the same natural disposition of the people still leaning to the viler sort, being impatient of peace and tranquillity, spread rumours, raise malicious slanders, repining whisperings, infamous libels, and others of that kind, to the detraction of them that are in authority; so as rebellious actions, and seditious reports, differ nothing in kind and blood, but as it were in sex only, the one sort being masculine, the other feminine.[161]

The rumour is an enemy of the state, the opponent of order. Everything would suggest that the royal family, on their visit to the theatre at the wedding reception for the Somersets, would have had just such an enemy of the state in mind when they saw the actor dressed as Rumor upon the stage. The sixteenth century was a century of popular unrest, revolts and uprisings, of the strenuous consolidation of royal power.[162] And the unsuccessful rebellion of the Earl of Essex in February 1601 gave Elizabeth I, who directly preceded James I, a real taste of fear. Before he published his digression about Fama in his *Wisdom of the Ancients*, the lawyer Francis Bacon, experienced in criminal matters and the business of the secret services, had at the behest of the queen, undertaken and won proceedings concerning high treason against his former patron, Essex. The death of Essex led to unrest and rumours, and Bacon himself gained dubious renown for his role in the demise of his young sponsor. When Bacon therefore wrote of the rumour as a form of "rebellious actions", there was a concrete political reference which all could understand.

In the English edition of *The Wisdom of the Ancients*, which appeared five years after this wedding reception, further groups had the opportunity of becoming familiar with this interpretation of the rumour as a ferment of sedition. It is a pity that a later treatment by Bacon of the same theme, an essay entitled *Of Fame*, remained fragmentary. As far as can be ascertained from looking at what was actually produced, he intended to systematise his thoughts on the rumour begun in the

The Many-headed Mass-murderer (England 1603)

Wisdom of the Ancients, expanding upon this book and producing a form of Machiavellian treatise. "Rebels, figured by the giants", he writes in 1609, taking up his previous line of thinking again, "and seditious fames and libels, are but brothers and sisters, masculine and feminine … wherefore let all wise governors have as great a watch and care over fames, as they have of the actions and designs themselves".[163] In the theatre this sister of sedition wears a tongue costume and winged cap, and King James I and his family will have noticed with satisfaction that they were not brushed by Rumor's cloak.

For the entrance of Rumor and his companions would have signified for the holder of worldly and ecclesiastical power in the kingdom not just an entertaining hour in the theatre. For a moment they played a part in a complex symbolic event: for Rumor is not just a theatrical figure costumed according to theatrical convention. In the reference system called theatre he represents the completely concrete "seditious" word as the brother of rebellious action. For a brief moment, perhaps between red wine and dessert, James I may have sensed the other, absent aspect of this play, and may have thought of the Earl of Essex as the paradigmatic rebel, whose brother is Rumor, the talk of the crowd, that "blunt monster with uncounted heads".

Campion does not let the entrance of Rumor last too long. Other allegorical figures appear, among them Eternity and Harmony, the latter accompanied by nine musicians; they expel Rumor and his conspiratorial entourage in order to re-establish the divine order, the order which the noble audience in Whitehall viewed as the true one.

However, this horizon of historical meaning is not fixed; it doubles in size if one views it from the point of view of Bacon's fragmentary essay. Like other essays, *Of Fame* is situated within the context of a compendium of the possibilities available to a statesman. Considering the sharp instincts of its author concerning issues of power, one can be certain that Bacon laid great worth in gaining recognition in the highest circles. That he does not merely stop at criticising rumours, also supports this. For he goes on to transport its mythical embodiment into an entirely new context: "But now if a man can tame this monster, and bring her to feed at the hand, and govern her, and with her fly other ravening fowl and kill them, it is somewhat worth."[164] In the hands of rulers, myths can become weapons.

Looked at in this way, the entrance of Rumor in Whitehall gains a second meaning. The sister of the giants threatens not only the divine order through the voice of the mob. Even if she is the sister of all the Earls of Essex on the earth, she can still be tamed. Falconry is the sophisticated art of hunting with hawks, a privilege of the privileged, an elaborate expression of social distance. This is the subordinate meaning of Bacon's political critique of rumour. Whoever knows how to use it has at his disposal what lawyers refer to as "power of decision", historians merely as "power". In Campion's singspiel, the figures of Eternity and Harmony quickly end the play of the dark forces and return the world to its divinely determined state. But Bacon, for one, knows that the magnificent set before which they act out their parts is the same one behind which Rumor is forever hovering, waiting for his cue.

Campion's figure with the winged cap, Rumore with his two arrows in Ripa's Iconology, the old man Hearsay – each of these figures, each of these images could be put in the place of the apparition which appears in Chaucer. Apart from a few external features, these sketches no longer have much in common with the Fama of renown. In different historical and medial contexts, in the theatre, as a drawing or in a novel, they sketch out historical experience with the aid of classical allegorical attributes. They symbolise, each in its own way, the phenomenon of polyphonic, anonymous talk which belongs to rumour. What is particularly apparent is the paradox of hearsay, expressed by Shakespeare with his "blunt monster with uncounted heads, / The still-discordant wavering multitude". Like the multitude, the rumour is one voice and many voices at the same time, a "pipe / Blown by surmises, jealousies, conjectures".

A wood-engraving from the time of Bacon and Shakespeare depicts this paradoxical speaker of the rumour, the multitude, the crowd, that relative of sedition, as a figure with strong legs and wings on its feet and hips. Instead of an upper body, a multitude of people grows from its waist. Beneath a sky in which an eye, an ear and a hand symbolise divine power, an inscription identifies this grotesque being: "The Swifte, Sharpe, Poysonable Tongued Monster of many heads that deuouereth men." This is perhaps what Chaucer's unnameable man at the end of his House of Fame may have looked like.

Whether King James I actually found himself thinking of the Earl of Essex or of the rumours circulating about himself when he saw the figure of Rumor in Campion's masque, nobody can know. However, what is certain is that Rumor appeared within a historically relatively stable and generally understandable symbolic reference system. In this system "real events" such as the rebellion of one Robert Devereux, Earl of Essex, appear as if they were merely metaphors in a mythically exaggerated reality. For whoever understands how to listen to and see power will see the "Tongued Monster" as a tameable bird of prey. In an age preoccupied with a new, rational conception of power, a conception that owed much to Nicolo Machiavelli, allegories such as Chaucer's man without a name no longer appear merely as ciphers for the multitude and their gossip, rather at the same time as pointers for those who steer.

Lucien Febvre believed that the "Kingdom of Hearsay" lost its power sometime in the eighteenth century. After centuries of unverifiable "as I have heard it" there arose a general expectancy of verifiable criteria, of comparability, of accepted standards. The beginning of this revolution of scientific paradigms is often associated with the work of Francis Bacon. It is ironic therefore that this advance of the rational against hearsay, this struggle against Fama, the sister of the giants, is a struggle for political hegemony. Power also implies the deliberately exercised control of the voice of rumour. The rationality of this control serves Bacon's interpretation of the myth of Fama. For whoever masters the social technology of the rumour, whoever can speak with the voice of hearsay, with the voice of the loophole, has mastered the high art of mastering. It is the art of being able to say something without being identified as the author, the art of being someone who can drive a stake into the eye of an opponent while remaining the one who remains without name.

4
Antiquity 1917: Modernity and Warfare

The Spy from Braisne – Colonisers of the Imagination – Censorship – The Zone of Myth Formation

The young volunteer hardly had any chance of avoiding the carnage. Naïve and inexperienced, he stumbled through the battlefield, which was shaking from the most modern technologies of war. Of what surrounded him he understood nothing. Yet still some form of guardian angel seemed to be hovering over him, taking care of him: "In vain did he look in the direction the shot was coming from, he could see the white smoke of the battery a great distance away and, amid the regular, continuous booming produced by the cannonade, he thought he could make out some volleys that were much closer", writes Henry Boyle, alias Stendhal, about the entrance of his hero Fabrizio del Dongo into the battle of Waterloo. "He could not begin to understand what was going on."[165]

In the battle scenes of *The Charterhouse of Parma*, Stendhal intensifies and ironises his own experience of the dilemma of witnesshood in war. What does the participant in battle experience of war? The author himself had travelled with Napoleon's army, right into the heart of the action. "From noon until 3 O'clock in the afternoon we saw everything that is to be seen of a battle, that is to say: nothing", he notes in his diary at Bauzen. War and battle have always drawn back from objective description.

The experience of this Stendhalian paradox, namely understanding "nothing" and seeing "nothing", and yet still actually being there, was something familiar, a century later, to the soldiers in the trenches of the First World War. The less they experienced, the closer they were to

81

the "actual" events of the war, the nearer they were to the battle, and the smaller, more haphazard and more personal seemed their experiences in their memories. Whoever was there had suffered; he had seen "everything, that is to say: nothing". This is the ground upon which the narrative interpretation of battles and history goes into action; the "witness of battle"[166] is also its interpreter. The soldiers knew this only too well, and many must have felt like the comrades in suffering of the hero of Stendhal's novel. "Was what he had seen a battle?" the convalescing Fabrizio asks in Amiens, after he has been brushed by the filthy hem of the cloak of world history: "And was that battle Waterloo?"[167]

The reality of the trenches exceeded the possibilities of explanation. Despite a mountain of descriptions of war and reports from battles, the great conflicts produce silence, a narrative vacuum. "Was it not noticed how, at the end of the war, the soldiers returned struck dumb from the field? not richer, but poorer of recountable experience", Walter Benjamin wrote in 1936 about the shock of the Great War: "What poured out ten years later, in the flood of war books, was everything other than the experience which travels from mouth to mouth. And this was not particularly odd. For never have experiences been shown to be more utterly false than the experience of strategy by trench warfare, the experience of economics by inflation, physical experience by battle of matériel, and moral experience by those in power."[168] And the fundamental problem of history would never be as clearly described as it was after this war, this "turning point in the history of the lie":[169] that each individual witness brings a fundamental lack of focus into the description of war and battle.

"An event lasts a couple of seconds, and the human faculties are not capable of recording all its fleeting phases as would a film camera. Each witness completes instinctively and in his own way the series, which is only partially grasped. He fills in the blanks and from then on forgets that there were ever any blanks in the first place. He then really does believe he saw everything he describes",[170] writes one of the great archivists of this war, Jean Norton Cru, about the problem of the witness. Man is a few steps behind the possibilities afforded him by his technology; he will never be as exact in his descriptions as the film camera. After he had evaluated more than two hundred and fifty personal accounts of the trenches by French soldiers, he saw it as "almost impossible to find just two accounts among thirty that even approximately resembled one another".[171] He saw the reason for this as lying in some form of Stendhalian paradox. His fellow soldiers during the war felt similar. They thought of Fabrizio del Dongo, whose adventure they

Vicenzo Cartari, Book Illustration (1647)

read at school. They knew that the reality they were experiencing was a part of the irreality which their generals, with the help of field telephone and aerial photography, held to be the "actual" course and "true" description of the battle.

This is the fundamental problem of the writing of the history of wars, wars in which rumours always play a role. A drawing from the seventeenth century shows the god of war Mars in his chariot, pulled by four horses, his lance jutting obliquely forwards. A small, winged female figure supports herself on the shaft of the weapon; in her left hand she holds a bow and some arrows. It is Fama, the companion of war. Wings and weapon symbolise speed and power; as the companion of the terrifying god she plays a part in his violence. The picture symbolises what a German phrase suggests, that "when war enters a land, lies appear like sand." This is just as true of Nicias' battle at sea in Sicily as it is for the Napoleonic campaigns or for the modern wars of the twentieth century. War creates that mixture of danger and insecurity with which questions, speculation and news can spread through whole regions and populations in the form of rumours. This is also a consequence of the particularly rigid control of information: "The state [in war] demands of its citizens the utmost obedience and sacrifice", Sigmund Freud writes in 1915, continuing: "However, it incapacitates them with an excess of secrecy and censorship, which makes them, intellectually oppressed in this way, defenceless against every unfavourable situation and every wild rumour."[172] The war creates rumours – but what do these rumours say about war?

The Spy from Braisne

September 1917: the European war is already being called a World War. The soldiers at the front, in the trenches, and in the rear are exhausted; the war is eating away at their nerves. Near the French village of La Malmaison the French army is planning an advance against German positions. North of the village of Braisne, in the department of Aisne, one of their infantry regiments waits for the call to enter battle. Yet the commanders do not yet know enough about the strength and formation of the enemy troops; and therefore they give the order for prisoners to be captured. Under the cover of artillery fire, the infantry mounts a surprise raid, attacking and seizing a German forward position in the village of Épine-de-Chevregny. They capture a German soldier. An intelligence officer asks the first question and learns that the reservist comes from Bremen; he is a "bourgeois de la vielle hanséatique de Brême", perhaps a shopkeeper of little note. The man is taken to the rear for further questioning – an everyday occurrence, nothing remarkable; the war goes on.

Yet the incident has an epilogue, albeit a short one, which the officer describes after the war. For not long after the capture of the soldier from Bremen, stories begin to circulate among the French soldiers about their dangerous and sophisticated enemy: "Those Germans! Such organisation! They had their spies everywhere", they exclaim. "We capture one in Épine-de-Chevregny; and what do we find? Someone who back in peacetime, being a shopkeeper, set himself up just a couple of kilometres from here, in Braisne."[173] Bremen, Brême, Braisne – in French this mix-up is easily made, for the *s* in Braisne is silent. If the unfamiliar, distant city in Germany is transformed into the similarly named village which is both familiar and close by, when circumstances suit this new version, then this helps explain not only the irrationality of the war but also the strength of the other side. What an enemy!

The officer reporting all this does not tell his story in order to demonstrate how lazily his fellow soldiers listened to what was said. Rather, he is trying to draw attention to the "travail d'interprétation"[174] which necessarily accompanies every act of perception, in the dangerous everyday reality of war as much as in the writing of history. This analogy does not come about by chance, for the officer who tells the story of the spy of Braisne is the great French historian Marc Bloch. As an historian and officer, he understands that for both social scientist and military man it is a question of indicating sources – whether they consist of historical documents or of questionable reports about German prisoners.[175] Bloch described what the paradigmatic power of uncertainty meant in modernity: the "crisis of the witness",[176] the end of the attempt to authenticate the historical by turning to an actual participant.

In 1921, three years after the end of the war, his *Réflexions d'un historien sur les fausses nouvelles de la guerre* appear, the sum of the experiences of an officer and historian. More than just a personal diary, these observations on the problem of the historical witness turn the attention of interpretative history to the issue of hearsay in war. Bloch compares his own activity as an historian to that of a "juge d'instruction", an "investigating magistrate",[177] and, as an information officer, he sees the rumours, horror stories and war myths not merely as phenomena peripheral to the military conflict, but also as circumstantial evidence and as the psychological-historical centre of the war. For the historian, war becomes the "laboratory" of history, since he can observe here the fundamental historiographic dilemma: namely that the increasing proximity of a witness to events threatens to render his account of those events less focused. "There are no good witnesses."[178] On the other hand, the experience in this "laboratory" represents a challenge for the historian. He makes no progress with the usual hermeneutic procedure of his profession, for the stories which rage in the trenches and beyond them, products of the "collective imagination",[179] give the urgent questions only symbolic answers, rather than the reliable information they demand. Only when they are viewed as symptoms of an insecurity brought about by censorship, fear and propaganda can the historian even begin to make sense of these often strange, puzzling or exaggerated stories from out of the darkness of battle. As with dreams in psychoanalysis, many of these stories also appear to have a hidden meaning, one which is lost on superficial listeners. What is close, history as it is forming, creates its own problems of mediation.

This complicates work with witnesses. At the same time it must also be remembered that many of these witnesses are themselves not "fixed", but rapidly change. For the war conducted with canons is also a war of words and rumours, with most of these originating in the immediate vicinity of the lines of battle. With his description of war as the "laboratory" of history, Bloch reveals, as Ulrich Raulff has shown, a further horizon. He suggests a new role for the historian and a new aim for history, one directed at the future. For the analogy of research and war, of historical and military activity, suggested by the word "laboratory", encompasses "an intellectual practice which promised a new way of going about acquiring knowledge: pragmatic, experimental, determined by the present, directed towards the future".[180] This represents a new conception of history; the investigation of the past and that of the present enrich one another in terms of subject and methodology. The historian begins today to unravel yesterday, and, as a mediator, reconstructs from its historical roots the genesis of the contemporary world.

The spy of Braisne was not the only inhabitant of the imaginary spaces at and behind the front. Whoever reads around in soldiers' letters, accounts of battles, war memoirs and diaries, which from 1914 on flooded the European book market, gains an impression of the way in which "fausses nouvelles" could grow into widespread and persistent rumours. While folklorists, social scientists, veterans and collectors go about sieving through the narrative material of the war, a great intellectual and archival endeavour also begins. It has been decided that the narrated war is to be transferred from the fragmentary storehouse of individual memories to a single, collective memory.

Yet the archivists of the Great War know only too well the Stendhalian paradox: The Battle of the Marne, for example, was "hardly more than an abstraction" [181] for those who had a bird's-eye view of it, writes Jean Norton Cru after looking at the witness accounts. Like the proponents of the still young history of thought, this veteran and critical archivist of the Great War also thought that "grand history" should concentrate less on strategic questions and more on other, previously neglected factors, on the "pain, fear, anger, hatred, longing, opinions and philosophy of war"[182] of front-line soldiers; he believed that these had been listened to the least in previous historical analyses of war. After the fighting had ended, the strategic and tactical aspects of the war remained the main focus of attention for historians. Yet historians also began to pay much attention to the history to be found beneath the surface of this "grand history". And the earliest beginnings of this interest are to be found with the likes of Bloch and Cru and their accounts of the rumour in war.

For despite the fundamental historiographic difficulties, historians and veterans on both sides of the Rhine, as well as in other countries, begin to develop this inexhaustible and overflowing "histoire des bruits de la guerre". Some of them, as they go about their work, have in mind a universal history of the rumour.[183] In Germany the work looks back to the initiatives of William Stern, whose research on the psychology of the witness represented the beginnings of social-scientific study of the rumour.[184] This investigation of rumours in war makes use of the most varied sources: the often extremely precise entries in diaries written in the field, the war memoirs which were published in great numbers in all the countries which took part in the war, the accounts of officers and common soldiers, and also the vast literature of letters home. In doing so, the historians of hearsay bring to light the countless *false tales* and *fausses nouvelles*, horror stories, "war fairy tales"[185] and strange rumours, which – usually for only a short time – whole towns, regions or nations believed.

Colonisers of the Imagination

And so to the invasion of the United Kingdom by the Russians. In August and September 1914, shortly after the outbreak of war, word begins to circulate in traditionally invasionphobic England that Russian soldiers are moving through the land on their way to Belgium to fight the Germans – an invasion of strange character. They are sighted everywhere, and are even seen kicking snow from their boots on station platforms. In Carlisle and Berwick-on-Tweed they demand vodka, and in Durham they jam a slot machine with a rouble.[186] It is estimated that around a quarter of a million of these round-faced, allied soldiers are travelling through England. They are mentioned in letters written in South Gloucestershire; they are spotted in the railway station at Oxford; from the Isle of Wight they are spotted on their way to the continent. Stubbornly this rumour remains in circulation for a few weeks, and it is clear that it is believed by many.[187] But as quickly as they arrived, the ghostly Russians vanish from the land. The slot machines swallow pennies again, and the landlords in Carlisle can peel the vodka labels off their bottles of whisky. A dream comes to an end, the nightmare of the uncultivated Slavs – or perhaps the projection of a wish for a strong ally?

The contents of the war rumours were mostly pretty brutal. At bottom, they reflected the fears, worries and needs of those affected by war: horror stories were the bread and butter of the times. In England, the nurse Grace Hume became a martyr-icon when it was reported that she had been the victim of alleged German barbarity in Belgium,[188] while in Montreal and Winnipeg the talk was of Canadian officers crucified by Germans. In the rumours that cropped up every day, there were often to be found quasi-religious motifs of martyrdom and salvation. As to the extent of their dissemination, no influence was exerted by the fact of their being shown to be false; quite the opposite, the only thing that determined the "success" or "failure" of these stories was whether they were capable of reflecting, in the form of a story, certain emotions, and of taking their place in the symbolic household of the collective imagination. Figures such as that of Grace Hume reflected the fear of the horrors of war: stereotypical, hard-hitting, producing empathy, in terms of both motif and structure they are paradigmatic examples of war rumours.

Between 1914 and 1918 similar stories crop up all over Europe, like that of the prisoners of war who, in their censored letters home, secretly note on the back of stamps the appalling truth about their plight, writing about cut-off feet, hands and, most often, tongues. Obviously none of these stories survive verification. Nevertheless, very similar anecdotes are told not only in Europe, but also in other parts of the world, such as in South Africa and Singapore.[189] In the Second World War they cropped up again, when horror stories about German soldiers, who were said to have carried out acts of brutality against Belgian infants with bayonets and knives, were just as popular. The more extreme the anecdote, the more stubbornly it remained in circulation. And with the modernisation of technology, these rumours developed further. In the Second World War Germans said of Poles – and Poles of Germans – that they threw babies from planes, and in the Gulf War Iraqi soldiers are said to have gone to work on premature babies in incubators. There is – or at least the trends and twists and turns of stories such as these would appear to suggest this – a form of international and transhistorical folklore of societies in war. Rumours play a special part in this usually grim thesaurus, for the stories of massacres carried out by the enemy, transmitted in hearsay, are particularly suitable for channelling fears and projecting negative emotions. Hearsay is a strategy for overcoming obstacles of communication. And rumours are therefore essential for the emotional economy of war. The psychoanalyst Marie Bonaparte, in her interpretations of just such "war fairy tales" (which are not necessarily false), again and again finds the same violent motifs. They are the mythical background-noise of world history, a murmur which can be heard in the present, as we leave the "century of the machine and the

Leaflet No. 4. For translation see Appendix, page 239.

AEROPLANE DISTRIBUTION OF COPIES OF AN EARLY LEAFLET PREPARED
BY THE FRENCH AUTHORITIES FOR THE GERMAN SOLDIER.

"It is not true" – French Leaflet from the First World War

heard in the present, as we leave the "century of the machine and the aeroplane",[190] just as clearly as it was in the time of Homer.

How do such rumours arise? As with the spy from Braisne, misunderstandings often set the "travail d'interpretation" into motion. And these were certainly the cause of many of the horror stories about German Soldiers which circulated in France, England, Russia and even China during the Great War. Near Koblenz there was said to exist a waste processing plant, the main purpose of which was to process whole shipments of soldiers' corpses into foodstuff for animals and into margarine and chemicals, such as glycerine, required for the production of munitions. Stories like these could easily achieve success because they gave expression to the general fear brought about by the new, industrial barbarity of the war. The origins of this particular rumour are probably to be found in press reports from 1917 about an animal carcass processing plant. An English-speaking journalist translated the German word "Kadaver", which stands exclusively for dead animals, as "corpse", and the rumour took off.[191] In 1925, with this rumour in mind, the American newspaper *Time Dispatch* suggested that in the next war the propaganda was going to have to be more subtle and much smarter if it did not want to appear unbelievable.[192] Rumours are interpretations; in situations of great uncertainty, they seem to offer coherence. Among the German soldiers advancing into Belgium in 1914 it was above all the partisan tactics of the Belgian rear guard which brought about fear and confusion. Often the enemy was not to be seen: ambushes, raids against communication stations and other installations, and swift, targeted guerrilla attacks saw to it that the advance guard of the invading troops found itself being opposed by an invisible civil and military enemy. And because of this, not only the Belgian military, but also the civilian population was transformed into a military opponent. Out of this situation there emanated the countless stories about atrocities committed by Belgian civilians against German soldiers. "The beasts in Belgium", "How I escaped from Belgium" or "From barbarous Belgium" is how soldiers headed their reports, verging on propaganda, from Antwerp and other places during the early stages of the war.[193] Pictures, letters from the front, books and plays also spread word of cut-off fingers and of the martyrdom of the wounded.

Whatever may have triggered these rumours, they led directly to the setting-up in Cologne of an organisation which had only one purpose, this being to take the sting out of one particular war rumour. For in Germany people were not just talking of beautiful, yet fatal, Belgian women who spent their leisure hours snipping off various bits of helplessly wounded German soldiers and plucking out their eyes and putting them in preserving jars.[194] Even the figure of the Catholic priest colonised the social imagination in imperial Germany. Some had heard that Belgian clergymen had incited civilians to commit horrific acts, others even said they had seen papal wearers of the cloth, knives in hand, themselves going about this gruesome work; the German press suspected the machinations of ultramontanists. Perhaps because of memories of the Kulturkampf between church and state in Bismarck's Germany of the 1870s and 1880s, German Catholic clergymen feared that the resentment directed at their Belgian colleagues could end up being directed back at them.

And thus the *Pax-Informationen* was established, a German-Catholic press agency, to go into battle against the rumours. In articles and commentaries it criticised the suspected anti-Catholic motives behind the spreading of these myths, and at the same time attempted to disseminate information which contradicted the horror stories – reports to the contrary, official orders and circulars given out by the army high command, and statements made by politicians.[195] The transnational solidarity of the Catholic clergymen was above suspicion of merely producing propaganda, a suspicion that most denials face at times of war. Yet no estimation exists of the success of this campaign. If today the last surviving veterans in German old people's homes were to tell horror stories about Catholic knives, nobody would believe them. Back then it was different.

These examples might give a sense of the way hearsay goes into overdrive at times of war. Its subjects and concrete circumstances change, its message remains the same, its audience, that is to say participants, also. For it expresses the thoughts and imaginings of entire groups. The rumour is a voice, and it usually makes no difference how exactly, from case to case, a story emerges from a snippet of information, and a rumour from the story. The problem of the human capacity for error is of secondary importance for the rumour. Much more important are the conditions which will allow it to extend in space – that is to say, in a particular social group – and in time.

For it is only the multitude of voices which constitutes the richness and power of the rumour and differentiates it from mere news. Apart from this, most of them are received and passed on as descriptions of curious incidents or as pointed, anecdotal stories, like the rumour of the spy from Braisne, that of Grace Hume and that of the murderous

Belgian priests. The Russians did not make their way quietly through England, rather boisterously poured vodka down their throats in Carlisle, stuffed their roubles into slot machines and stamped snow from their boots on station platforms. This is how rumours inhabit the diffuse space of the collective imagination, forever turning to new, impressible figures and symbols, images and stories; some of these even grow into "war rumours", which straddle national boundaries and often persist for long periods of time.

Censorship

However, some actively provoke rumour myths. The impressive story of the passage of Russians through England has a very real kernel, one which commentators usually overlook in their enthusiasm for the strange rumour. Instead of one hundred or even two hundred and fifty thousand, there were in fact six or seven thousand Russians, who, hailing from the USA or Canada, were stationed in Edinburgh before being transported south and shipped from England to the battlefields of Europe. Fama is not always stranger than the convention referred to as reality. Every English newspaper which suspected that it would almost be more surprising if the rumour were false than if it were true, as some did,[196] understood the fog of hearsay better than then may have been realised. Under pressure from the military censor and massive propaganda, the criteria which, in peacetime, would have been used to verify a piece of news disappear. Hardly anyone remains able to differentiate between rumour and news; and this contributes to the silence of the returning soldiers. For who would believe them?

Attempts were made to interpret the myths and stories of the war psychoanalytically, as if they were dreams. According to these interpretations, particular motifs in these stories conceal deep-seated emotions: the latent dream thoughts of society. Where rumours circulate, there is, if one believes these dream analyses of the social, a shift and intensification which enables the communication of even "forbidden" fears, without at the same time reducing the fighting spirit. Victor Soklovski remembered a rumour about Russian soldiers which, in a way, answered the English rumour about the Russians' passage through the United Kingdom. It transferred the fear of being taken in by propaganda into a grotesque image: "The English had landed a herd of monkeys which had been trained militarily. It was said that these monkeys were immune to propaganda, that they mounted attacks fearlessly and would defeat the Bolsheviks."[197] Only monkeys are immune to gossip and rumours.

War rumours bypass and, at the same time, reflect a double censorship, the official control of information and the turning into taboos of certain emotions. With all this pressure of censorship, the typical motifs of horror and victimhood are stirred up, which Marie Bonaparte in her psychoanalytical study of "war rumours" was one of the first to describe. As interpretations of a diffuse reality, these rumours and stories, for their part, provoke further consideration and interpretation. And because none of these interpretations brings the hermeneutic game to an end, rather drive it on, new versions and variants continually arise. Strictly speaking, when the talk is of rumours, the back-and-forth of these multiple sketches and stories must also be considered. For rumours are not just texts, rather also sequences of varying narrative situations. Series of narratives are transported along them. Decisive for the "success" of a rumour is not just its "plot", rather also its extension in space and time, its speed and the number of people participating in it. At the end of the day, rumours are not literary creations.

And if it is that they react to the censorship of certain information during war, rumours can still not be understood as a medium for information. They do not satisfy the requirement of "prompt verifiability";[198] its authority is of an alien kind and lies in its establishing a realm of everyday story-telling this side of an experience which transcends the possibility of description. This realm is delimited and dynamic: with its motifs it tends to concentrate on several particular subjects; at the same time, however, its narratives lend themselves to being passed on and modified by those who hear them. It is precisely because of their anecdotal, cutting and brusque qualities that war rumours can compensate for the silence of those who have been struck dumb by the inexplicable reality of this war, which Walter Benjamin observed in those returning home. For war rumours are not always just stories of what others have experienced, rather, at the same time, they seem to do away with any need for explanations, as every good story should – they are themselves the explanation. In the spring of 1915 the story spreads throughout England of the miraculous rescue of a British unit in Belgium, near Mons, by angels. German cavalry had just cornered the English soldiers and had begun to charge at them, when suddenly a row of white figures appeared between the attacking cavalry and the exhausted infantry. Completely confused, the Germans paused long enough for the British troops to escape.[199] Some even said they could see how the German horses stamped the ground uneasily when they saw the angels.

The Zone of Myth Formation

But back to the appearance of that other phenomenon, of the spy from Braisne. This and other rumours, believes Marc Bloch, are founded not on one single misunderstanding or the partial deafness of a front-line soldier who was too close to an exploding grenade. They arise much more often from "collective ideas",[200] which require perhaps only a chance event or insubstantial incident as their trigger. Braisne – Brême: it is not difficult to comprehend how the rumour about the Germans' deftness at spying could arise. Like the "fausee nouvelle", for Bloch the rumour is also the mirror in which 'the collective consciousness' sees its own face. This mirror, however, arises, according to Bloch and other witnesses of the time, not in the front lines, rather in a particular area of interpretation behind the front: in the lines further back, made up of field kitchens, logistics units and camp-followers.

For here soldiers with different functions and units meet and swap stories about what is going on at the front. Even the soldier from Bremen questioned by Bloch is brought from the front to these lines. The story about him travels in the other direction; somewhere behind the front he is transformed into "the German spy from Braisne" and then travels with the rest of the supplies and infantry units back to the forward positions – evil, cunning and extremely dangerous.

Thus can one imagine the path of myths and rumours. They come into being before and after the battles and skirmishes, in a "state of permanent curiosity",[201] in the boredom of waiting, where soldiers give up the isolation of the front, where they meet others, where military personnel encounter civilians. In these moments of comparative leisure, what Gottfried Keller observed in a much more peaceful world, the fact that "men who constantly see each other talk each other stupid",[202] also happens in war. Typical war rumours seep out of the soldiers' quarters and out of what Marc Bloch calls the "agora"[203] of the world of the trenches: from field kitchens, letters from the front, soldiers on home leave, and soldiers returning from it then spread throughout the land what rumour's kitchen has prepared, and the press do their bit to supply the land with news of the mythical front.

The First World War was also a war of perfected communications. The generals got their reports of how battles were progressing over the telephone, photographers took pictures of enemy positions from the air and leaflets fell from gas balloons which had been fitted out as propaganda machines, scattering over the trenches. The British dispatchers of these consignments were taking up and further developing

HOW LEAFLETS WERE ATTACHED TO THE BALLOONS

English Propaganda in the First World War

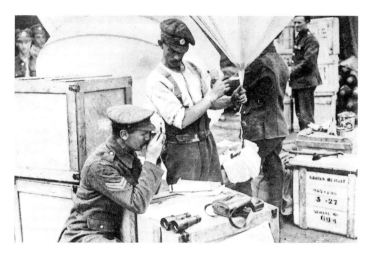

REGISTERING THE DIRECTION AND VELOCITY OF THE WIND
IN ORDER TO JUDGE WHERE THE LEAFLETS WOULD FALL

a method of mail distribution which had already been tested extensively in peacetime. Its material traces are on display in the Frankfurt
Museum for Post and Communication. In the museum one can also
find a fifty-pfennig piece lying next to a postal airdrop bottle, which
German Zeppelins occasionally released before the war. Whoever found
the bottle, which was made of oil-paper and held together with a strip
of fabric, was asked to take it to the nearest post office. The British
proceeded without the accompanying coin. In the last three months of
the war alone they showered their German readership with thirteen
million of these balloons' leaflets; Fama volat. As obvious propaganda,
or disguised as German counter-counter-information, these leaflets filled
the information vacuum of the front-line soldiers in their trenches –
with facts and food for though. The guiding rule of *Crewe House*, the
British propaganda organisation in the war, was that "only truthful
statements be made".[204] "You are not fighting to protect your fatherland
because it never occurred to anyone to attack Germany" is the message
of the suspected first leaflet produced in October 1914, for which the
author H. G. Wells, as leader of the Germany Division in Crewe House,
was responsible. As a specialist in the literary genre of invasion literature,
he had a few years previously had the United Kingdom visited by
Martians. Now he was writing about the background of the massacre
on Earth for his continental public: "You are fighting in order to satisfy

the bellicose ambitions of the those who seek war ... This whole affair is rotten to the core."

With quite what expenditure this war of words was waged is made clear by a few lines written by Sir Campbell Stuart, Vice Director of *Crewe House*, after the war. At the start of the war three leaflets were produced each week, each with a print run of around a thousand copies. Towards the end of the war the print runs rose from around one and a half million in June 1918 to a good four million that August, and in the last ten days of the war, before the weapons fell silent, 1.4 million sheets sought German readers – full order books for the English printers Messrs Harrison and Son.[205]

The German soldiers at the front, with this airborne literature, had the choice between the little paperback books of field pack literature and the weekly, German-language trench-news, produced specifically for them by the British – with the German Kaiser as its logo: *William, Made in England*. If written media is indeed viewed as more reliable than oral communication, which nobody ever has in black and white, this special reading-matter certainly went some way towards disconcerting its readers. Which was exactly what it was supposed to do. Thus the hunger for news and rumours, brought about by the danger and insecurity of the front and the area immediately behind it, received additional nourishment through the most modern means of distribution.

The soldiers took the war very seriously as a war of interpretation (and reading). This is shown by how precise and with what sensitivity they differentiated between the graduations of the factual within the broad area of "soldier news".[206] For every nuance there was a special expression: "As-tu un perco?"[207] ["Have you got a perco?"] was how soldiers often greeted each other in the French trenches. "Perco" was short for "percolator" – and at the same time the nick-name the first airship crews gave their balloons, the shape of which was very similar to that of the coffee machines of the time. For this reason the soldiers understood with the word "perco" a piece of news which, to play on Virgil, "had wings instead of feet" and which was therefore "uncertain while at the same time important".[208] The phenomenon of the rumour could hardly be better described.

Similarly there was talk of "bac" as in "bac à rab", the name given the hole in the ground for kitchen waste. Where food and drink is prepared, Fama begins her flight; in war the field kitchen is the harbour of rumour, and the cook is barber and messenger. As with "perco" and "bac" the

DISPATCHING THE BALLOONS

name for the cook "maître nouvelliste" points to the kitchen as *the* reloading point of news in the war: The cook gets to hear about everything and knows all the news, be it "ragot" or "potin", "perco" or "bac". "Kitchen news" is therefore the name given to any information of uncertain origin.

Thus idle talk and gossip are everywhere, nestle in the smallest communication trenches, in dug-outs and soldiers' tents. For, as Lucien Graux puts it, the hunt for news, and particularly for good news, is one of the most important occupations of the soldier, and the front is a great market-place for gossip; whoever has no tip, no snippet of information, is no comrade. Along with the interrogators and cooks, prisoners and deserting enemy troops also bring new wares to the market. And apart than these, soldiers returning from leave are a regular supply; letters from home do the rest: "Qu'est-ce-qu'on dit à Paris?", "Was gibt's Neues aus Berlin?" If one adds to this what trickles down

from the officers' circles to the common troops and also what the telephonists, the cyberneticians of the front, have to tell, one gains an
impression of the fog of the oral in which each soldier stumbled around.
In a continuous back and forth, "fausses nouvelles", hearsay and
rumours stream from the front to the rear, from home to the trenches,
from leaflets into the press and back again.

On a map of the front, Bloch contended, there should be marked out
an area from which rumours hail: the "zone of myth formation". Present-
day theoreticians would perhaps speak of an "interpretation
community", something not restricted to its current location. German
and French soldiers tell very similar stories, only with different characters
and elements. Cut off from reliable information and controlled by the
military censor, the soldiers at the front on both sides exist in an insuperable incontemporaneity. As modern as the communications of this
war are, and with them also the instruments of propaganda and
censorship, the discrediting of information through this censorship and
manipulation leads the soldiers back to a time before modern communications, to a time before the newspaper, the book and other printed
media. For in the trenches they suddenly find themselves right in the
middle of another age. This asynchronism is, for Marc Bloch, the
signature of battle; it leads to a "massive renewal of the oral tradition,
the antique mother of legends and myths".[209] This expresses what Freud
meant when, looking at the whole of society, he spoke of the incapacitation of its citizens by the state during war. The media also have a role
in this incapacitation, for the conversations of the trenches travel behind
the lines in soldiers' letters, are printed, spread, gain the authority of the
written, without ever being checked for their accuracy: "The report is
fixed in writing, objectified in print and finally materialised in a
book."[210] Thus the chain of hearsay reaches for the media of letter,
newspaper and the ever quotable book.

Marc Bloch's reports from the zone of myth formation revolve around
the fundamental problem of the historical witness. With his observations
of the slaughter he sees an ignored territory. He extends the historical
paradigm to include informal phenomena such as hearsay, idle talk,
rumour and events which are temporally close.

In the changes which hearsay makes to a rumour, Bloch sees the interpolations of the collective imagination at work. Braisne-Brème-Bremen:
A syllable, a "little word", a misunderstanding suffices, and the rumour
enters in the text of everyday conversation: "Those Germans! They had

their spies everywhere!" Here social fears produce their all-encompass-ing text. The rumour says "what simply could not be said in any other way". If it races from the troops in the rear to the forward lines, it first has to pass through something like a pre-censor, a collective editing procedure. What remains is the spy from Braisne. The power of this "spy" is given to him by the voice of hearsay.

What historians like Livius or Tacitus looked into in Roman antiquity, that is to say, *rumores* and *famae* as indicators of the psychological state of the people, again come to the fore with Bloch, although in a slightly different form. Like Thucydides, Bloch is concerned with a history which is near, with battles which he himself experienced. And Bloch derives this developing history from oral sources. The historiographic dilemma, that proximity does not imply clarity, is a repetition of the classical problem of sources. The oral descriptions given by eye- or earwitnesses are "the oldest form of tradition" wrote Ernst Bernheim at the beginning of the twentieth century in his *Einleitung in die Geschichtswissenschaft* ["Introduction to History"]: "We call it 'rumour' when what is at issue are events of the present which the speaker has not himself witnessed and whose report has passed through the mouths of many unfamiliar people. We call it 'legend' when what is at issue are events of the past which have been transmitted just like the rumour, only are both the common property of the memory and the narrative of a larger community."[211] What "has passed through the mouths of many unfamiliar people", forces the historian to think seriously about his role as investigator and writer of history. For in war he finds himself faced with the "everything, that is to say: nothing" which also envelopes the author of *The Charterhouse of Parma* and its hero.

In the zone of myth formation, modernity, the era of automatic weaponry, tanks, aerial photography, field telephone, large-circulation newspapers and propaganda machines, also proves to be an era of hearsay. This experience has the officer Marc Bloch revise his under-standing of himself as investigator and historian. "History", he will write a few years later, "is the science of a change and, à bien des égards, a science of differences".[212] Those affected by war myths are a long way from this dialectical understanding of their situation. In the same way as they believe in the spy from Braisne, so too will soldiers in wars to come tell each other about massacres, battles and skirmishes, stories far removed from written history.

While killing, logistics and war communications[213] are being perfected, the "antique mother of legends and myths" will remain hovering over everyone who remains in the zone of myth formation. In this historical discontinuity, those participating in rumour and gossip can never make any advances in understanding their own situation. On the contrary, while the Enlightenment shows its other face in the industrialised war, rumours unleash a similar power to that of myth in antiquity. Whoever says what he has heard did not experience what he is describing, and everyone who listens to him hears what could have been intended also for him. Whoever in war asks about the truth of history is taught by rumour the myths of battle.

5
Stigma or the Poetics of the Rumour

The Maids of Orléans – Trient, Dormagen and other Roots –
Stigma in Schroffenstein – Makah in Russia –
Trobriander on the Weser – The Poetics of Culture

"I noticed it for the first time when people began to gather into a mob outside the shops", the twenty-four-year-old student says in her statement. "It was the first Saturday in June, a lovely Saturday, and many people had travelled in from the countryside to do their shopping. Hundreds were on the streets. Crowds had formed, blocking the entrances to the some shops, including the entrance to my parents' shop: 'Don't buy anything from the Jews, they traffic in girls.'"[214] When Monique A, on Friday 4 July, gives her account of the rumour of Orléans, the nation already knows all about it. For weeks the story of the anti-Semitic occurrences in the capital of Loiret has been reported in the newspapers. But, as yet, nobody can find an explanation for the rumour of Orléans. Is the great nation populated by anti-Semites? Or did a frenzied rumour arise on its own? The shock is triggered by the contents of the rumour, by a Jewish caricature. Some see this fiction as a form of collective mirror in which what is repressed stares back at the people; they sense the poetics of the rumour's transmitting another, until now inaccessible, truth behind the lie.

The Maids of Orléans

On 10 May 1969 a boutique selling women's clothes opens in the central French town of Orléans. Its main attraction is its changing rooms. They are styled on dungeons of the Middle Ages, which give the shop its name: "Aux Oubliettes". Almost immediately word goes round that girls are being anaesthetised in the changing rooms, locked up in the cellar, and then sent off to oriental brothels during the night. There is even talk of submarines. It is said, by way of explanation, that the dealers in clothes and women are Jews.

The rumour was probably hatched in the Collèges Religieux Saint-Paul or Saint-Charles or in the local Jeanne-d'Arc secondary school. Out of these closeted worlds it quickly enters the spheres of other girls of Orléans: schoolgirls tell it to their friends, young employees have soon heard the news. And then it leaps into the world of adults; mothers warn their daughters, teachers their students, the public prosecutor is called. On the surface, Orléans remains calm, but soon everyone is saying: the Jews, the shopkeepers, are up to something. No smoke without fire. Then, at the month's end, in the short moment of tension between the referendum and the presidential elections, during the political vacuum in France, the situation erupts. Fathers and husbands storm the boutiques to rescue their daughters and wives, anonymous callers make anonymous telephone calls, and whoever came along just to do some shopping, stands and watches; tumult. On Saturday some shout: "Don't shop with the Jews!" And that evening, when everyone starts returning home, the rumour, ever mutating, keeps the gossip going on the buses. Only very slowly does it begin to fade.

Then, thankfully, comes Sunday. But on Monday the newspapers pick up and react to the story. The bishop, political groups and parties make declarations; meetings and conferences are held. After two weeks the rumour has been dispelled. When Edgar Morin and his team arrive from Paris, countless mini-rumours and fragments are still swirling around, myths and anti-myths, obviously aftershocks of a *rumeur sauvage*. Or has there been some form of intentional conspiracy? people ask themselves in Orléans. And if so, by whom and against whom? Did anti-Semites put the rumour into circulation? Was it "the Jews" themselves in order to gain sympathy? Did the press direct it all? What remains is suspicion and distrust – and people's shock at what they have done. No smoke without fire.

Morin and his group composed the detailed diary of a rumour, as far as that is possible. Origin, dissemination and the threat of mob violence, these were the three stages of this rumour. The researchers could find no evidence of a conspiracy. On the contrary, the rumour of Orléans seemed to have emerged from unruly talk – an unsettling finding. It directs attention to the terribly banal, to sexual fantasies, and to an anti-Semitism lurking at the back of society. In a country which, a quarter of a century after the end of the Second World War, bases its moral self-understanding upon the myth of the *Résistance*, the armed opposition to the German invaders, completely different myths suddenly spring up and transform what is "real".

This result alone is worth the cost of the research. At first Edgar Morin was confused about his sociological adventure. All the conversations

UNWORTHY OF YOU! Poster in a Berlin Factory (1950s)

and research, the sociological detective-work and searching around for clues had exhausted him: "I cannot go on, I don't want to go on", he wrote in his diary on 26 July. Field research is strenuous and never comes to a satisfactory end. Yet finally, on the last Sunday in August, he gets there: "Editing finished", everything is completed, the grotesque rumour has been analysed. Reason to be happy. Nevertheless, he has misgivings: Morin recoils in the face of the *fait accompli* of the successful analysis. He hesitates before putting the lid of theory on the events: "I have" he notes in his diary as a concluding remark, "looked for the versatile and polymorphic scheme of which the shaking of one element affects all the others, changing the image of the whole. In this respect I am satisfied with the analysis. But I ask myself", he continues, "whether the most essential aspect has not in fact slipped through its net, this *poésie fabuleuse*, which mixes up dream and reality and, in a mystical way, fuses the one with the other, a *poésie* which will always escape sociological study". There is a puzzling remainder, a gap between cause and effect. The more one knows of the rules and motifs of this uncanny *poésie fabuleuse*, the more difficult it is to say what constitutes it.

The Parisian field researcher out in the provinces also finds literary origins for the rumour of Orléans. In the previous years and months many similar stories, some with accompanying illustrations, had appeared in diverse obscure magazines and in other basic reading-matter of the "little people". In Paris, Toulouse, Tours, Limoges, Douai, Rouen, Le Mans, Lille, Valenciennes, as well as, simultaneously with Orléans, in Poitiers and Châtellerault, similar rumours appear. It therefore appears as if the rumour of Orléans projects a collective "idea", be it a literarily transmitted one,[215] onto an actual social situation.

This *poésie fabuleuse* immediately gives rise to new stories, as which it continues to circulate. It is therefore not *poésie* in the usual, exquisite sense of the word, rather, on the contrary, only as a repeatable and variable oral piece of news does the rumour reveal its power. The poetics of the rumour fuses handed-down legends and anecdotes with a modern social occurrence. In Orléans, in the interaction of written and oral media, have the neighbours of yesterday suddenly become their mythical doubles of today. The roots of these rumours go back a long way into the cultural history of the West: for hundreds of years Jews have been defamed as murderers of children and murderers of God. Even the rumour of Orléans of the second half of the twentieth century plays a role in this fatal poetics of culture.

Trient, Dormagen and other Roots

What happened in Orléans was not a spontaneous occurrence. The rumour came from a deep stratum of collective memory, and was supported by a structure that has endured for a long time. Since late antiquity, and reinforced since the Middle Ages, accusations of ritual murder levelled at Jews have been part of the everyday reality of the Christian West. These myths spring from Christianity's blame of the Jews for the murder of God, and certain narrative elements of these myths highlight this. Repeatedly, myths of ritual murder and their like transfer Christian religious stories into the contemporary world; at least, this is how they are interpreted by the religious. Jesus dies again and again, and it is always decided "that Jews are the culprits".[216] And at the end of these myth-productions there are often riots, pogroms, torture, trials – everything that the nineteenth century covered with the word "Judensturm" ("Jew storm").

From 1144 onwards, that is to say from the death of William of Norwich, myths of ritual murder have played a major role in Christian life. The pattern and context of these stories are always the same: a child disappears, the parents look for it. When it is found, its corpse displays peculiar wounds. It is concluded that the child has been ritually murdered by local Jews. Many different rumours about an actual situation can accommodate this one plot. What is set down in chronicles, letters, proceedings of trials, later also in printed tracts and anti-Semitic pamphlets as "proven" reports, sustains, with its exemplary cases,[217] the everyday gossip of the common people right into modernity. For a long time it was the case that "it is known" what Jews are capable of getting up to. At the end of the seventeenth century people still have detailed memories of what is said to have happened in 1237:

At around the time of the festival of the apostles Peter and Paul, the Jews of Lincoln in England stole a boy of 8 called Hugo … Now they began to act out the tragedy, and to start with they selected one of their number as judge, the Pilate character. According to his demand as the judge, the poor child was lashed until blood flowed, crowned with thorns, mocked, scorned and spat at. One of them approached him and stabbed him with a knife. They then drenched him with the contents of their bladders, all the while calling him Jesus. Finally they nailed him to a cross and split open his side with a spear, right down to the heart.[218]

The Christian child in the role of the crucified, the Jews as murderers of God: an implicit understanding by both common Christians and the elite which corresponds with this narrative pattern arises. People start saying what they have always known, indeed what everyone has always known. Often there is interplay and feedback between literary and oral descriptions and visual representations of similar events. In the course of a several hundred-year period of transmission, cults grow up around the bodies of victims of supposed ritual murders. For the Christian inhabitants this pays, and indeed does so twice over: dead believers do not demand fees, and the martyrs, stirring so many a heart, stimulate the local tourist industry.

The most significant case is certainly that of Simon, a boy from Trient, who in 1475 drowned while playing in the river Etsch and whose body happened to travel through the canal system and come ashore at the house of a local Jewish family. In order to escape the threat of blame, the family reported what they had found to the local authorities. Yet soon they were arrested and interrogated. Hearsay became their undoing, setting in motion a spiral of accusation, torture, confession, retraction and renewed torture. The cycle of exemplary stories, current rumours and associated violence came to life as a repetition of religious-narrative structures. Through this the punishment is transferred into the present, the Jews experience their hell in the here and now. Torture sees to it that this cycle is not threatened by facts which contradict it. It projects onto the accused the anti-Semitic implicit knowledge of the myths of ritual murder.

With inquisitorial tenacity, the excited and engaged judges and their servants force "confessions", until finally one text emerges from the "polyphony of the proceedings",[219] from the hither and thither of the acts of brutality, agonies, fabrications and retractions – the protocol. This will later be fed back into the cycle of implicit anti-Semitic knowledge in other villages and towns in the form of chronicles or "newspapers". The miracles brought about by the "holy martyr Simon" also help spread word of the events. In the first fifteen months after his death alone, Simon apparently works 129 miracles, a sequence of rumours which prove to have positive economic consequences for the region, for they attract hordes of pilgrims. Also beyond Trient the pilgrims travelling home spread word of the martyrdom and miracles of Simon, which in turn leads to a huge wave of anti-Jewish attacks throughout Northern Italy. The pictorial representations and written reports about Simon finally transform the story into a fatal *poésie fabuleuse*, driving on the spirals of rumour and vilification. When the first of these writings appear, the torturers in Trient are still at work. Brutally they eliminate the difference between reality and rumour. The accused Jews pay for this levelling, after all their agonies, with their lives.

Following the same pattern, children will again and again be murdered for use as martyrs with which to attack local Jews. Foreknowledge and rumours symbolically co-ordinate an actual event and transfer it into another context. From the dead child there arises "an historical metaphor in mythical reality".[220] Reality confirms and renews myth. The consequence is the violent infringement of rights, staged or spontaneous outrages, plunder, torture and murder.

The case of the seven-year-old Marie Catharina Bloemer from the German town of Dormagen, on the Lower Rhine, demonstrates how the mechanics of the rumour operate. On the Tuesday of the *Kirmes* festival, the girl disappears without a trace. After two days of searching in vain for her, the enlightened town chronicler reports:

> The child has not yet been found, despite all the effort which has been put into looking for her. The opinions as to what might have

happened to her can be counted in their thousands. The opinion which holds most sway is that Jews seized the child because, according to an old saying, they sometimes require Christian blood. And since the disappearance of the child coincided with the end of the Festival of the Tabernacle, there can soon be found witnesses who saw the Jew Sekel with a sack, or the Jew Schimel at midnight lurking around houses.[221]

Three days pass before the body of the abused child is found. Now it is demonstrated what rumours are capable of: in Dormagen and the neighbouring towns and villages in which *Kirmes* is also being celebrated, people gather into mobs; there is tumult in front of the houses and shops of the Jewish inhabitants. Hundreds make their way to Dormagen to see the child. Such an occurrence suits the autumn festivals, with their brawls and suspended mores. One day the crown dramatically increases in size:

The common saying that the blood had been drained from the child by Jews had drawn thousands here. Many had come from three hours away, from Straberg, Nievenheim, Worringen, forming little processions, which prayed loudly. Because it was Tuesday, the church was full to bursting. The saying had spread everywhere that the blood had been drained from the child and that it had bled from 700 wounds.[222]

The laid-out corpse of the child even influenced the down-to-earth chronicler. The rumour "that Jews are the culprits" just seemed too plausible in a time when all manner of strange and incredible things were having such a determinative effect on reality. For example, in the chronicle one can read of the unsettling "prophesy" that on the following day "from Vienna to Amsterdam, mountain and valley will become levelled".[223]

The official post-mortem concludes that the girl was the victim of a sex crime. Her numerous wounds were the result of her fighting back during her ordeal. This finding takes the pressure off the Jews of the town, as did the Prussian legal officials from Cologne charged with investigating the affair. They and their heavily armed guard are all that stand between the Jews and the drama which was ready to unfold. Only now does the rumour begin to die down. The myths about ritual murder which formed its basis disappear into the latency of collective knowledge. The next rumour will call them up again, be it on the lower Rhine, or on the Loire.

Both rumours, that of 1819 and that of 1969, are based on the interplay of mythical, implicit factors with actual, real elements. The population of the region of the Lower Rhine know the "old saying" of alleged Jewish ritual murders, and in Orléans one could read illustrated articles on the subject. Whether it is deliberately set in motion to eliminate despised opponents, or whether it arises of its own accord, in each case the rumour projects these stories from the latency of collective memory onto actual reality. The boy Simon drowns while playing and becomes a martyr, the poor Marie Catharina is transformed into a saintly figure by rumour and the pilgrims it attracts, and later, at the time of the sexual revolution, the young women of Orléans become defenceless objects of lust. The aggression these fantasies bring with them is demonstrated by the other side of the role play: there one finds "The Jew Seckel with a sack", Schimel, who was seen "at midnight lurking around houses", but also the owners of the boutiques *Dorphé, Sheila* and *D.D.* in Orléans, Tobias, Samuel and Engel from Trient, and all the other Jews throughout history whom rumours have stigmatised and turned into scapegoats.

The rumour is the voice of stigma. It gives the cue, that "word spoken by an actor, at the end of which another is to start speaking himself, enter onto the stage, or carry something out".[224] How the play proceeds, however, is determined by the distance of political power from the anti-Jewish myth. The smaller it is, the greater the stigma. These rumours do not just follow some general anti-Semitic principle, rather are themselves anti-Semitism. "Anti-Semitism", Adorno writes, "is the rumour about Jews".[225] Its fictionalising power, the *poésie fabuleuse*, remains virulent. In February 1970 a woman faints in front of a clothes shop in Amiens. An employee of the shop rushes over to help her, and soon afterwards the old rumour has started moving through Amiens also. It tells the same story – of girls, cellars, submarines and sex, the same anti-Semitic colportage.

Stigma in Schroffenstein

Looking back at the earlier, folklorism-inspired years of Russian linguistics, Roman Jakobsen, now an old man, regretted that he had never carried out his plan "to study one of the most widespread and animated species of folklore, namely gossip and above all fictions in the oral narration of events".[226] What he and his colleague, the ethnographer Petr Grigorevic Bogatyrev would have found, we cannot know. Today, since "archaic" forms of life throughout the world are on the retreat and their populations which were earlier called "primitive" are disappearing, ethnological research tends to seek out what remains of archaic and authentic forms of life in the so-called First World. In the tautologies, contradictions, and iterations of oral culture, anthropologists, sociologists and folklorists now attempt to trace the secret of myth.

Long before the first anthropological journey to the land of hearsay took place, long before microphone and tape recorder, topi and field diary became the standard instruments of the ethnographer; writers reflected on "fictions in the oral narration of events". When in their stories or plays they wished to show the fictionalising power of hearsay and rumour, they developed ethnographic models of the oral and of the poetics of the rumour. In dramas, stories and novels of the psychologically insightful nineteenth and twentieth centuries, rumours appear as the voice of the collective. In fiction's reality, the flywheel of the rumour drives the narrative on; voices contrast with and comment upon one another. Their chatter becomes the subject-matter of the narrative. Aesthetic refraction allows for the demonstration of the processes involved in the fictionalisation of reality; it shows how the "they" raise their voice.

In Tony Richardson's film *Mademoiselle*, the screenplay of which was written by Jean Genet, some farmers are sitting together drinking a beer. Dusk is falling; the faces of the men can only be differentiated with difficulty. Outside the cattle are dying from drinking poisoned water. Something must be done, especially after one farm after the other has gone up in flames, and another has been flooded. But what? For a long time the men have watched Manou, the Italian forester whom all the women adore. They do not know that the well-respected village schoolteacher, the title character of the film, has been spreading water, fire and poison over the land. Something must be done. It must have been Manou. Was it Manou? "Everyone is saying it", one farmer says. Another asks: "Who is everyone?" – "Nobody in particular", is the answer. "But there's something in the air." In the air lie the fictions of the *poésie fabuleuse*, of an all-too-lively rumour. This demands a victim. In the end the farmers kill Manou behind the houses.

As a phenomenon of blame and fictionalisation, stigma, in ever renewed, exemplary narratives, produces definitions of the other. It is a literary act.

In drama it also speaks with the voice of hearsay. In Heinrich von Kleist's tragedy of 1803[227] the two antagonistic branches of the family Schroffenstein have been bound together "since olden times" by a testamentary contract. The contract stipulates that after the death of all the members of the one branch, everything owned by that branch shall be transferred to the other. Even from a great distance, the voice of hearsay travels with the power of an oracle. On both sides it tells the same story of the hostility of the other.

This double rumour has the same dramatic power as the oracle of a Greek tragedy. Both voices inescapably determine what happens: Oedipus fulfils the prophesy of Delphi and the Counts Schroffenstein both end up with something of which they are truly guilty, something that far surpasses the fictions made up by the other: each kills his own child. Neither escapes rumour, the voice of stigma. Both fathers prove to be "heroes of adjustment",[228] adjustment, that is, to the dictates of hearsay. Each tragically becomes what he accuses the other of being. Where there was at first only smoke, there is now fire. Like the oracle in Sophocles' play, spoken words here also hinder the eyes' capacity for witnessing. At the end of the play the fathers recognise their own blindness; this blindness resembles that of Oedipus.

"Everyone is saying it", therefore it must be true. Where the two branches of the noble family compete for economic, political and symbolical resources, the rumour effects the decisive transfer from the latency of the negative stereotype to its bloody manifestation. "The normal and the stigmatised are not persons but rather perspectives", writes Erving Goffmann. "The stigmatized and the normal are part of each other; if one can prove vulnerable, it must be expected that the other can, too." That is the fate of the Schroffensteins, the dramatic heroes of adjustment to a rumour. "Bring wine! Fun! Wine! You can laugh yourself to death with it! Wine! The devil rubbed coal over the faces of both of them in their sleep", Johann exclaims at the end of the tragedy. "Now they know each other again." The "fictions in the oral descriptions of events" conquer reality. Only once they have done this do the two agents of rumour recognise one another for what they are: one the mirror image of the other, both a part of the other. Hearsay projects identity in two directions.

In the tragedy this has tragic consequences. Even if today ethnology celebrates orality, not without pathos, as the El Dorado of its discipline, they nevertheless abstract it from its content, from what is actually said. In Kleist's theatre every member of the audience can take part in what they see. They can observe the destruction of the Family Schroffenstein, can see how the oral, how the voice of rumour produces the intensification and enchantment emphatically conjured away by ethnology. The characters in the play will feel little for the emphasis of ethnologists for the culture of the oral. Hearsay and rumour do not just produce ethnological paradises.

Makah in Russia

When the unfamiliar collegiate councillor Pavel Ivanovich Chichikov arrives with his coachman Selifan and valet Petrushka in the provincial town of N., the strange literary machinery of rumour is set in motion. The "not handsome, but neither ... particularly bad-looking"[229] hero of Nikolai Gogol's 1842 "Poem" *Dead Souls* disturbs the inhabitants of the Tsarist province. For he wants – nobody knows why – to buy up the "dead souls", that is to say the dead serfs whose names still appear on the government census, of whom the owner is liable to taxation. The town, which was "in no way inferior to other provincial towns", is in all respects an ideal cross-section of everyday provinciality: "The houses were of one, two, and one-and-a-half stories, with the everlasting mezzanine which provincial architects consider to be very beautiful." In this somewhere, which we know does not lie too far from either of the two capitals of the tsarist empire, the charming rogue and apparent man of the world ends up providing for ample gossip and incessant rumours. What is Chichikov up to with the "dead souls"?

"They've been merely invented to cover up something else. What he is really after is this: he wants to abduct the governor's daughter",[230] divulges Anna Grigorievna, a "lady agreeable in all respects" without family name, to her friend Sofia Ivanovna, an "agreeable lady", who is not identified in any greater detail. "This conclusion was indeed quite unexpected and in every way extraordinary", the narrator explains, and from this moment on, in the pale blue drawing room "with a sofa, an oval table and a little screen with ivy winding round it", the ludicrous rumour about Chichikov's amorous intentions increases its triumphant progress.

At first Gogol has his two gossiping ladies blur the trail which could lead from this piece of news to the woman who made it up. While her curious listener displays the hoped-for reaction – on hearing it she "turned pale as death, and was certainly alarmed in good earnest"[231] – the author of the rumour vanishes: "I realized what it was about as soon as you opened your mouth." The subject was hanging in the air, now it has been expressed, soon intensifying into certainty, until it became the case that "both ladies finally were at last absolutely convinced of the truth of what they had at first regarded as a mere supposition of nothing". And this, the narrator laconically clarifies, was "nothing extraordinary".

The fantasies about Chichikov, who since his arrival has been the object of erotic projection and speculation, arise in a situation of economic uncertainty. What does this landowner, this outsider, want to do with the dead souls? Should one suspect a particularly ruthless capitalist ruse? And thus the rumour comes to contaminate every conversation in the town. Soon it divides into two versions – a male version and a female version. Both are suitable for creating distance. The women hide their longing when they, over a century before 1969, give a particular form to the ubiquitous myth of the stranger as seducer of girls, namely that of the erotomaniac Chichikov. Among the men the image of Chichikov as a forger of bank notes gains increasing currency, something aided by the insinuation of his being a notorious swindler. Many even take him to be Napoleon.

Gogol's rumour has, like that out of Orléans, three phases: the period of incubation in the blue salon, then its profusion through all strata of society and finally its breaking out in the form of social activity; the rumour becomes action, it demands a victim. "All these discussions, opinions, and rumours for some unknown reason produced their greatest effect on the poor public prosecutor. They had such an effect on him that on returning home he began to think and suddenly, without rhyme or reason, as they say, dropped dead." This accelerates the events. The inhabitants of the town close ranks in front of Chichikov, and as a consequence the atmosphere changes. At first Chichikov does not sense this; the rumour is an open secret known to everyone but him.

In 1942, a hundred years after the publication of Gogol's ethnography of the Tsarist province, the anthropologist Elizabeth Colson travels to another sphere of talk, to the Makah, the native inhabitants of the northwestern coast of the United States. Her ethnographic excursion turns into a journey to the Kingdom of Hearsay. [232] Studying the Makah, Colson discovers a form of reality built upon gossip and orally communicated fictions. Other than this, their society has no definable identity. At least, this is how it appears to Colson. The Makah is down to about a fifth of its size at the end of the eighteenth century – to two thousand members, this decrease having been caused by diseases and other influences of non-native America, and the Makah's cultural institutions have almost all fallen victim to rigorous assimilation. Nothing religious, linguistic or ethnic any longer obviously indicates who belongs to the Makah and who does not.

The last ties of this dying culture, Colson argues, consist in a complicated system of scandal and gossip. This binds the Makah to their cultural tradition and at the same time serves the purpose of defining social roles and regulating claims of status. And its defining property has concrete applications – in the distribution, for example, of shares in the Makah land which is up for sale: only someone who is Makah can profit from this. And whoever speaks about the Makah like a Makah is Makah.

And the Russian province is similar in this respect. By means of satirical overdrawing, Gogol shows that it has particularly serious consequences for the subject of gossip when the gossips form a collective. The guest, who has been well received up until then, is suddenly shunned, his social and private contacts slip away from him: "They refused to receive him or received him so strangely, talked in so constrained and incomprehensible a manner, looked so embarrassed, and altogether everything was in such a confusion and muddle that he began to have doubts as to whether their brains were quite in order."[233]And when finally he finds out what is being said about him, he decides to take flight.

This moment of departure is described with care. Chichikov is approaching the edge of the town: "At a turning in one of the streets, the carriage had to stop because its whole length was occupied by an endless funeral cortège."[234] The public prosecutor, the victim of all the gossip, is being taken to his grave. The funeral procession marks the circle that the rumour has drawn around Chichikov. "Full of unpleasant sensations, he at once hid himself in a corner, covering himself with the leather apron, and pulled the curtains over the windows." Only once the cortège has passed does the carriage of the buyer of dead souls set off again, leaving the town behind it. This is the moment in which the focus of the story leaps from the talkative inhabitants of N. to the person of Chichikov. His double, though, the collective projection, remains behind in the town, together with Fama and the gossip she incites.

Gossip collectives like this one also seem to withstand history: "The rumours about him kept getting worse and worse"[235] Bulgakov writes decades later when he resurrects Chichikov in his satire about Soviet bureaucracy. "Uneasiness entered the hearts of all. Telephones started to jangle, conferences began ...", and once again the suspected rogue flees the, this time Soviet, gossip collective, its mouth full of curses, its stomach full of diamonds. But that is another story.

Twenty years after Colson's journey to a realm of gossip, Max Gluckman based his anthropological theory of gossip on her report. Gossip, he proposed, is a culturally controlled game with important social functions and one of the most important social and cultural phenomena.[236] For it is above all gossip and related phenomena which bind a society together; the more advanced the society is, the more important is its gossip for it. It stabilises the group in that it formulates social norms and controls their observance. According to anthropological theory, it enables the gradual review and reworking of social rules. Gogol's inhabitants of N. have no time for thoughts on this matter; for them it is just a question of shutting out Chichikov. Their gossip is, in the final analysis, everything but reciprocal. The supposed erotomaniac and swindler has no opportunity to partake in the gossip, rather must hurry to leave the circle of this culturally controlled game, of this discreet indiscretion. When gossip turns into rumour, when in the end "everyone is saying it", the fictional double replaces the person. And then it is a good thing if that person has a coach and horses.

Trobriander on the Weser

The necessity of a figure of projection is something learned by the ward of the Westphalian authorities, Cord Horacker, in July 1867. On hearing the (false) rumour that his beloved, Charlotte Achterhang, has been unfaithful to him, he breaks out of the detention home and hides in the forests, more precisely, in Solling, and restlessly circles his home town of Gansewinckel. He hopes to get news of his darling. The power of attraction of love and the fear of punishment balance each other, leaving him to orbit. Horacker becomes the desperate satellite of Gansewinckel. The theft of a little food turns him into the bogeyman of the region, gaining him notoriety as a brigand, bandit and murderer. His finds his Makah in the original inhabitants of the little town beside the water. Yet what for the anthropologist Colson was gossip, is, for the chronicler of this story, the rumour.

Wilhelm Raabe's *Horacker*, published in 1876, the twentieth of his thirty-nine books, takes the name of its main character. And titles are teases: the less they give away of their texts, "the better",[237] writes Lessing, and reading this story about the telling of stories, one notices

George John Pinwell, *The Gossips* (19th Century)

that the title means "the blind spot of the matter". "Horacker was rampant in the land",[238] it is said when the reader first reads his name – as if it was a cattle plague or fever that was being discussed. One of the many meanings of the word "Horacker" is the hungry boy roaming through the forests. At the same time it also names his imaginary double, the one spoken of in the rumour, the savage brigand and murderer, and therefore also a myth which feeds on history. For savage beasts, at least since early modernity, have belonged to the landscape of the European imagination. Even now, in the age of television, one still hears such stories; the monster out in the forest, even nowadays, seems to produce a slight shudder and arouse feelings of cosiness indoors – at least this is the conclusion reached by researchers into the oral traditions of the countryside.[239] And in *Horacker* these fictions reflect the fears and feelings of aggression to be found in the collective imagination.

The meaning of "Horacker" is therefore ambiguous. The difference hidden in the title determines all the events of the book. These are constituted by rumour and hearsay, which mobilise the usually hidden, dark sides of the inhabitants of this province of the Kingdom of Hearsay. Ironically, Raabe's narrator has the antique divinity appear: "Fama, as we know from mythology, has many thousands of tongues at her disposal",[240] he pontificates:

> From house to house, from lane to lane rumor flew, though now and again, like a conflagration in a strong wind, it leaped over a house or an individual. But she who watcheth and sleepeth not, she, the youngest daughter of Earth, born of her in angry revenge upon the gods for the murder of her stalwart sons, her dearest Titans, she, Pheme, the goddess of sagas and reputations, espied our friend Hedwig Windwebel at the right moment, too, and whispered this most recently engendered nonsense in her ear.[241]

This playing with Virgil's allegory has an alienating effect. Placing antiquity and modernity together like this produces a narrative situation of deeper, secondary meaning. On the first page of the book the dialectic of truth and lie is already presented as a leitmotif when the narrator tells us that he is going "to write an amusing story", one in which he is going to allow himself to lie "devilishly believably". The reader is constantly reminded that he is reading a book. This method of creating distance, this black humour,[242] shows the story to be a literary experiment. It has a happy ending. One wonders whether this could possibly be the case in real life. Out of the distance arises a form of ethnographic experimental set-up to look into human weaknesses, an ironic psychogram of an all-too-normal provincial society.

Raabe's rumour profits from curiosity, vanity, subconscious brutality and similar emotions and sentiments. As an ethnographer of his fictional Gansewinckel, Raabe gives an example of how hearsay functions as a strategy of anonymity. This game of quotation eliminates the agents of speech. Where there is no longer a named speaker, Fama unfurls her wings:

> "Horacker has murdered again! A man from Gansewinckel just told the dyer Burmeister all about it at New Gate! … Horacker has slain an old schoolmaster! … Horacker has slain two schoolmasters!"
> "Were they carrying papers identifying themselves as schoolmasters, friend?…"
> "Can't tell you, friend; perhaps you could tell just by looking at them."
> "Yes, they found them in a thicket with their heads bashed in – it was horrible! And the murderer left a note on a bush making fun of them."

"An old woman from Dickburen found them while she was out pilfering firewood. And then they brought them into the village on stretchers. – They say one of them lived for a quarter of an hour, and the chairman of Gansewinckel parish himself rode into town with the awful news just now, and the mayor and the court officials already know about it. Oh, wouldn't I ever like to know what they're saying right now. I mean, can you even call something like this human?"

This is what wild stories sound like: the gossip substantiates itself as it did on the squares of revolutionary Paris. The ethnographic narrator reasons that this is what is so enchanting about rumour, that it can be left to itself. It is merely by chance that anybody becomes the bearer of a rumour. Not only the person whom the talk is of is missing, but also the witnesses to the events described, and here there appears a hole, one in which literature expects to find the agents of the corresponding reply. This absence of so many is what constitutes hearsay. Where everything is quotation – event, witnesses, speakers – the medium of rumour unfurls its umbrella of total anonymity. What keeps it taut is the increasing dynamism of an exciting piece of news, until finally the notabilities of the town – the vicar, his wife, the vice-chairman of the parish – each in their own way, clear away the fog of rumour.

These snippets of conversations demonstrate how the number of Horacker's victims increases. His fictional acts become ever more gruesome, the facts change. A mixture of interpretation and interpolation gives Fama wings. And at every step the alleged witnesses gain in both detail and prestige: a man, the dyer Burmeister, the chairman of Gansewinckel and finally the court officials. This is how the fiction of gossip handles the figure of the witness.

In the compilations of contemporary myths, of urban myths, put together by folklorists and sold in huge quantities in the form of popular literature and books designed as gifts, there is again to be found this type of structure. In order that the gossip become news, the rumour-monger alludes to someone who appears close, for example to "a friend of my mother" or "my colleague's sister". And even if, from case to case, region to region, version to version, the actual contents of this convention change, suiting the particular needs of the speaker, the plot of the story in question nevertheless remains relatively stable.

Wilhelm Raabe shows the tautologies, contradictions and iterations of oral culture which ethnology attempts to describe systematically; the situational, rhetorical and narrative context of rumour:

'What sort of civilization is this? Is it even conceivable with the taxes we pay? And the education in the schools? I ask you, what good are police and government to me if it may very well seem to them to be a joke that something like this can happen to someone in our century? Sure, but you just don't sweep in front of your door at the right moment, and you'll certainly have no doubts about there being authorities whom the Lord hath set over you! ... Well, in the end I for one don't lay the blame on Horacker if he keeps on getting wilder and wilder!"[243]

And the unmentioned counter of this gossiping replies: "'You're probably right about that. And when all's said and done, a person feels jealous of his own dog, because once it has got a license tag dangling around its neck, it can at least go for a quiet walk in peace! ...'" And with this the story within a story of Horacker is given a moral. A narrative situation of "X said" is transformed into a moral one. Rumour forms the blob of fat that floats on the soup of everyday resentment, and it is a technique in the art of self-reassurance that we belong to a different species. The narrative process of rumour develops and shapes fundamental social norms. Literary reflection highlights the other side of stigmatising rumour, what sociologists call "in-group conformation". A rumour is more than just what it says.

This is just as much the case in Gansewinckel, Raabe's little town on the river Weser, as it is on the Trobriand Islands off Papua New Guinea. There the anthropologist Bronsilaw Malinowski observed that the "primitive", that is to say oral – as opposed to written – language of the inhabitants, was used merely as a means of conveying information. [244] Through his work he came to the conclusion, which was to have such a profound effect on the study of language, that the view of meaning as being *contained within* an utterance is false and untenable, and that the meaning of an utterance is determined by the situation in which it is made. And Malinowski did not think that this was restricted to the language of the Trobrianders, seeing all language as being fundamentally a tool, a vehicle for information, not an instrument of reflection. And what is more, as a tool, Malinowski argued, it bound people together in their everyday activity, fulfilling a social function.

The anthropologist therefore revealed an aspect of language which Roman Jakobson takes up thirty years later in his model of speech functions, that of "phatic communion".[245] Jakobson counts among the phatic all those aspects of speaking and language of which the purpose is to bring about and maintain communication.[246] Malinowski's phatic communication determines the gossip of Gogol's women just as much as it does the idle talk of Wilhelm Raabe. "For in this use of speech the bonds created between hearer and speaker are not quite symmetrical, the man linguistically active receiving the greater share of social pleasure and self-enhancement. But though the hearing given to such utterances is as a rule not as intense as the speaker's own share, it is quite essential for his pleasure, and the reciprocity is established by the change of rôles." Gogol's woman turns "pale as death" when she hears what she must hear. And to compensate her for what she has heard, the gift of speech is given her.

Adriaen van Ostade, *Two Gossiping Women* (17th Century)

And thus she speaks all the more convincingly when she then passes on the story herself. The rumour is formed from the series of exchanges of role that then arises: one has heard something, one therefore passes it on; the receiver becomes transmitter, the ear mouth, *ad libitum*. The asymmetry of conversation must be maintained, and one therefore embellishes, invents, interpolates, as does the next receiver / transmitter, and so it goes on. The system of hearsay offers both parts, that of the hearer as well as that of the speaker, possibilities of resetting the social balance; all human speech is phatic.[247] Malinowski must certainly have considered, when he came up with the term "phatic communion" – a "demon of terminological invention"[248] – what "phatis" means in Greek. In Homer it stands for talk, legend, rumour, posthumous renown, for reputation both good and bad; in effect, it means something similar to *pheme* or *fama*.

The talk in Horacker also forms the phatic link. Raabe paints a portrait of Ühleke as being a specialist at doing things with words. He has just frightened and worried a young woman with some alarming news about Horacker. Did the fiend come across her spouse in the forest? she asks herself. "Ühleke was the man's name, and he has every right to be satisfied with the effect his news had",[249] the narrator writes of the gossiper, and describes him as having a "comfortably benevolent and insidious face", the face of a man who is only too aware of what he is up to: "Well, I myself still consider the whole story utter foolishness. People are simply too gullible!" By spreading his "grisly tidings, with all the commentary arising therefrom" he puts up the umbrella of hearsay. As a rhetorical strategy, it replaces the witnesses with the "they" of the "they say", about whom Martin Heidegger will, half a century later, write that "it can always bear the weight of having 'them' base what 'they' say on it. It can provide the easiest answers because it is not something which needs to stand for anything else."[250] Yet while Heidegger, in his critique of modernity, the public and above all the temporal forms of the social, condemns this existential "they" on account of its ignoring "all differences of niveau and sincerity", Raabe develops the social and historical contradictions of the figure of speech of the "they". These paradoxes are what have people, as individuals, sometimes lose their way in the realm of the social.

In an "excursion through the little word 'they'"[251] he demonstrates the social force expressed with the formula "they". "They" are where external norms are determinative, "they" mean lack of freedom, the lack of the ability to determine one's own course. "But they have been here – strangely enough! And now and then they bear the name of Cord Horacker or Lotte Achterhang, and even when one hears it said in the village everyday that it would have been better if they had never been born, they are a long way from believing it; but, for all that, they know what grim hunger is and that everything they see, except for their own hide, belongs to someone else."[252] To be understood as simultaneously both collective and individual, "that wonderful, that sublime little word 'they'" indicates the gear change between norm and deviation, between power and marginality. The narrator poetically names all aspects of the aporia of the word "they": "It is the darting, lustrous foam upon the waters; it is the stagnant black of the deep." It is precisely this game of surface and depth that is an essential characteristic of hearsay. It pervades the anonymously communicated exaggerations, commentaries and commonplaces of the rumour; but it also determines the manner of appearance of the individual participants in the conversation. If Ühleke, self-satisfied, says what he himself may not believe but which frightens out of her wits the person with whom he is speaking, for a moment he gains a new role. "By helping to spread a rumor, an ass always has the opportunity of suddenly becoming an interesting fellow – and of feeling like one as well."[253]

Raabe's Swiss contemporary and colleague Gottfried Keller, in his short story *Das Verlorene Lachen* ["Forlorn Laughter"], goes into greater detail about the way in which the art of spreading rumours is governed by laws. In this story the hero Jukundus Meyenthal comes across a witch-like figure who is ill-famed as a expert of rumour and intrigue, of whom it is said that she is capable of "filling the land with a rumour in just a few days".[254] He asks her about the tricks of her trade of blackening names, learning that it requires

> to begin with just a particular, in itself perfectly innocent quality, a state of affairs, a certain characteristic of the person in question, an incident, the taking place of two circumstances or coincidences, just about anything, that in itself is true and unquestionable, something that can provide the kernel of truth for a whole host of fictions. And one need not make do merely with fictions, but may advantageously take the misdemeanours and atrocious acts of the one person and attribute them to another, making use of any superficial similarities, or indeed may pin on someone else what one oneself always fancied doing or perhaps has even dabbled in a little.[255]

Montage, projection, invention, inversion are the names of the rules in regard to which rumour is formed. That Keller's rumour-witch gains a "divine pleasure" in her activity indicates the cement of the phatic ties which is strengthened by rumour.

Like Gogol and many other authors of the nineteenth century,[256] Raabe characterises the inhabitants of Gansewinckel with recourse to what Malinowski sees as a communion of words. The stories of Raabe and Gogol treat the subject of "fictions in the oral narration of events", that is to say gossip, idle talk and rumour. At the carefully constructed chain of talkativeness in N. or in Gansewinckel, at the oral customs of their characters, the narrators take a similarly ethnographic look as does Malinowski at the "primitive" Melanesian inhabitants of the Trobriand Islands. Here, as in the fictional towns, there is to be found every form of speech "in which ties of union are created by a mere exchange of words".[257] The writer confirms the findings of the ethnologist and vice versa. Both develop models for the context of the *poésie fabuleuse*, both see the rumour as a social catalyst and as a provocative element of literary or theoretical fiction – the mountain landscape of the Weser also lies in the Pacific Ocean.

The *poésie fabuleuse* arises from the chatter of the people, and it feeds on this. The literary locations presented by Raabe and Gogol are full of characters like Ühleke – gossips, fine ladies and others who invent and spread rumours. As a rule, these are normal, everyday people. A great person, Aristotle writes in *The Nicomachean Ethics*, "will speak neither about himself nor about another".[258] It is not only in the *Familie Schroffenstein*, in *Dead Souls* and in *Horacker* that these great people are seldom to be found. It is precisely this that highlights so clearly the ethnographic character of these works of literature. For idle talk and gossip, rumour and hearsay are part of the social world in the most diverse of societies. Precisely the manner in which they literarily reflect this omnipresence of talk, this phatic tie between people, constitutes the realism of Gogol's and Raabe's stories. They are themselves anthropologists; for the Greek word for a person who speaks about people is "anthropologos"; the word suits Heinrich von Kleist, Nikolai Gogol and Wilhelm Raabe just as well as it does the twentieth century experts of the phatic. For the literary anthropologists also speak about people and describe how they hear and what they say, about themselves and about others. "Everyone is saying it." – "Who is everyone?" – "Nobody in particular. But there's something in the air."

The Poetics of Culture

The "poetics of rumour" has many faces. Aesthetic and literary images shape the fictionalisation of reality through the voice of hearsay. Kleist, Gogol and Raabe give form to hearsay with literary models of stigma, with which both aspects of this projection appear to belong to one another. In so doing the *poésie fabuleuse* of projective rumours such as these can drive the literary characters so far as to commit acts of violence.

Yet Elizabeth Colson's expedition to the Makah demonstrates that idle talk, gossip and rumour are not necessarily to be equated with stigma. From 1942, the same year in which Colson was with the Makah, originates another mention of the rumour. It clearly shows that context determines what direction hearsay is going to take, what it speaks of and what it can set off. The path to this other side of the rumour leads to the concentration camp Sachsenhausen bei Oranienburg. In the inmate's kitchen, which now serves as the museum of the camp, articles and relics from Sachsenhausen's history are on display. On one of the walls with documents dating back to the time of National Socialism, the archivists of the document centre have put up an extract from the camp rules. Together with grainy photographs, the prisoners' uniforms and other props of the terror, the words again hammered up on the wall allow an unexpected view of the reality of life in the camp. With the choice of these sentences the organisers of the exhibition allow a glimpse at the near-absurd lengths to which those who ran the camp went in order to control the inmates. The passage is taken from the first section of the "General Camp Rules", which was displayed in the camp, and is dated 6 November 1942; it reads: "*Political discussions and the starting and spreading of rumours are forbidden,* as are card games, games of dice, and above all gambling."

That those in control wanted to govern as much as possible every social excitement of their victims indicates the logic of their apparatus. Rumours are forbidden because resistance, conspiracy and insurrection can take shape in them. They can spread unnoticed by the sole central power over the prisoners by means of unmonitored talk. In attempting the most extensive regulation of every manifestation of life, the strict control of informal talk is intended to put an end to every difference, every sign alternative to the power of the camp, be it political or playful. Obviously those running the camp saw the "starting and spreading of rumours" as an act tending to subversion.

The forbidding of this activity held among thousands of prisoners, and also for a little boy whom the National Socialist forces of extermination had, after several stations of deportation, finally sent to Sachsenhausen. He was born in the Polish city of Lodz, official date of birth 30 September 1937, although this date was probably brought forward by his father in order to improve the boy's chances of surviving in the ghetto by thereby qualifying for elementary work. From 1939 the child lived with his grandparents in the Lodz ghetto, was separated from them, afterwards came to Ravensbrück, later to Sachsenhausen. His time in the ghetto and in the camps he could, as he later said, as an adult no longer remember. Nevertheless he wrote a novel which treated the theme of survival among the conditions of the ghetto. In 1969, the year of the events in Orléans, Jurek Becker's *Jakob the Liar* was published, a book about hope.

The book is at the same time the biography of a rumour. For the piece of news picked up by chance by the hero and then passed on, that the Russians are on the advance and that therefore liberation is in sight, spreads in the blink of an eye around the society of the ghetto.

Jakob Heym heard what he knows on a radio in the station house of the German command. It is only because of the good mood of a soldier that he survives the visit he is ordered to pay it. He could never have allayed the suspicion that he might have been spying. But, unverified, nobody would believe his news, something that Jakob must recognise in his listeners. And therefore out of need he reaches for a lie, and in doing so sets the unstoppable mechanics of the rumour in motion. "I have a radio!"[259] he says. At first only Mischa hears of this, then Kowalski, and then just about everyone. "News exists to be passed on. On the other hand, you know how it is, with the informant being held responsible for all the consequences", the narrator considers at the beginning of the novel.

There are, to be precise, two pieces of news: the gossip that Jakob has a radio, something strictly forbidden in the ghetto, and also the rumour of the ever closer approach of the Red Army. Both pieces of information have different circles in which they are passed around. Those who have heard of the radio continually pester him for more news and demand to know more about the concrete existence of the source: news like this without a source is worthless, is just a rumour, the reader is told. Jakob accepts the complication of his life by the lie[260] and gives them what they want, invents news, right to the end, kilometre by kilometre, of the Soviet advance, makes "a tonne of hope" out of "a few grams of news":

"I would do it for you, for you and for me, I'm also doing it for myself, for one thing is certain, that I cannot survive on my own, only together with you".[261] For those closest to him, then, he requires the lie of the radio; the rumour captivates more distant circles, however, without this aspect of the lie.

For the new knowledge affects everyone in the ghetto, even those who know nothing of its supposed origin. With the rumour comes hope, and with this hope culture gains entry into ghetto society, which has been without a future for three years: "Anyone who does not know it must be a hermit, not everyone knows the source of the news, the ghetto is just too big, but the Russians are on everybody's mind. Old debts being to play a role again, embarrassedly they are called in, daughters turn into brides, in the week prior to the festivities of the New Year weddings are to take place, people are crazy with joy, the suicide figures sink to zero."[262] The rumour invents an aim; in the midst of certain death there arises a messianic structure. Whoever is shot this close to the end, the narrator tells us, has lost his or her future. But the saviour does not come, the desperately anticipated end of the story remains a fantasy of hearsay; they have all lost the future.

This rumour emphasises the other aspect of the *poésie fabuleuse*. Instead of proclaiming destruction and danger, it brings news of salvation. While the rumour in Orléans speaks of barbarity, Jakob's lie, acting like a religious prophecy, sets the collective mechanics of hope in motion. It follows the logic of a game. Each individual step, act of dissemination, embellishment, protest and demand for more is performed in the context of an "as if", and with a playful awareness of the expected roles of speaker and listener. In the light of the hope, everyone again suddenly has a part to play – be it merely the proud spreader of good news. The first to be infected is Jakob Heym; he "dreams up an innocent little game",[263] the result of being so close to a dozing command post that he finds himself coming away with a little sunshine from it. The game continues with the brusque or timid, apparently nonchalant or craving, greedy attempts by his friends to get something new out of Jakob. Into the everyday life of the ghetto enters a new dimension; it is the dimension of role-play, which is what the social realm is founded upon. "And suddenly, just before noon, Kowalski, the barber, poses his perfidious question. Without any preparation, and in an insultingly innocent manner, he says: 'And?'" With this 'And?', as with every unmentioned but perceptible 'And' in this book, the vision of a future runs alongside the clear everydayness of certain death as a form of game.

Where before there was the certainty of death, the future now seems to open itself up, and against the sombre finality of the facts a web of speculation and interpretation weaves itself into existence. Reality again has a symbolic dimension; since Jakob Heym has begun to play the part of the owner of a radio, play has threaded its way through the machinery of extermination.

When he goes into the cellar with Lina, for whom he acts as a substitute father, in order to play her his "radio", Becker opens up the ethical dimension of this game and rumour. Jakob sits behind a stone wall and imitates the sound of a radio; the child is told to sit where she is and not to look, just to listen: "'Can't I see it?' – 'Definitely not!' says Jakob sternly. 'When you're as little as you, you're not even supposed to hear it. It's strictly forbidden.'"[264] Yet Lina discovers the truth about the radio when she does what she has been told not to do and watches the radio imitator: "Lina cautiously puts her head round the corner. Out of sight of Jakob, who is sitting sideways on to her, with his eyes tightly closed, an indication of the greatest efforts of body and mind, and, forgetting himself, is emitting a noise, following rules which only he knows." But rather than being disappointed, Lina plays along with the game. She senses the secret of this piece of theatre: that there is hope as long as it is played, that there is truth as long as there are liars like Jakob Heym.[265] And therefore all the greater is the disappointment in the ghetto when the game of the rumour finally comes to an end. Jacob's friend Kowalski is the first victim of this new reality of no hope; he kills himself. When the camp is cleared this is at the same time the moment at which the story has its origin. On the transport the narrator learns from Jakob the truth about his lies.

Rumours interpret, and they themselves demand interpretation. They can be true or false. In every case they have a meaning. For they are symbolic and public "systems of construable signs".[266] Only in terms of how a rumour relates to its context is its meaning defined. In Orléans the rumours project feelings such as fear and hatred; in the ghetto of the novel it reflects the hopes of those captive within it. Whether true or false, rumours play a part in a "poetics of culture";[267] they form a type of hinge connecting an historical and a mythical reality. They suffuse what is referred to as "reality" with that *poésie fabuleuse* which Morin sensed in Orléans. And they can contribute that the historical event itself appears as the metaphor in the system of a mythical reality and is experienced or suffered.

Whoever is touched by rumour and hearsay plays a part in a process of interpretation. The lies set hesitantly and reluctantly into the world by Becker's Jakob Heym, the pensive laughter of Raabe's Ühleke, the gossip in the fictional Russian province, all these are the practices of those who take part in the development of collective meaning. "Play is what sets the player on his path, which entangles him in the game, traps him within it",[268] writes Hans-Georg Gadamer in *Truth and Method*. Participation in the rumour is similar to this. It is like the game of the collective; almost everyone can take part, everyone knows the rules of hearsay. And what Gadamer says of play, is often true of the rumour, namely that it becomes master of those who take part in it.

This is demonstrated also by the logic with which the "camp rules" of Sachsenhausen lists the "starting and spreading of rumours" between "political discussions" and the playing of games. For as with card games, games of dice and gambling, it is true also of the system of hearsay that it is something that cannot be predicted or controlled, is itself, in this respect, a form of game.[269] And it is here that one finds its small moment of freedom. But the truth of the camps remains the final, brutally stark reality. And therefore whatever could establish an – even only subjective – distance from this principle of absolute control is not tolerated. Here and in the ghetto nothing is to take place "of its own accord"; in the eyes of absolute power rumours even have, with their possible glimmer of collective hope, the character of insubordinate conduct. They could put in question the monopoly of violence, when, with their rhetorical power, they spin a web of interpretations. That however would represent the end of definiteness and the beginnings of difference; one could call this "culture".

6

"Rumor Clinics" and Other Forms of Control

Hotline – Rumor Clinics – Rhetoric –
Control Centres – Limits of Control

Did the President of the United States have sex with an intern? This was the question the American public was asking in the middle of Bill Clinton's second term of office. As the rumours about the goings on in the Oval Office became ever louder, the White House set up its own hotline, a sort of emergency telephone number. Whoever phoned up learned the truth about *Monicagate* – at least, the official version of that truth. The hotline indicated how seriously the government took the rumours, even among the little people. By means of direct conversation, Clinton's image-managers intended to clear their boss's name of the accusations that were appearing in the Internet and being picked up by the media, and from the ever more widespread rumours. Personal contact with the callers is a stratagem of the complex art of denial. Whether this contact had any success is something that cannot be measured with any accuracy; the continued circulation of this self-willed instrument of political opinion-formation demonstrated ever more clearly that people were not satisfied with the "big" denials that Clinton had repeatedly given the press and their cameras. Indeed, this was a clear demonstration of how the negative rhetoric of denial often has exactly the opposite effect from the one intended.

Bill Clinton's problem with *Monicagate* was not a new one. Statesmen and politicians have always sought to control stories and rumours circulating about them in order to protect their reputations. Presumably without realising it, they are following the advice of the philosopher Francis Bacon, who wrote that "all wise governors" must carefully watch and follow rumours in order to be able to make use of their dangerous power instead of being damaged by it; for rumours are "often the shadow of approaching events".[270] What in Roman antiquity was resolved by the *Delatores*, namely through the relaying of news from the people to the authorities, is now dealt with by teams of advisors and specialists who concentrate wholly on public opinion. They also pass back information about the state of the president's image.

Political rumours often react to secret politics. This is another reason why it is difficult to control political gossip. An attempt to exert some control over what people are saying is a good indicator of the rationality of the government. Bill Clinton's hotline as a strategy for just such rumour control has a rich ancestry – and some direct precedents in recent history. One might think of the "mouches", the "flies", the spies who, in Paris of the late seventeenth century, listened out for what the people were saying and noted down what they heard. Usually their hunt for words led them to public places, to the Palais-Royal or to the Tuileries, often to the drinking dens of the city. Sometimes the *mouches* turned for information to "domestic servants or other people who had access to the relevant house"[271] and could therefore also eavesdrop on private conversations. For decades these word-police spied on what people were saying. Acting for the lieutenant general of the police, they were paid to write reports on the gossip they had heard, the so-called *gazetins de police*. In these was presented "what they had heard in its raw state",[272] to be evaluated and archived, secret *faits divers* of hearsay. Already here one can find the principal elements of rumour control of the twentieth century. The spoken word is transformed into the written word; what at first emerges at the periphery travels to the centre of power, and simultaneously with their change of media, rumour and gossip undergo a social elevation. "Ludwig XV was madly keen on the reports and very much liked his private secretary to read them out loud to him."

On the other hand, this centralisation of hearsay indicates a politics of opinion on the part of those in power, one which works with rumours offensively. For while there are agents who report to the king what people are saying, there is also a staff which distributes rumours,[273] a procedure that demands a high level of secrecy, a secrecy which always places this sort of politics in great danger of itself becoming the subject of rumours. The *mouches* are also able to monitor this situation and to report back to the lieutenant general of the police. This critical point, at which the rationality of power collapses, demonstrates the difficulties with which any system of rumour control is faced. Already in the

Johannes Sambucus, *Fama and the Printer* (1566)

Encyclopaedie of 1751 the connection between rumours and control by the authorities is evident; from the point of view of the Enlightenment, the rumour is a potential source of irrationality, against which all that can help is the "vigilance of the police".[274] For political rationality, the rumour maintains its reputation for subversion, for inciting anarchy, for being a weapon in the struggle against the monopolistic control of information; to the powerful it appears as the "ammunition"[275] of the unarmed. And these they understand as being most willing to mount a targeted action against them upon gossip, a real conspiracy of political opposition.

It must have appeared much the same to Bill Clinton when he had the *Monicagate*-hotline set up to have an "entrenchment to protect against the darts of the slanderous tongue of rumour".[276] In the more recent history of the United States, there have been two institutions which can be seen as direct precedents of this medial intervention in the idle talk of the little people, the so-called "rumor clinics" of the Second World War, and the telephones of the "rumor control centers" with which the authorities attempted to quell the riots that flared up after the murder of Martin Luther King. Set up under different historical and medial conditions, both institutions, clinic and control centre, demonstrate the status the state gives informal talk, the status of a particularly dangerous ferment of anarchy and insurrection.

Rumor Clinics

When, after the catastrophe of Pearl Harbor in December 1941, the United States entered into the war against the Axis powers, not only was the production of weapons, munitions and other war products speeded up, but rumours also propagated in huge quantities, as is usually the case in times of war. Be it of an early victory over Germany and the end of Hitler, be it that someone had heard of terrible horrors, be it that someone knew of the deaths of some prominent figures, or indeed of the destruction of the entire navy and army, the rumour-mongers splashed out with rationed goods – Fama always offers her own version of official history. Rumours had their high point in the days and weeks immediately after 7 December. Since the American leadership at first kept quiet about the extent of the losses, Americans were dependent upon hearsay for information. When the first official (and, as it happens, palliative) reports were published, confusion and fear grew, and the population's imagination went into overdrive. It was believed that the entire Pacific Fleet had been sunk and that thousands of planes had been destroyed on the ground.

In the end, President Roosevelt felt it necessary to intervene personally. In his war address of 23 February 1942 he at least partially clarified for the nation the extent of the losses. Surveys of attitudes showed that he influenced a good quarter of the population with what he had said. Twenty million Americans closed their ear to Fama, empirical psychologists estimated. Nevertheless a few months later across the country there could be counted over a thousand rumours pertaining to the war. A good two-thirds of these were directed against the allies or against particular population groups: blacks, Jews, government officials, the British, the army and the navy. A good quarter of the rumours caused fear; these rumours were of tortured American prisoners, of illnesses spreading among the troops and the like. Only about every fiftieth rumour spoke hopefully and illusively of the dreams of the nation in their first summer of war: of victory and peace.

With this enemy on the home front, it was soon a question of some form of regulation of the dissemination of information and rumours, of a supported programme of American psychological enlightenment. An "Office of Facts and Figures" (OFF) and the "Office of War Information" (OWI) fought against it with (apparently) hard facts and real disinformation, there being a general acceptance that it was primarily a lack of information that produced rumours. On the other hand, OFF and OWI sought, like their counterparts in England, Japan and Germany, which operated with very similar methods, to put into effect a curfew on speaking. In the United Kingdom the humorous *Careless Talk Costs Lives* poster from the pointed pen of the Punch caricaturist Fougasse brought the population to silence, while in Germany "Feind hört mit!" – "The enemy is listening!" slogans were posted up everywhere.[277] On the American posters the Führer, the Duce and the Japanese emperor were depicted as nosy triplets, ears cupped, above the line "Enemy ears are listening"; a man drowns dramatically because "Someone talked", and Uncle Sam placed his finger on his lips: "I'm counting on you. Think before you talk."[278]

Silence serves secrecy and combats rumour. This is something the Germans and British knew as well as did the Americans: "Be ashamed" was what "loudmouths" were told in the Third Reich as they looked up at "shadow man" and "Pst!" posters. Garish red posters from 1944 with slogans calling for silence: "Do not corrupt mood and outlook by passing on rumours and exaggerated descriptions of events" are more prosaic examples of what Germans were being told.[279] And on the other side of the North Sea, the injunction to remain silent was put into verse: "Whether alone or in a crowd, / Never write or say aloud, / What you're loading, whence you hail, / Where you're bound for, when you sail". In America people were implored not to gossip with an even catchier rhyme: "Zip Your Lip and Save a Ship."[280]

This also became the catch-phrase of Mrs Frances Sweeney, the citizen of Boston without whom there would never have been any rumor clinics. At the beginning of 1942 the *Queen Mary*, a civil ship in the service of the American Navy, secretly anchored in Boston's harbour. Although or, indeed, precisely because the local media had been bound to remain silent about this, people soon began whispering about secret goings on in the harbour. It was said that there were apparently only blacks on board, volunteers for a suicide mission, others had managed to find out that there was not a single Jew in the crew, and others spoke of a cargo of wounded; some others had even managed to get hold of enough information to speak of a mutiny. When a few nights later the torrent of rumour was still circulating, a new rumour sprang up that the ship and its suspicious cargo had left. But it was not until the following morning, in broad daylight, that the *Queen Mary* put to sea, leaving Boston's quays and a fog of rumours, gossip and hearsay in her wake. And with this departure came the hour of Mrs Francis Sweeney, a woman renowned for her sense of community. In order to put an end to the anti-Semitic, anti-British and, above all, defeatist rumours that were circulating in the Irish community of Boston, she organised a meeting for members of several administrative bodies and other people of influence. Among others, police officers, teachers, social workers and businessmen took part in this citizens' initiative against Fama. The *Queen Mary* was however just the starting shot; the engaged citizens and officials agreed to rid Boston completely of all rumours.

Working with Gordon W. Allport, professor of psychology at Harvard University, and his doctoral student Robert H. Knappe, Frances Sweeney established the first rumor clinic in March 1942 – not long after Roosevelt's address. This rumour-hospital placed a weekly column in the local paper, the *Boston Sunday Herald-Traveller*. The intention here was to report on and eradicate rumours pertaining to the war. This rhetorical search-and-destroy campaign in the matter of the rumour, which by the end of 1943 had at its disposal a network of more than forty inter-connected American and Canadian clinics for its surgery on the open heart of the collective imagination, served as a model for further operations. Its perhaps greatest success was forcefully to spread the idea throughout the country that rumours are a matter for control by the authorities.

The person officially charged by the "Massachusetts Committee of Public Safety" with the task of looking into ways of controlling the rumour, the doctoral student Robert H. Knapp, defines his adversary Fama as "a proposition for belief of topical reference disseminated without official verification".[281] He views it as a primitive medium, imprecise and extremely unreliable. The rumour is therefore the distortion of functional communication. The rumor clinics are intended to fill the realm of hearsay with their own, credible information. Teams of specialists and people in authority are put together for this purpose. Alongside journalists and psychologists, to these teams also belong figures from public life: representatives of the church, trades unionists, businessmen, policemen, representatives of various cultural groups, blacks and whites. They work in close co-operation with representatives of the army and navy, of the FBI and other federal organisations; out of the citizen's initiative grows a concerted action of the highest reputation. The rumor clinics soon become institutions which people feel they can trust.

The work of a clinic is carried out in three steps: anamnesis, diagnosis and therapy. To begin with, relevant rumours are tracked down and collected by so-called "rumor wardens" or "morale wardens". These consist of volunteers who through their professions come into contact with many people. They form a type of network of eavesdroppers. More than two hundred Boston bar employees,[282] for example, supply the local rumor clinic with the necessary material. These warders of the rumour keep their ears to the ground and their eyes wide open, writing down what their neighbours and colleagues are saying.

The rumour front also runs straight through the middle of the armed forces. In a parallel action to that of the collection of rumours at large in the civilian population, the American military begins stalking Fama among its own. In the routine monthly reports filed by military intelligence personnel, information is now to be supplied about rumours circulating in the army. Upon hearing a rumour, an intelligence officer would usually write it down within an hour, each noted upon a separate sheet, together with information about the immediate source, the

G. van Kampen or A. Nicolai, *Fama with Wings, Fanfare and Reed*

estimated extent of the rumour's spreading, and an estimation of the credibility of the source and of the source's own source.[283] Such was the psychological labour of war. At the demobilisation of the unit, the military censor confiscated all the documents of the rumour collectors. Also in the military, at the front, the voice of hearsay is considered dangerous. Security is the absence of rumours; what comes with war belongs to the war.

In civil America rumours were apprehended with methods very similar to those used at the front; special questionnaires and lists were used by those charged with gathering up the rumours in order to get to the heart of each rumour from the many variants in circulation. The results were then posted to the rumor clinic. Yet were they, when the envelopes were opened, after this change of media, after this social elevation from the people to the elite, still the same rumours?

At least they were now readable, quotable and criticisable texts, ones between which the rumour doctors had to make a choice. This was the second stage of their work; a small number of the stories were fed to co-operating organisations, such as to the Red Cross, while a much greater number, after diagnosis, were fed straight to the waste-paper basket. Yet even the rumours that remained after this initial selection, the most dangerous ones, were then further sieved out. However if a rumour is both "substantially true" and "harmful", Robert Knapp's committee for public security recommended in retrospect that, "it is best not to give it still wider circulation".[284] In these cases it would have been impossible to trust even the rumor clinics' own methods, and the waste-paper basket took the place of the censor.

To the around only 10 per cent of the submitted rumours which the agencies saw fit to attack, belonged the WAC rumours. The way these rumours were handled is a paradigmatic example of the third stage of rumour control. The United States had several Women's Army Corps stationed in North Africa. A rumour started to circulate back home that five hundred of them had become pregnant and been discharged. They had, it was said, followed their inclinations under the African sun more than their orders – whether with friend or foe is not recorded. The *Syracuse Post-Standard*, which had fifty rumour wardens assigned to it, got to work on this rumour, and shortly afterwards had it printed. The *Post-Standard* quotes the story in many variants, supplying it with the warning, in bold type, "RUMOR". "Over 500 WACs have been discharged from the service because of illegitimate pregnancy" – "500 pregnant WACs have been returned from North Africa" – "General

Eisenhower says the WACs are his greatest source of trouble and are of no value to him." That was all false, the rumor clinic stressed. Since it is difficult to confirm the contrary, the newspaper could only set one statement against the other in a wholly apodictic manner. It reported that the number of WACs stationed in North Africa was less than five hundred and that Eisenhower thought very highly of them. There was of course "not the slightest shred of evidence to support such tales as these".[285] After this rumour was set straight, there followed the advice to the reader to question and consider critically every similar piece of information, every rumour.

But this was not the whole story. The main work of the clinic lay in fathoming the psychological background of these sorts of rumour, such as sexual inhibitions, suppressed fears and the mechanisms of psychological projection. Displaying a sophisticated talent for writing, the author of the piece about the WAC rumour shifts from the "you" of informative address to the inclusive "we" of description: "We human beings are complex creatures."[286] This is an eternal truth. Nobody, he writes, is invulnerable to the power of the rumour and all the "juicy" stories. For they "are not made merely by incidents, nor by the false and careless words; nor by Axis agents; they are a part of the stuff which is inside those who listen to them". Potentially every American could become a patient of the rumor clinic; everyone must work on themselves, asserts a professor of political psychology at Syracuse University in his capacity as Professor of Political Psychology.

His battle in the Sunday newspapers is that of light against the dark forces of the subconscious, and what he has to say acts like a sermon from the front line running through the soul of every American. Politics and war become a question of the ethical maturity of each individual. What the enlighteners about the rumour either do not know or are silent about is that German propagandists are secretly putting into effect targeted whispering campaigns to direct the voice of informal talk along the lines that suit them. Financed by American Nazis, rumour propagandists have been at work since 1940, that is to say, since before the American entry into the war (propagandists whose methods will quickly be adopted by advertising strategists for sophisticated advertising campaigns[287]). They spread word that Germany will win the war and that the information about German atrocities are just rumours. Apart from this, they also distribute their stock of anti-Semitic ideas.[288]

The clinics are intended to take away the rhetorical and mnemotechnical potency of rumours, such as that of the pregnant WACs. Particular care is called for when individual population groups become the subject of a rumour, since there is a danger that slogans and turns of phrase may remain in the memory of those who hear them, even after they have been refuted. So dangerous are the form of words of the rumour. For this reason the instructions at one rumor clinic recommend breaking up memorable sentences into their constituent parts. In this way forgetfulness is encouraged. But when all other media are utilised in the struggle against the "rumor virus" – cinema, posters, slogans, songs – the doctors explicitly warn of the dangers of an incorrect and dangerous deployment of that powerful instrument of manipulation, the radio. Howard Koch and Orson Welles' broadcast of the latter's *The War of the Worlds*, an account of a Martian invasion on Earth, still figures large in the minds of the social psychologists. For radio broadcasts are often only listened to fragmentarily: "People tune in late and tune out early",[289] report the specialists, reducing the phenomenon to a catchy formula.

Rhetoric

The campaign of the clinics is above all a rhetorical operation. Theoretical essay and complex explanation are put into action against mnemotechnical verse and aphorism, against parataxis and ellipsis, against the constant "it is said that". For this reason the rumour is shifted in the clinics from main clause to subordinate clause and indirect speech: "Rumour has it that ...". Hearsay is repeated in that it is cited. Not just syntactic, but also graphical means attempt to make Fama appear alien. Thus the whispered stories are presented incarcerated between inverted commas, such as in the Boston *Sunday Herald* of 18 July 1943: "RUMOR: *Some minority group (Negro), (Jew), (Catholic) (or other) is not loyal to America, but is (planning a riot), (plotting to get control of the government), (evading military service)*."[290] The rumour as construction kit, a victim to mark with a cross.

A rumor clinic operates with the strategic aim of influencing political opinion formation; for this purpose it makes use of medial, rhetorical and literary methods. In a similar way to how the Brothers Grimm collected together the fairy tales of their time, they gather up spoken rumours and put them in writing; they give them new contexts, demonstrate their impact and, through analysis and interpretation, demystify and explain them. They oppose the fleeting, ephemeral and intermittent text of the rumour with the relatively constant – that is to say repeatable and recognisable – medium of centrally printed text. The space of writing stands against the non-spatial, uncontoured and mobile principle of hearsay,[291] which only lasts a moment before disappearing, and then perhaps reappearing shortly thereafter. In the place of the mobile web of drifting variants, versions and quotes, in the place of the anonymous series of voices, it publishes a single, reproducible text.

The clinics demonstrate also their authority with their high print runs. Authority can be detected in the way their articles are set out, always headed in bold with the title "THE RUMOR CLINIC", and also in the language of these articles, for example in the use of talk of "us" and "them", in the emphasis placed on academic positions and titles, in the author's competence as a specialist, and in "real world" close friends and advisors mentioned within them – in short, authority speaks through all means with which the text "points to this figure that, at least in appearance, is outside it and antecedes it",[292] which is the description Michel Foucault gives the author.

With the proliferation of new rules governing discourse, among these, for example, directives not to talk, war secrets, military censorship, and other aspects of the culture of secrecy that led to a scarcity of information, the war of the rumor clinic against rumours seems like a conflict of enormous transpersonal and transepochal forces. But people continue to spread rumours, despite the social scientists, military personnel and politicians in their rumor clinics. People know only a little about the effect of the clinics on the public at large. In Syracuse the activities of the rumor clinic are, from the very beginning, monitored by a scientific research programme; the researchers, some of whom are themselves active in the anti-rumour programme, discover that white-collar workers and teachers constitute the group that most avidly reads the clinic's output.[293] Obviously reading the articles about the rumours demands a certain critical competence on the part of the subjects of the research, who mainly consist of members of the families of the social scientists conducting it. Such questionable results were to be expected since the relatively elaborate clinics indeed appeal to a more educated readership. What alone is interesting is the finding that men are more liable to believe the American war rumours than women.

The success of anti-rumour campaigns like that of the rumor clinics cannot be measured. Details about the amount of anti-rumour literature published says little about the effects of analysis, censorship and attempted control. Yet the clinics will have had an effect. Indeed, the fact that the clinics were themselves the subject of a rumour intimates the attention paid them by the American public. For it was soon announced that anyone caught spreading the rumours against which the clinics were combating would receive a fine of ten thousand dollars or a long prison sentence.[294] At least, that was what people said was now the case.

The unregulated dimension of talk provokes those who wish to control it to make use of the measure that can be thought of as constituting propaganda, the instrument which, ever since Pope Gregor XV attempted to counter Protestants and pagan Americans with more than just the sword, has been used to persuade people to believe what others have wanted them to believe. The rumor clinics stand in the tradition of the Sacra Congregation de Propaganda Fide. For they do not just wish

THINK BEFORE YOU TELL ANYONE! Poster in a Berlin Factory (1950s)

to disseminate information, but are explicitly battling for the "trust" and "faith" of the people.[295] Yet this is perhaps something that cannot fully be achieved merely with newspaper articles and posters.

Somewhat enviously the American engineers of manipulation therefore sometimes look across the great divide at their German counterparts. There they find the German population being encouraged to avoid "idleness, monotony, and personal disorganisation",[296] it being considered that these allowed sufficient time and reason for rumours to spread. However, the Third Reich had no such programme, and Germany was anything other than Fama-free. An entry in Victor Klemperer's notebook also shows this. The Dresden philologist and sensitive chronicler heard the rumour about a rumour "that the Gestapo put out a rumour in Berlin and monitored how quickly and by what route it made its way to Munich".[297] Klemperer's observation shows how in Germany people were also conscious of the power and origin of rumours and believed that the authorities had an interest in the exchange of unofficial chatter. And they were right: for precisely the talk and gossip of the little people on the preferred themes of "home" and "front" carried – and gambled with – a spirit of virtual resistance.[298] For this reason state and party took great interest in it. With their reports on the mood of the people, the organs of the state responsible for security and various rumour agencies of the Reich propaganda ministry and army took pains to get on the trail of the flight of words on the "home front"; chains and networks of rumours appeared to the authorities as "centres of resistance" which had to be destroyed. The word "faith" also crops up here, something the state wanted members of the population to possess in order to be "immune" to the rumour, that potential catalyst of unrest.

And it was no different in Japan. Already before the American airforce, taking off from aircraft carriers and secure bases in the Pacific, began in 1943 systematically to destroy the military capability of the Japanese Empire, the unanimity of the Japanese was coming under strain. Graffiti in all manner of places, even slogans scribbled on bank notes, reminded the Japanese in their everyday existence of the wartime shortages and of the fall in the standard of living. In a country in which "it was a rare toilet or factory wall or lamppost" [299] that escaped the scrutiny of the "thought police", gossip and rumour were also carefully noted and combated. At least, this was attempted, for it was suspected that they expressed a form of dangerous power: the honest opinions of people who had had enough of war and its privation and suffering.

Yet in Japan the campaign against verbal sabotage through hearsay was difficult. One knew of rumours which spread in the circles of those who were entrusted with the task of making them safe. From August 1937 to April 1943, the relevant Japanese authorities brought cases against 2139 people because they had spread one or more of the 1603 rumours that contravened the military code. In around a third of cases, the flight of Fama also had legal consequences for those who had taken part. Between December 1943 and May 1945 alone, the military police identified over 8000 rumours; more than half of these concerned military matters, the others concerning living standards and questions of domestic security. And the longer the war went on and the quicker emperor and government lost credibility, the more rumours began to circulate. With the increasing uncertainty they quickly gained weight as constituting an alternative level of reflection. As everywhere in times of war, they reflected the mutual hopes of people who were scared and in need. Just the local colour varies the motives of these stories. Thus it was reported towards the end of the war that policemen had, in their battle against the black market in rice, taken their knives to sacks which in fact contained children; and attention was also turned to the Koreans living in Japan, who, it was said, were guilty of rape and cannibalism.

War rumours therefore surfaced in both camps of the Second World War. Even the neutral Swiss discussed whether penalties should be imposed or whether people should be allowed to talk freely.[300] When, in the face of this world-wide dissemination of very similar rumours, the American domestic propaganda specialists looked around to see what their enemy counterparts were up to, was it really just to gain some short-term tactical advantage over them? The further development of rumour control in the United States would suggest that there was more to it, that this newly systematised approach to the rumour operated within a wider framework. For with the victory over National Socialist Germany, the battle of the rumour doctors did not even pretend to be coming to an end. Looking back at the experience of American propaganda abroad and of enemy propaganda in the United States, American social psychologists soon recognised how easily what people say could be influenced by the techniques and strategies of manipulation perfected during the war.[301]

Control Centres

The professional rumour-killers and researchers of the Forties saw the war to a great extent as a test-run for the civilian years to come: "The danger of the rumour will not be over when the shooting stops."[302] After having managed, for the first time in history, to go a long way towards controlling the virus of the rumour in wartime, Knapp believed, new paths would open up into a brave new world without rumours. That was the vision of the technocrats of communication. And at the end of the war, the struggle against rumours and the research into them did not come to an end. In the Forties and Fifties social psychologists conducted numerous studies in close financial and personal co-operation of the scientific and military communities. They were trying to understand the psychological dimensions of war as well as the rudiments of the psychological conduct of war. The years-long interdisciplinary "Project Revere" alone, sponsored by the US Air Force at the Public Opinion Laboratory of Washington University, produced a flood of around one hundred articles and reports, which alongside various aspects of the psychological conduct of war, also examined the effects of rumours.[303]

The blind spot in the system of rumour control is something, however, which none of the rumour doctors can fill; they cannot move beyond the limits of their discipline, they cannot place themselves outside the framework within which they operate. At least, this is the impression one gets when one observes the subduers of the rumour at work: a child of the rumor clinics, shortly after the war the most important social-psychological study of the rumour is undertaken. Gordon W. Allport who, together with Leo Postman, was the author of the book in question, was the spiritual father of the clinics.

The two researchers from Harvard University began by stating that their work concerned enlightenment, that is to say, the destruction of the power of the false and stupid rumours by means of knowledge: "In the summer of 1945 the atomic bomb was the subject of many rumours, especially among the uneducated",[304] they wrote in the book which appeared in 1947, using this example to show what it is they stand against with their work: "It was rumoured that lethal radiations hover for a long time over an area hit by an atomic blast." Propaganda is mightier than science; and even the fight against rumours sometimes finds itself clambering around on rumours. In the second edition of the study, published in 1965, that is to say, at a time when the American government can no longer claim that there is no risk from radiation, this book demonstrates this dialectic of scientific enlightenment about rumours. It now looks as if the attempt to bring enlightenment has been infected by the "virus" of rumour. And because it itself, probably without knowing it, has been struck down by just such a virus, it unintentionally demonstrates the historical framework of just such a fight against infection. When it is not the illness, but rather hygiene, that causes infection, when it is not the rumour that is ideological, rather the enlightenment about it, then the therapy itself is the disease.

Thus the war can be seen as the father of some strange things. Some of them, such as the rumor clinic experiments with children,[305] follow closely on the heels of the anti-rumour practice of the war, others, such as the so-called "rumor control centers", telephone centres geared towards dealing with rumours, make a grand entrance a good twenty years after its end.

Their pre-history, however, begins much earlier, namely on a hot day in that summer which, because of its race riots, has been logged in North American history as the calamitous "Red Summer". The weather was good on 27 July 1919. The sun shone above the American Mid West, and girls and boys made their way to the beaches along the edge of the lake. The seventeen-year-old Eugene Williams from Chicago packed his trunks and towel and went, like hundreds of blacks and whites of his age, to swim. Throughout America, racial segregation determined even the lighter sides of life here on Lake Michigan. An invisible line of demarcation divided the beach into a white zone and a black zone. It was this line that would cost Eugene, wading into the "black" water, his life.

Whether a ball from one side of the line got thrown into the other, whether someone whistled at the wrong girl or a funny look spoiled a bather's fun, somehow, on that sunny day, the beach erupted in violence as Chicago's white and black youths fought a pitched battle among themselves. First a few exchanged words, an argument, a few shoves, and suddenly the beach descended into pitched battle, with fists soon turning into stones and bottles. When Eugene, away from the trouble out in the lake, turned to come back to shore he must have noticed that he had drifted over to the "white" side of the beach. Perhaps he was not a very proficient swimmer, perhaps he was seized by cramp – whatever the case, he found himself unable to get back to his side of a beach which had turned into a battlefield. He drowned. When shortly afterwards his body was retrieved from the water, the wildest rumours were already in circulation. Swift as the wind, the rumours flew through the city, and they proved to be enough of a spark to set off the powder keg of Chicago.[306] In a few days thirty-eight people died on account of the racial unrest, twenty-three blacks and fifteen whites; nearly two-thirds of the five hundred injuries reported to the police were injuries

Hans Weigel the Elder, *Fama* (c. 1546)

thirds of the five hundred injuries reported to the police were injuries to blacks.

What differentiated this race riot from both earlier and later ones were six hundred pages of printed paper, the report written by a commission set up in the wake of the disturbances. This report, with a title typical of its era, *The Negro in Chicago*, can perhaps be seen as the beginning of the modern age of American research into the rumour. It emphasised that rumours played a decisive role in the riots. And ever since this report was published, it has been generally accepted that in order to hinder riots one must fight against rumours: no fire signal without Fama, no flying stones unless words have themselves flown first.

But can it be said that rumours were responsible for the deaths of nearly forty people? And what should be done to stop them? Half a century later, while American cities before and, particularly, after the murder of Martin Luther King on 4 April 1968 experienced disturbances approaching the intensity of a civil war, the considerations that these questions raised had tangible consequences. The Kerner Commission, set up that same year to look into the events, reported that 65 per cent of the rumours that accompanied the unrest significantly aggravated tension and disorder.[307] And with this, the war against unofficial talk became an issue of utmost concern throughout the States. In almost a hundred cities in North America – and also in some Irish and British cities – rumour control centres once again take up the work of the rumor clinics over twenty years after the demise of the latter.

According to a report of the US Department of Justice, a "Rumor Central" was "an office responsible for the collection, evaluation, and countering of rumors which could lead to civil disorder".[308] In principle these centres work along the same lines as the rumor clinics of the Second World War. Citizens report what they have heard, the information about the rumours is analysed and compared with the known facts in order that the rumours can then be neutralised systematically by the modern rumour doctors before being placed back into civil society. But these clinics do not have to rely on Gutenberg's genius in order to be able to do their work: Alexander Graham Bell is the person to whom they must be thankful. Yet before they turn to his invention, they have tried all manner of other means of getting their message across, including educational films, the employment of street-workers in Washington in 1967 or even, in several cities in Indiana, the use of a special anti-rumour guard.[309] Yet it is soon noticed that all these are not up to the task of fighting modern Fama. Since rumours made use of modern means of communication during the race riots, it makes sense, in turn, to make use of these means to fight them. Everywhere in the land citizens' organisations, public welfare agencies, student clubs, chambers of commerce, churches and, naturally, local administrations and police forces set up telephone-based rumour control centres. They are called "Verification Centers" or "Rumor Clarification Committees" and thereby encourage people to get in contact with them to get filled-in on recent events. Whoever comes across a rumour simply needs to pick up the phone. Some towns even have two control centres, and in the capital Washington, four rumour phone lines divide the work up between themselves; one of these is rigged up exclusively to set the minds of edgy senators at rest. A slogan of the time exactly sums up what the authorities were trying to do: "Kill a Rumor Today."

That sounds easy, and it was often cheap, if nothing else. The telephone strategy in San Mateo cost 126 dollars a year, while San Bernardino spent yearly forty thousand dollars on the battle against Fama. It was all a question of the size of the town. Some centres operated with volunteer staff, others, like those in Boston, Chicago, Detroit and Los Angeles, with paid employees, some even employing teachers with whom to drain the swamp of wild chatter.

Alongside thirty-five other rumour centres, the centre in Chicago, held in great repute by the authorities and media, is, in 1974, still functioning throughout the day, every day. It has at its disposal ten telephone lines to take calls from the public, lines which handled forty thousand calls during the riots that followed Martin Luther King's death and which still find themselves overburdened by the demand for information, a telephone line that links the centre directly with the fire service and the police and also a special line for research and confirmation. During the disturbances at the end of the Sixties, the members of staff have to mark out the problem- and rumour-zones of the city: black for sealed-off streets, blue for where marksmen are operating, and red for where the entire urban crisis is flooding along the telephone lines into the rumour control centre.[310]

Limits of Control

The effect of centres such as those just described cannot be estimated with any degree of accuracy. Unlike the rumor clinics of the Forties, it is clear who has set them up: in the vast majority of cases white suburbanites. They want to know whether black vandals are on their way to their suburb or whether their Cadillacs are safe. The official rumour-telephones only very rarely take calls from black communities. Quite the opposite; the distrust that so many blacks felt for the state and urban authorities went so deep immediately after the murder of Martin Luther King that they viewed the centres as precisely the mechanisms of social control that they were. The unspoken dictum of the rumour phones was "Keep Quiet and Prevent a Riot."[311] The centres could not close up the divide between the races. In practice, they used their influence for the most part to balance out the actual information deficiency of the white majority. It is no wonder, then, that so many blacks were distrustful of an institution with which, entirely in accordance with guidelines, there worked bastions of authority and control such as governor, mayor, national guard, white press and other suspected agents of their social misery. For not everyone would have been too comforted when, on the other end of the line, they were greeted by a terse "Sheriff Flanagan, rumor phone".

Rumours speak of the direct cause of, but never the underlying reason for, social tension. There is no truth in falsity, and the events after the death of Eugene Williams in the "Red Summer" and the Harlem riots of 1943 had already shown that those attempting to bring order to the situation, and indeed politicians, can themselves be supremely effective spreaders of rumours. Where police stations become places of reshipment of risky information, the trust of whole population groups is not so easily won. Since the rumor phones are seen as hotlines for whites, they themselves become an interpretable factor in the battle for information, gaining symbolic value.

The centres stand or fall depending on nods given by a social "middle", a centre of local power and respectability that speaks in the name of everyone. The main rule of a centre of power like this is sober pragmatism: "Avoid philosophical discussion at all costs"[312] is the first commandment in an official directive for rumour centres. Unlike most American social researchers, according to whom rumours simply spring from a lack of information, the telephonists of the rumour did not think it a good idea to mention the black, blue and red zones to their flustered callers. Campaigners against the rumour recommend countering rumours with common sense. The question is whether this sort of attitude can do anything to help social cohesion. The anti-rumour pamphlets that circulated in the affected regions read like little lessons in social trust in a landscape of social distrust. This literature warns gravely against setting up the centres within police stations, a piece of advice that was ignored often enough. Every member of a centre's staff should keep the procedure anonymous, remaining silent about their own identity and the location and address of the telephone centre. It is not the personal authority of a named author, as with the clinics, that stands up against rumours, rather an anonymous ensemble of specialists, functionaries and "decision makers", which remains hidden behind the voices of the telephonists. How the rumour phones are to be viewed as a universal information service, an umbilical cord between citizens and the local authorities, when those who run them hide their identities with such great care, remains a mystery. As houses burn in Chicago, Boston and elsewhere, these dreams also go up in smoke.

While the people on the streets reacted to what they heard and saw, to the realities which were the cause of so many rumours, in the centres the phones were near melting point, so little did so many know about what was actually happening. Perhaps the burning cities demonstrated the failure of an attempt to protect a presumed centre of society against an assault by the periphery. It must be recognised that with the telephone centres' pragmatism there was never any hope of counteracting the centrifugal forces in a society that was disintegrating ever more rapidly. The periphery proved to be more real than the centre, and the disturbances took place regardless. In the face of the disappearing chances of measuring the ever growing media and those who control them against some form of reality, the dreams of the control centres seem somewhat ludicrous. What effect did the telephone centres set up In Los Angeles in April 1992 have after the acquittal in the Rodney King trial, or when the trial was conducted again a year later? Who believed Bill Clinton's information managers at the end of the *Monicagate*-hotline? These initiatives do, however, demonstrate one thing, namely the faith that those who operate them have in the remnants of some form of social centre. At the same time, though, they show precisely how this centre disintegrates into many centres.[313] For even the centre is just a rumour at the periphery.

This can be seen already in the historical modernisation thrust from rumor clinic to rumour control centre, in the leap from the medium of print to the medium of the telephone. The printed medium stands in a hierarchically arranged system of centre (editorial, printing) and periphery (reader); the telephone, on the other hand, allows much more complex exchanges of information in various directions, which is precisely how it was used during the broadcast about the invasion of the

Martians. It is not without reason that we speak of "telephone network". And the rumour against which Bill Clinton's rumour centre did battle came from the network to end all networks: the Internet.

The medium of print's conception of itself rests on its verifiability, on the unchanging existence of the texts that are disseminated by means of it. And this is something implied by a large German daily paper, in its advertising literature offering subscriptions, when it explicitly recommends itself to potential subscribers as a print strategy against rumours: "Dissatisfied with 'half measures'? Fed up with half truths and rumours? – Well then we should finally get to know one another"[314] it writes. And the president of the German journalists' organisation warns about the Internet as a medium of rumour: "The stream of information has become much faster. Rumours, erroneous reports, but naturally also correct news are sowed much more quickly than before" he says in an interview, "and in the Internet often it is not at all possible to tell whom a piece of information came from".[315] And it is certainly the case that the Internet has exactly the same structure as hearsay; and information sent through it is often picked up and amplified by the medial system of television, radio and finally also the press; there gossip from the Net mutates into news, even if only the news of an anonymous fragment of hearsay. The news channels broadcast "as directly as possible; increase the tension with live broadcasts, evaluate, dramatise and follow events minute by minute. News is made to appear more important than it is, press conferences are an integral part of the spectacle – a self-infecting circle of pomposity arises."[316] The mass media end up merely representing publicity rather than producing it.

As regards the Internet, its supporters stress, it is the democratic uses to which precisely its uncontrollability can be put that is what is so wonderful about it. Among the documents to be found at the "Drudge Report" website, which let the cat out of the bag about the Lewinsky affair and set the rumours about it in motion, there can be found conjectures as to the genesis of this great media event. One of these texts appears under the heading "Invisible Ink": "The ethics cops who patrol newspaper and magazine newsrooms can't control the rumors and unsubstantiated stories that people post to the Web … If the Web prints it and television goes with it, print must follow."[317] For the online journalist Matt Drudge and his supporters, the real danger does not come from the "virus" of unverified Internet stories, rather from censorship; the hygiene, not the illness, is what is seen by them as infectious. Control of the Internet would only be possible from a point outside the Net, it would have to encompass the whole Net and encounter it as a single entity, and would have to be the equivalent of some form of total blackout or computer virus.

Considering the possibilities for manipulation and simulation afforded by modern technology, reality appears – as in the recent film *Wag the Dog* – increasingly as a playground for the flood of data of which the modern world consists. On the homepage of the Drudge Report one can find a point at which to enter the water and swim in it. Everyone is invited, be it by submitting some commentary, a new story or a new version of an old one or some other information, to play a part in the hearsay: "Confidentiality guaranteed!" The Internet offers confidentiality and secrecy. Never before has a medium been so well described by Virgil's description of Fama, for like his monster it is to be found "thriving on movement, gathering strength as it goes";[318] and the digital Net also "never closes her eyelids in sweet slumber".

But the prototype for cyberspace is not to be found in the twentieth century, rather in Ovid. His description of the House of Fama reads like an analysis of the possibilities offered by digital communication. Like Ovid's construction, the Internet is also everywhere, and like Fama's house, it too has "a thousand apertures"[319] and "countless entrances"; "It's open night and day and built throughout / of echoing bronze; it all reverberates, / Repeating voices, doubling what it hears" Ovid writes

CALL IN A STORY TO THE DRUDGE REPORT

Confidentiality guaranteed!

[Type and send from box below]

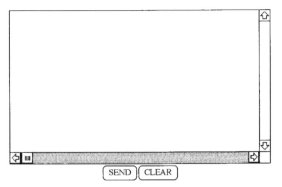

about unregulated communication. "All things everywhere, however far, / Are scanned and watched, and every voice and word / Reaches its listening ears." And finally "Rumours everywhere, / Thousands, false mixed with true, roam to and fro." What is true, nobody can say, but everyone can make their contribution.

The echo chamber of hearsay is a small rectangle on the screen: "Type and send from the box below", the Net asks its users, who can then choose between two commands: "send" or "clear". It could not be easier. The simple arrangement makes apparent that in the age of electronic mass media, the story of the rumour has not come to an end. Quite the opposite: it perfectly suits the medial possibilities now available. The Internet is hearsay in digital form; the great age of Fama has just begun.

7
The Search for the Formula for the Rumour

The Click in the Region of the Heart – Virus? – Formulae,
Functions – The Solution – The Spiral of the Rumour

When, a hundred years ago, the Harvard professor Hugo Münsterberg carried out an experiment in Idaho, he had no idea that he would soon become the star of a global rumour. He had travelled to the West to carry out tests on the accused during a trial of a criminal called Harry Orchard – "a depraved murderer of eighteen human beings"[320] – using association tests and other exotic psychographic methods. He looked into "false memories, illusions, suggestions" and entrusted what he found to a few legal journals. He refused interviews with the press since his experiments "were merely carried out in the service of science", as he put it, and because the proceedings against Orchard were still under way. Yet the newspapers were insuperable. In the *New York Herald* appeared the first lengthy, hypothetical article about Münsterberg's experiments with Orchard. His invention, a young colleague speculated, was a machine made up of three parts: "the automatograph, which records involuntary movements; the pneumograph, which records the rate and rhythm of breathing; and the sphymograph, which, attached to the wrist, records the heart beats". All three machines together would clearly show, he argued, whether the witness was speaking the truth or lying. Had Münsterberg really invented this psychological wonder machine? people asked in New York. In Boston this hypothetical article reappeared as a statement of fact, and shortly afterwards it was cabled to London that the famous professor's "'crowning life's work' was the invention of an apparatus by which he could detect lies". The question of truth and lies in the legal sense seemed at last to have been answered.

The news swept back to America, was embellished, altered, exaggerated. It sped to France, to Germany, and soon it was reported in three hundred newspapers around the world: Hugo Münsterberg had invented a "lying-machine".

Yet this rumour about the forensic solution to the problem of bearing witness was false. At least, this is what Münsterberg insisted. After his trip to Idaho he sent countless denials and explanations, in which he denied the existence of his lie-detector, though without success. He was unable to silence the murmur of rumour. Years later Münsterberg was still being connected with the lie-detector. The dreamed-up machine designed to force truth out of a criminal had, in fact, forced truth out of the picture; hearsay was mightier than the witness.

The rumour about Münsterberg's wonder machine was a cultural phenomenon and also an event. And like every event, this example of hearsay is not without a background and context. Max Weber argued that events do not just take place, do not just happen, but have a meaning and happen because of that meaning. What this meaning is in the case of rumours is something to which poets, politicians, historians and other social scientists have all put their mind. Whether with or without "sphymographs" and their like, while the still young social sciences are in the process of developing their modern conception of themselves, they do not find their objects of study just in established social institutions. "A social fact", wrote Emile Durkheim in 1895, "is any way of acting, whether fixed or not, capable of exerting over the individual an external constraint; or: which is general over the whole of a given society while having an existence of its own, independent of its individual manifestations".[321] What could better fit this description than rumours?

In their search for an equivalent language, social scientists define the rumour within the limits of their discipline with the help of experiments, formulae and models. While they measure, compare, sketch and analyse, they develop systems to which hearsay as an event relates. In doing so, most sociologists, psychologists and academic lawyers approach the peculiar social phenomenon of rumour with the categories of norm and deviation, truth and falsity. They are particularly interested in the question of the truth value of the rumour; its medial circumstances and above all its particular rhetorical structure play only a subordinate role. This is how many researchers into the rumour look for the independent existence of hearsay. The testing procedures, developed for this purpose and sometimes extremely involved, concentrate on

Georg Pencz, *Rumor* (1531)

questions of content, reference and variance. What is the rumour saying about what, and how does it mutate over time?

The Click in the Region of the Heart

Winter 1901/02: in the criminology seminar of Berlin University professors and students are discussing a legal text. The debate is coming to an end. The day has been long, outside it is dark, the clock says that it is a quarter to eight. Yet before trained and student criminologists alike can go and enjoy the rest of the evening, something most out of the ordinary takes place:

> At the end of the debate about Tarde's book Privy Councillor von Liszt asks: "Would anyone like to add anything before I say the final word on our reading?"
> Dr K. stands up.

von Liszt: "Colleague K. would like to speak."

K.: "I would like to consider Tarde's theory briefly from the point of view of Christian moral philosophy."

Leh. loud enough to be heard: "Oh, to think we nearly missed out on that!"

K.: "Be so good as to be quiet when you have not been asked!"

Leh.: "How dare you say that to me?" He stands up.

K. "If you open your mouth just one more time …" He approaches Leh. with fists raised.

Leh.: "Get away from me, or …"

Leh. takes a revolver and presses it up against K.'s forehead.

von Liszt hits Leh.'s raised arm. The revolver sinks to the level of K.'s chest. When it finds itself in the region of K.'s heart, the lock clicks.[322]

"K." survives the click in the region of the heart, "Leh." also; nobody is injured – and neither is anyone arrested. For what looks like a scene in a play is in fact just that. The performance is part of a psychological experiment with which members of the faculty of law at Berlin University, under the direction of Sally Jaffa, sought to test the accuracy and reliability of witness statements. Apart from the "actors" taking part in it, nobody is informed beforehand, yet many of the witnesses, who had been startled out of the serenity of the seminar, were detained and asked to write down what they had seen: some that same evening, some a day later, others some time after that. The lawyers wanted to ascertain what role personal background, the temporal distance from an event and other factors play in memory. The idea for Jaffa's experiment came from the Breslau philosopher and psychologist William Stern, who was born in 1871 and was the pupil of Moritz Lazarus, the founder of ethnopsychology. Among Stern's teachers and colleagues can be counted, with the likes of Hermann Ebbinghaus, Wilhelm Dilthey and Georg Simmel, some of the truly progressive philosophers, sociologists and psychologists of the time. In the context of forensic psychology, he opened up with his work the social-scientific inquiry into the rumour.

1902, shortly after the "murderous attack in the lecture hall", he devises a strange experimental set-up. He wishes to clarify the question, "to what extent the average statement of a normal, flawless witness can be considered a correct account of the objective facts".[323] What does a witness say when he speaks the truth? This question interests the courts as much as it interests history, which is why contemporary historians carefully observed the research of Stern and his colleagues.[324]

Stern works with "first-class human material", namely with "educated persons at the most receptive age". Already "on account of his job" one could with him "expect a certain amount of practice in the observation and in the self-criticism of the memory".[325] The subjects undergo different memory tests, and Stern arrives at the perhaps not exactly surprising conclusion that a mistake-free memory is "not the rule, rather the exception"; mistakes are an integral part of memory, and "even an oath is no protection against fallacious memories". Memories too lead their "own lives". A similar conclusion is reached by the directors of the Berlin lecture hall performance: "An action, even the most concise, leaves its mark on the memory also not better than a spoken word", those who carried out the test ascertain, going on to note that the manner and content of a memory assimilate to the "normal, often experienced".[326]

No memory is without mistake. When every memory is wrong, what then happens when several people are involved? William Stern answers this question with a further psychological laboratory experiment: with an "experimental rumour". Stern himself, as "Person A", reads the following crime story to "Person B":

A strange discovery was made a few weeks ago in a small town 6 miles from Lyon. In a respectable house in the town lived the widow of a civil servant. Of her two children, the son died a few years after the father, while the pretty daughter had disappeared from the house immediately after the death of her brother, something that greatly confused the mother, who had the vanished searched for with all means, but without success. In the course of the years, the pain of the young woman ebbed away; she had sought forgetfulness in a busy social life, at the same time with lively benevolence. – An anonymous tip-off to the police suggested the inconceivable, that the daughter had not vanished, rather had the whole time, that is to for say 3 years, been held as a prisoner by her mother. The police found a secret jib door that led into a wretched little room. Here the poor girl lay unkempt upon her bed of straw. The unnatural mother, who was immediately arrested, refused to give any information about what had happened. Of the many conjectures that sprung up everywhere, only one was voiced which did not seem at all plausible: it was said that perhaps the son of the widow was killed by his mother, who wished to inherit everything herself, in order to remove him from the picture, and that the daughter, who had by chance been witness to the crime, was then in this way rendered harmless by the criminal.[327]

Stern makes this rather detailed, "original" account the starting point of a sequence of versions recounted by different people. Subject B later notes what he remembers; this is then read to C, and so on. Each experiment, says William Stern himself, is a "fiction". And a rumour that is based upon a narrative, upon a fictitious crime story, itself produces more fiction. This can be seen when one compares the first, fourth and last versions of this murder story. The final version of the anecdote is more gripping, more concrete, harder-hitting than the original. What before was vague is now definite, out of suspicion emerges certainty, the obviously disturbed mother of the first version mutates into the "dehumanised" murderer. And finally the secret door no longer leads into an anteroom, rather down through a trapdoor into a "dark, eerie room".[328] The first laboratory rumour in the world develops and demonstrates its own rationality. It reduces complexity and adapts its narrative according to moral criteria. Good and evil come strongly to the fore, and the whole gives an idea of a "dark, eerie room" under the ground of the "facts".

Other scientists emulated Stern's experiment. They explored diverse parameters of memory, and in doing so also touched on the question of the "declarative accuracy of the sexes".[329] In November 1908, the Breslau psychologist Rosa Oppenheim repeated the experiment with the same "crime story". As with Oppenheim, the last recorded version of the story is the shortest:

> A family was made up of father, mother and some children. The father and the children, apart from the youngest, died suddenly. The mother seemed to be extremely upset, yet soon she had forgotten everything and became cheerful and happy again. Then the youngest child also died, yet soon after that a rumour arose that this child had not died, rather had been held prisoner by the mother. It was looked into and the child was found locked up and in a wretched state. The dehumanised mother had done this to shield herself from the suspicion that she had poisoned the son.[330]

There now appears a new factor: instead of the anonymous tip-off, a rumour emerges. Even if Rosa Oppenheim is convinced of the "variability and of rumours",[331] the rumour that is introduced into the story is obviously correct. Oppenheim however, like all empirical researchers into the rumour, measures the rumour as a form of misdirected message that becomes more erroneous the further that it travels from its origin. The degree of departure of a piece of information from its original form indicates correspondingly the radius of its dissemination and also its age.

Most of the early explorers of the rumour proceed in a similar manner. As sorts of lie detectors they measure the pulse and rate of breathing of Fama. But in investigating rumours as sequences of departures, they are presupposing the existence of an "original". What they can then reveal is the false collective memory of it. Already in the social experiment it is clear the "original", the origin, is a composition – a story. "Person A",

M. D. LXXI.

Jost Amman, *Fama with a Fanfare* (16th Century)

as the person conducting the experiment, who places himself at the beginning of the chain of information, is called, is nothing more than a practical tool. It forms a degree zero of gossip, in order to be able to measure from this a distance along the axis of information change. This construct of the degree zero can, without further ado, be transferred to a reality outside the laboratory. The episode with the clicking revolver alone has several witnesses, whose versions of the events complement and contradict one another and can feed back on one another in diverse ways, if so allowed. Stern, Jaffa and Oppenheim all fail to spot the issues here raised; their metaphor for the rumour is the chain with a beginning and an end. It is precisely the construction of the "original", upon which the entire experiment is based, that appears as the actual fiction of this experiment. Later researchers will, with much more sensitivity to the actual machinations of the rumour in reality, eventually settle on the model of the net, which has no beginning and no end, at most a centre and a periphery.

Despite such opposition to Stern's premises, the scientific exploration of the rumour begins with his experiment. For the experiments staged and inspired by him exposed the rumour for the first time as a subject for the social sciences. Up to the present day, researchers into gossip operate with similar methods to Stern, and experimental sociology still considers the rumour to be a form of misdirected message. Everything becomes, when it is possible, ever falser, ever more fictional the further it is in space or time from its origin. Where however is the point at which the variation comes to a halt? And according to which rules does this happen?

Rumour is a voice that mixes up the true and the false. This is something that William Stern also knew; modestly he viewed his experiments as initiating the first considerations of Virgil's Fama, who grows in that she spreads. What also grew was the number of rumour experiments. For several decades psychologists and sociologists attempted, with similar fictions, to find out all the rumour's tricks. Again and again students in Berlin and Breslau had the opportunity of experiencing strange performances during their law or psychology lectures. Masked figures would dash through the auditorium brandishing weapons and shooting each other in the head, or getting up to some other nonsense. Men dressed as clowns and white men with blackened faces would rush in, hurl insults at each another, perhaps reach for weapons, and then disappear as abruptly as they had appeared. At the genesis of research into the rumour are to be found crime stories and scenes from street theatre. And it ends with the numbers with which those conducting the experiments evaluated the reports of their surprised subjects: between 20 and 50 per cent of the reports, it was found, could be relied upon to contain errors.[332] But nobody made any real progress beyond that of the pioneer Stern.

Virus?

But just what is it that makes a rumour a rumour? This is something about which even the most appealing piece of criminal drama says nothing. Rumours are difficult to classify since they are always both the medium of hearsay and the news that is mediated; the word "rumour" means both things simultaneously. Because they wish to do justice to this paradox, not only writers, but also scientists use metaphors when the talk is of rumours.[333] They describe the rumour in everyday language, as a being that somehow has a life of its own, which runs, slithers, gradually spreads or jumps from place to place.

Metaphors such as these influence research and its results. In 1928, one and a half decades before American rumour controllers in the Second World War fought against the *rumor virus*, the Russian sociologist L. A. Bysow conducted some research on an historical rumour from the time of the Tsars. He differentiated between three types of progression, three velocities of the rumour: "the dark, mischievously passed-on, secret ones" have "a creeping character" and are "very slow" and "dangerous"; others spread "most wildly", are "particularly colourful and often lead to public shock" through fear or through joy; "submerged rumours" from time to time disappear "from the surface of public life", but always obstinately return.[334]

Whether creeping, flying or submerged – however the Fama virus may move, it is dangerous, for usually when it circulates, according to Bysow, there is an "increase in emotions".[335] A similar social fever was also diagnosed by the American campaigners against the rumour during the Second World War, discussed in the previous chapter of this book. They also monitor the pulse and rate of breathing of their patients in order to differentiate between truth and lie "automatographically". Their image of the rumour as virus suits the present day in the same way as the gods and chimeras suited antiquity. But is it then not simply a revision of the mythical attitude which created the divinity Fama out of gossip?

The metaphorical themes of infection, epidemic and pathogen have been around for a long time. In Wilhelm Raabe's story *Horacker* it is said of a rumour that it "raged" – as if it were a fever. The literary play with such images may have ironic sides; yet this is only possible because people understood and today still understand the rumour precisely as a type of fever, an illness, a plague. This is a result of its speed and its suggestive voice. And rumours and plagues do actually resemble one another in the nature of their spreading through direct contact. At least in its oral form the rumour is founded upon the temporary simultaneous presence of speaker and hearer. This simultaneous presence can be replaced and the possibility of its occurring increased by means of distance-shrinking media such as letters, the telephone, radio, television and the Internet. The analogy of rumour and plague also holds in the context of rumour's dissemination through these media. Even the mathematics that attempts to model the rumour adopt this analogy in its language. "There is a certain probability that with contact between an uninfected and an infected person this rumour or, as may be the case, illness is passed from the one to the other, that is to say, spreads",[336] explains the Aachen mathematician Harald Günzel in a radio interview.

The decisive aspect of the metaphorical model of the virus is the idea of a living, fundamentally active phenomenon. "Small living creatures that move most gaily" [337] is the description which the caretaker of the town hall of Delft gives the microbes he was the first to see under the microscope that he had made himself in the year 1675. Do the researchers who in our microbiological age view rumours as viruses have such "living creatures" in mind? Today there is for us no more striking image for the dissemination of the rumour than the plague. Epidemics find their carriers and circulate until, exhausted, they collapse; when everyone knows everything there is no longer any reason to pass on what has been heard. For this reason, specialists in dealing with hearsay sometimes recommend, as an emergency brake, their total dissemination.

Whoever takes the virus metaphor seriously and considers the rumour to be an external force must also determine precisely how rumours "break out" and become "epidemic", how people becomes "infected" by them. Bysow proposes the following "epidemiological" diagnosis:

1. The event that serves as the starting point for a rumour is witnessed in a particular manner of interestedness by one or more persons ...
2. The event is assimilated by the witness or witnesses (individually or collectively); it is valued in terms of its significance to public life.
3. News of the events is passed on ... The individual links of the rumour combine in the course of their reception and transmission and form a chain. The individual links of the chain are not themselves

rumours; only the chain in its entirety or, better, the whole network of chains forms a rumour.[338]

To the model of rumour as syndrome belong therefore various factors: firstly the pathogen, that is, the relevant news of an event – whether it actually took place or not; secondly, a first case of infection, that is to say, the witness, and finally, a specific population that picks up the infection and passes it on. And it is precisely at this point that the theoretical weaknesses of this, in essence, strictly functionalist picture become evident. The people involved are presented as mere "black boxes", as mere factors who react automatically without any will of their own, without the ability to protest: as one-dimensional. From a mathematical point of view, it makes no difference if one is speaking of rumours or of viruses: "The formula doesn't care."[339] But as soon as this model is applied to reality, its limitations become clear, for there is no form of immunisation against rumours as there is against viruses.

Nevertheless, mathematical models of the dissemination of rumours do have their usefulness. Harald Günzel differentiates between three possible scenarios: "First scenario: Right from the start the rumour grows in terms of its dissemination, eventually reaching the whole population. Second scenario: The rumour grows, reaching a local maximum – which would then be its global maximum – and then drops back in terms of its dissemination to nothing. Or the rumour has from the very beginning no chance and immediately falls back to nothing."[340] Rumours, like plagues, either spread far and wide or "die" immediately. In the jargon of mathematics this is what is called a "birth and death process", which means that: "Medium sized epidemics have a very small possibility of arising."[341] What is of significance for mathematics is now whether the threshold that decides between success or failure of a rumour can be determined, and how many "rumour corpses" there are, that is to say "people who hear the rumour but do not pass it on".[342] The whole mathematical model is based upon four short equations. But as soon as real-world imponderables are gathered up into mathematical reality, the rational image of the rumour changes: for now rumour turns out no longer to be calculable. That is to say, under certain conditions it is "entirely conceivable" that chaos arises, "that the rumour jumps around chaotically, and that it cannot be predicted how it will behave the next day, or the day after that or in a year's time", explains the mathematician. On the one hand chaos, on the other an all-or-nothing situation. The clearly visible contradiction in the theoretical models of the dis-

Anja Eckert, *Fama* (1985)

semination of rumours gives a taste of quite what tricky objects of study they are. The mathematical picture of chaos reinforces the impression of hearsay as a dark, difficult-to-control force that always throws up something unexpected.

When in the year 1546 the Veronese doctor Frascatoro was the first to differentiate between three different forms of infection, these being through touch, through polluted surroundings and at a distance, scholastic medicine suffered a defeat from which it was never to recover. The discovery of "living creatures" also fatally undermined the Hippocratic doctrine of humours and constitutions.

Yet it is precisely the antique medical knowledge killed off in this way that presents us with the precise image of a phenomenon that suddenly concerns everyone: "When many people are struck down by an illness at the same time one has to ascribe guilt to them, which is equal, in the broadest sense, in all of them."[343] Whoever spends much time looking at the rumour comes to the same conclusion as that reached by the Hippocratics regarding plagues; they are what hangs in the air.

Formulae and Functions

Under laboratory conditions, the instigator of the American rumor clinics during the Second World War, Gordon W. Allport, in the late Forties again takes up his research into the rumour. Together with his colleague, Leo Postman, he repeats and modifies William Stern's experiments. The two researchers come up with the same conclusion as Stern: the further a rumour travels from its origin the more self-willed it appears to become. But unlike Stern and Oppenheim, they are not satisfied with ending their work on the theme of rumour merely at the registering of such mutations. In the light of the results of their experiments they in the end come up with three rules according to which rumours behave while altering the information they convey. They call these rules *levelling, sharpening* and *assimilation* – and they may remind some of Stern's three-aspect pattern of news modification of the rumour: omit, modify and add.

Levelling stands for the leaving out of details, the ironing-out of particulars. According to this, names of people and places, and regional details are only loosely connected to the news; they can be dropped with ease or, depending on requirements, can be replaced by others. After five stations nobody knows any longer with certainty where an event took place. *Sharpening* is the editing down of the piece of news to something concrete and above all easily remembered. Out of suspicion grows certainty. Finally the news adapts itself to the circumstances of its present narration: depending on narrator and listener, different aspects are emphasised. For example, Allport and Postman noticed that white subjects interpreted descriptions of racially-motivated conflicts differently from black subjects. This adjusting of a story to the subjective situation of its speakers and hearers is something researchers refer to as the law of *assimilation*. Emotional and rational factors exert influence on the rumour: "Rumor is set in motion and continues to travel in a homogeneous social medium by virtue of the strong interests of the individuals involved in the transmission. The powerful influence of these interests requires that the rumor serve largely as a rationalising agent: explaining, justifying, and providing meaning for the emotional interest at work. At times the relationship between the interest and the rumor is so intimate that we may describe the rumor simply as a projection of an altogether subjective emotional condition",[344] contend Allport and Postman. Rumours therefore hint at the psychological motives of those who spread them.

But how does it come to such projections? Allport and Postman develop a formula for the conditions without which no rumour can arise. It reads: $R - I \times a$. This means that R roughly corresponds with i times a. The strength of a rumour ("R" for "rumour") corresponds according to this formula to the importance of a rumour ("I") multiplied by the uncertainty about the situation ("a" for ambiguity); the more indeterminate the general situation and the more significant the news, the stronger the rumour. If any of these factors approaches zero, then no rumour can arise. Although some researchers, on account of empirical test results, object to the conclusion that it is precisely rumours that are viewed as not being important which are transmitted more easily and more often, several experiments in the Fifties confirmed Allport and Postman's results, at a time that is when even the most primitive experimental set-up could reach for technical instruments which Sally Jaffa, in her memory experiment at the beginning of the twentieth century, missed out on: film and audio tape.[345]

The often cited formula for the rumour set out by Allport and Postman appears plausible, even if it completely ignores the significance of the communicative network.[346] It is lacking in many ways. It suffers from what all functionalist models in the social sciences suffer from: their inability to comprehend groups and individuals other than as unconsciously-reacting stages in the model. This methodological and theoretical limitation significantly reduces the usefulness of these models' results. What they find out corresponds all too comfortably with their premises and is presented as holding true like a commonplace, and equally seamlessly for every communications system. All that appears halfway new and important is worth communicating.

Other researchers sought to supply what was missing in the model by introducing a subjective factor into it. They expanded upon the formula, increasing it to R – I x a x 1/c, with "c" representing the critical competence of those involved in the hearsay.[347] If it is a high figure, then the rumour has a tough time, yet if the rumour descends upon uncritical hearers then it can be sure of a swift dissemination. Alertness protects against rumours.

But even this model sees rumours as a pathogen introduced into a population which beforehand was "healthy". It is, however, actually the case that rumours arise in the midst of groups, as if all by themselves. Insecurity, confusion and unwakefulness are not qualities of the rumour, rather are external to it.

The Oxford anthropologist Peter Lienhardt investigated a rumour about a vision of a saintly apparition in Islam and came to the conclusion that

Hieronymus Sperlin, *Fama with Soap Bubbles and Snow Balls* (c. 1750)

rumours "generally represent complexities of public feeling that cannot readily be made articulate at a more thoughtful level".[348] With this representational character, this acting as substitute, he touches on a second aspect of the rumour, for in standing for something else, a rumour *signifies* something. Its structure alone demonstrates its representative character: not "I say", rather "people are saying". "The rumour has its associations much less in the field of logical thought than in the field of metaphorical thought", emphasises Peter Lienhardt: "It is not found by rational speculation. It is figurative." Expression is given to complex collective feelings and in the image in which they are composed. The rules and forms of such composition constitute the cultural-historical dimension of the rumour.

Since Virgil, the rumour has been described as an inventive rhetorical force. Where sociology and the social sciences with which it is closely related, at its borders, grind to a halt, there begins the cultural history of the rumour. It is not enough simply to gauge and classify rumours. For perhaps they are something quite different from a substitute for information or an outlet for social tensions. Whether rumours distort reality is of secondary importance for researchers; what is decisive is that they construct symbolic realities. Rumours work by deferring, that is to say, metonymically; poetically they construct metaphors. They express what cannot be formulated in other ways: hate and fear in Orléans, horror in Rome, chaos that arises from order. Perhaps they are something like a collective fantasy: the dream of society from outside itself. Perhaps rumours, like dreams, also get past a form of censorship. But then they can only be interpreted like a dream, like a literary text, a strange collective literature delivered in the mode of indirect speech.

The description of hearsay as information that is gradually transformed as it makes its rounds by whispered post, of the interplay of the "body" of society and "virus", is not an exhaustive one. Rumours have a special part to play in the emergence of meaning, namely as meaningful events. They belong neither in the sphere of the individual nor in the realm of "objective", material institutions. Whoever interprets rumours, interprets interpretations. Information, news, messages: all these form the connection of witness, event and conveyor – be they true or be they mere allegations. And this is why the social sciences always devote their attention entirely to the witness and how what he or she says is disseminated and changed. But precisely at the point where the rumour starts to differ from other forms of media and information, a systematic loophole of the social sciences emerges. Understanding the rumour begins with the insight that it is founded upon hearsay, in other words, that it is self-referential.

The Cue

In 1909 or 1910, that is to say shortly before William Stern's experiments, a young Swiss psychoanalyst is assigned the task by an educational authority of writing a report on "the mental state of the thirteen-year-old schoolgirl Marie X". The girl has been suspended from her school because she has been blamed for a malevolent scheme. Apparently, Marie tried to defame her teacher as a paedophile, something that neither the teacher nor the educational authority wished to see tolerated. Also in the interests of Marie's parents, the report is to clarify the matter and give the rebuked child the chance to go back to school. As a sort of psychological investigating magistrate, the psychoanalyst C. G. Jung questions witnesses and those involved, and it soon becomes clear to him that two forces are exerting an influence on the matter of the man and the girl: dreams and rumours.

"Indirectly a rumour had reached the ears of the teacher", writes Jung, "the girl had been telling an ambiguous story about him. Research revealed that one day Marie X had described a dream to three girl-friends."[349] Jung managed to go some way in reconstructing this dream, which had an erotically charged increasing closeness of teacher and girl as its buried content. He was helped to this conclusion by a few drawings made by the girl and by her mother and girlfriends, whom Marie had only recently told of her dream. Jung placed great value on being able to reproduce, at least approximately, the so important psychological "original story". For with its elements that obviously lead back to a dream – not to a thought-out story – can it alone establish the innocence of the child. The teacher at first did not want to accept that it was all just a case of a dream. He suspected much more than this; that she had made it up. He had to say however, that the harmless dream narrative did now appear to be make sense, and for a while he vacillated between these two hypotheses, before finally accepting that it did indeed boil down to a harmless dream that had been turned into something sexual by the girl's classmates, realising that it would be wrong to attribute to the child the sophistication required to make up such a sexually ambiguous story. Thus the "original story" obtains the character and status of circumstantial evidence. The unconscious truth of this story exonerates the child of the accusation of having schemed, and weakens the charge. The teacher can now see things in a better light.

The dream of Marie X was not something invented; with its syncopations and leaps it has basic features of dream-work. The contents of the latently sexual dream are projected into the real world. Everyone who can remember back to being as young as Marie X will be familiar with the motifs: disguises, transformations, swimming together in a lake, ambiguous remarks etc. The analyst finds with those who have heard this different version of the story that, apart from a few details and interpolations, their descriptions so strongly resemble one another that Jung has no problems identifying the "original story" as the origin of the rumour. In his psychoanalytical research he also makes use of the teacher's own preparatory work. The teacher had, as soon as he got wind of the gossip, made the girls who were spreading it write down what they had heard. Jung divides these depositions into those given by the earwitnesses, that is to say, by those who heard Marie relate her dream, and by those who heard the gossip. With those who heard the dream narration, that is to say Marie's friends, there are clear differences: detours are cut out, a small alteration of detail changes the meaning, where the dream contains "syncopations", interpolations are made, it comes to "imagined details and events used to paper over gaps in the memory",[350] people are duplicated or replaced by others – all variations come about because the witnesses partake in the dream.

In the second group of witnesses, that is to say, with those who know Marie's dream from hearsay, this sympathetic further dreaming of Marie's dream continues. The different versions of the narrated and further narrated dream shift individual elements, motifs and images, partly into hints, partly into holes or into an area of explicit inexpressiveness. Thus the stories become more metonymic and at the same time more clear-cut than the dream. Seven of eight girls mention an inexpressible incident which is hidden in formulations pregnant with meaning, with one witness even refusing to continue with so "indecent" a story.

It is not surprising that the analyst sees with this dense ensemble of dream and collective continuation of it an unconscious libidinal impulse at work. What Marie dreamt was "le vrai mot de la situation", the "automatograph", the fitting expression of something that was already in the air. With her dream, Marie gave the cue for her friends to give free rein to their subconscious; told and told again, the story became, in an extremely tense situation, an instrument of hate directed at the once admired teacher. With the smoke of the ambiguous rumour of Marie's erotic dream, it was easy to imagine that there was fire that accompanied it. To the teacher, the gossip that arose from this was as embarrassing as it was understandable, which is why the schoolgirl was punished so severely. Luckily it found in Jung a clever assessor. With his detective work he was able to illuminate the background to the events and exonerate Marie; in the end she was allowed to attend her lessons again.

Jung's analysis and interpretation of the rumour follow – he emphasise this himself – from the experiments of Stern, Oppenheim and their followers. He makes clear that he does not see himself as a lie detector of the rumour. As an analyst he investigates much more the psychical transformations first made possible by the rumour, that is to say the context and the process in which the collective meaning of this rumour arises. Jung sees the rumour as an interpretation, as a symbolic treatment, as an answer to a question, as the solution to a problem. And when he therefore describes it – as he does dreams – as a "cue for the subconscious", he is drawing a more precise picture of the rumour than the norm-and-deviation based formulae and laws of empirical sociology ever could.

The Spiral of the Rumour

The attempts described at the beginning of this chapter to uncover the rumour's tricks all share the feature of starting out with an original version, from an event witnessed by someone. This is no surprise, for at the end of the day, the relevant experiments hail from the context of forensic science and psychology. With the rumour, however, this reliance on the rumour is wrong-headed: its bearers and those that take part in it are only ever witnesses of gossip, not of events. This difference is important: "The rumour is always contained within a subordinate clause, always of the form: 'have you heard, this and that is said to be the case', or 'people are saying that she did this and that'. Nothing is confirmed, merely presented."[351] "It is said", "People are saying" or "It's going around" – it is with such self-referential formula as these that rumours identify themselves. Whoever passes on a rumour has a sense of or knows what he is doing, for he confirms and repeats the rhetorical pattern in which it was passed to him.

Various mechanisms set in without which the rumour would never become the cue which awakens collective emotions, pushing them in a certain direction.[352] To this must be added the essential factor of its repetition, and the variations it undergoes while being repeated. And if there is rarely any understatement, then still its opposite, hyperbole, is a standard feature. All this can be found in the indirect speech of the "It is said that". Only what fits into this complex machinery of rhetorical rules can have the necessary trenchancy, clarity and seductiveness to effect a piece of news' transformation into a cue, a suspicion's transformation into hearsay, and a question's transformation into a rumour.

Jean Luc Cornec, *TribuT* (1989)

Jung puts all this to good use in his analysis of the rumour in the girls' classroom. He was able to determine the direction from which the rumour came. The relevant psychical forces, some working on the level of the individual, some working on the level of the group, cannot be thwarted, rather must be understood. In seeing the rumour as the collective interpretation of a dream, Jung could reconstruct the dynamics of hearsay and determine the one point which is equivalent in all of them and upon which everyone looks, regardless of whether they have, as a primary earwitness, experienced the rumour early on, or whether they, as a secondary earwitness or even later participant, heard it and passed it on. For each individual, hearsay soon becomes lost. It comes from somewhere and hurries on to who knows where. Whoever comes into contact with the rumour can feel the dynamics of its dissemination. The geometrical figure that best represents it is not the line, not the chain and not even the net. The fitting graphic symbol is in fact a curve that circles around a point again and again, forming ever new coils: the spiral. It too has no beginning and no end, no origin and no destination, and yet it goes on, carries on twisting, ever at a distance from the point about which it turns.

The rumour, as a cue, a rallying cry, issued by the "they", that strange authority in which the positive and the normative coincide: "Everybody says it and what everybody says, must be true", James Fenimore Cooper's novel *Miles Wallingford* tells us. A rumour is an offer to class oneself alongside this "they", to play along with it, to put another twist in the spiral. A rumour is a cue like those found in the theatre: "a particular word or phrase ... which serves as a signal to another actor to enter or begin a speech",[353] a beacon.

The witnesses of gossip do not experience hearsay merely as a wildly narrated substitute for missing information. They see themselves as conspiratorial participants in a collective rhetorical operation of confident uncertainty. They all look towards the central point of the spiral. If Jung is right about hearsay, then it stirs complex emotions in the collective subconscious, emotions that could not be expressed in any other way.[354] It is a mirror in which society catches sight of its hidden self. This sight causes pain, a pain that is usually felt by the weak, the outcasts and defenceless, sometimes also by those who once were powerful. Francis Bacon recommended that we should "watch and care"[355] when it comes to dealing with rumours. Social science may offer tools for this carefulness, but, without a careful understanding of the background of the rumour, even they only manage to scratch around on the surface.

The rumour is both complex structure and single piece of news, in a strange way both scandalous and seemingly plausible at the same time. It comes from Ovid's House of Fama, where there is "no peace, no silence anywhere",[356] and where whispering voices can always be heard. After a hundred years of the scientific pursuit of rumours, they have, despite all "automatographs", retained their power. Their symbol is the spiral, of which only a small section can ever be seen, its organs are mouth and ear, in the cochlea of which the physical resonance transforms into a psychical impulse. Rumours can be as swift as fear, as cold as hate and as sweet as the voice of the sirens. Above all, though, they are as close as if they do not come from outside, rather from that distant and undisturbed inner part of us that is only perceived by the person who holds a shell to his ear, being not a bellow or a scream, but the murmuring of quiet voices, like the swelling of the sea heard from afar.

Notes

1 Febvre 1990a, 13. [Translated from the German]
2 Sahlins 1992, 150.
3 Apart from a few studies of the motif of Fama, to which I also turn in the third chapter of this book, literary criticism has yet to offer up a coherent treatment of the peculiar phenomenon of the rumour. This gap becomes all the more apparent the more questions about the connection between orality and literary aesthetics – roughly within the framework of "skaz" research – become part of the canon of this discipline. See Ong 1985, Bachtin 1971, Banfield 1982, Ejchenbaum 1988, Vinogradov 1988.
4 Bergmann, 1987.
5 Against the all too obvious uniformity of cultural histories, Dietzsch's *Kleine Kulturgeschichte der Lüge* stands out from the crowd. Ever since Harald Weinrich's answer to a prize question set by the Deutsche Akademie für Sprache und Dichtung, ever since his *Linguistik der Lüge*, adherents to linguistic pragmatism, inspired by Searle and Austin, have undertaken research into the laws of "linguistic errors" (see Falkenberg 1982) – with mixed results. There has been, however, no comparable research on the rumour, and even philosophy appears to be avoiding this theme – unlike the theme of the lie. This systematic avoidance is certainly a result of the rumour's transpersonal dynamism. For, in contrast to the lie (see Giese 1992), the rumour is usually anonymous, with an origin which is difficult to locate or define, and only ever "intentional" in special cases.
6 See above all Kapferer 1987. See also Evard 1989.
7 See Bergson 1993.
8 Popow 1995, 283. [Translated from the German]
9 For the origin is no "beginning that satisfactorily explains everything" (Bloch 1993. Translated from the German: Bloch 1974, 47).
10 "Sorting material is what makes the scientist a scientist", writes Ossip Mandelstam (Mandelstam 1994, 101). In terms of procedure, I am taking heed of an observation made by Paul Veyne, who in his inaugural speech at the *Collège de France* declared that "history exists only in relation to the questions we pose it" (Veyne 1988, 8. Translated from the German). In terms of interpretative selection, my procedure follows that outlined by Szondi (Szondi 1978).
11 In some contributions to the currently booming genre of cultural history, a stale historicism, for which everything in the past is necessarily and undifferentiatedly a part of history, seems to be flogging itself to death. In the face of everything gathered up, all too often without much thought or any scruples, by this form of history one feels like the singer Nina Hagen in front of the television: "Everything is so colourful, I can't make up my mind."

12 Cassirer 1988, 51. Cassirer sees in the comprehension and presentation of these features the task of the philosophy of culture.

13 Pointers on theoretical questions are presented in the endnotes along with brief mentions of methodological problems, for theory also has to prove its value in analysis and interpretation – and not "in itself" – if it is to serve literary and historical research as a "critical activity" (Peter Szondi).

14 Braudel 1958, 747.

15 Plutarch 1939, 435. Following: 435.

16 Plutarch 1939, 435. Following: 437.

17 But "even though the actual soldiers who had escaped from the action itself gave a clear report", the Athenians at first did not want to believe this news, writes Thucydides (Thucydides 1923, 191).

18 Geertz 1993b, 9.

19 Hunter 1990, 302.

20 Hunter 1990, 306.

21 Winkle 1997, 625.

22 Aeschines 1919, 105.

23 Theophrastus 1993, 83–85.

24 Plutarch 1939, 437.

25 It could be that the barber understood the real events merely as an historical metaphor in a mythological context, in a way similar to the inhabitants of Hawaii in the Eighteenth Century: Captain Cook appeared to them as an embodiment of the god Lono, something that was later to be the undoing of the, at first, honoured explorer. See Sahlins 1992a, 23.

26 Plutarch 1939, 437.

27 See Pausanius 1918, 83.

28 Plutarch 1939, 437.

29 Homer 1998a, 20.

30 Homer 1998b, 295. For a discussion of the historical supersession of *ossa* by *pheme*, see Wassermann 1920, 10.

31 Aeschines 1919, 103.

32 See footnote 2, Aeschines 1919, 102.

33 Pausanius 1918, 83.

34 Hesiod 1936, 59.

35 Wilamowitz-Moellendorf 1955, 17.

36 Hunter gives examples. See Hunter 1990, 321.

37 Rhianos, Tiberius' favourite poet, composed a poem about *phéme*, and like this work, a declamation of the Greek grammatologist Helladios has also been lost, as has the section on *phéme* in Iohannes Stobaios' great book of excerpts, fragments of which have been preserved.

38 At least, this is argued by Flacelière (Flacelière 1959, 114).

39 Barthes 1993, 109.

40 Vernant 1974 [Translated from the German: Vernant 1987, 207]. Vernant is here echoing Schelling. For the Greek scholar Marcel Detienne mythical images are tasked with "expressing a part of immediate experience that is of itself enough to repeat itself and reproduce and, in so doing, to resist

intellectual interpretation, which seeks to decompose its unity (Detienne ˙1984, 27. Translated from the German).

41 Sophocles 1994, 107. Following: 121, 125.
42 Sophocles 1994, 341. Following: 341.
43 Pindar 1997, 165.
44 Pindar 1997, 47. Following: 199.
45 Böttinger questions the identification of *pheme* of Athens with Fama of Rome. See Böttinger 1850, 374.Wassermann argues along very similar lines. See Wassermann 1920. Detienne, on the whole, identifies the Greek and Roman divinities. See Detienne 1982.
46 Aeschylus 1956, 41. Following: 41, 60.
47 Aeschylus 1956, 60. Following: 60, 60, 52.
48 Aeschylus 1956, 59.
49 Plato 1926b, 159.
50 Gill 1993, 71.
51 Plato 1926a, 127. Following: 129.
52 Plato 1926b, 157.
53 Detienne 1984, 37. [Translated from the German]
54 Vernant 1984, 9. Following: 9. [Translated from the German]
55 Detienne 1984, 42. Following: 42.
56 In *The Odyssey*, *pheme* is at one point to be found in a hidden place, in the innermost part of a house. The chthonic moment is something to which Virgil refers when he describes Fama as the daughter of the earth.
57 Thucydides 1919, 39–41. Following: 35, 37, 39.
58 Thucydides 1919, 39.
59 At least, this is an opinion expressed by the melancholy and inebriated protagonist (who is in some respects very similar to the author) in Schmidt's story *Schwarze Spiegel* (Schmidt 1997, 87, 85); he sees Weber's picture in the Hamburg Kunsthalle, which he visits on his tour of what remains of the West after the world's atomic destruction. Schmidt did in fact view an exhibition of etchings in which Weber's picture was also included.
60 The formula in question was "immune through trust", and by this was meant trust of the National Socialist state. See Max 1943.
61 Dröge 1970, 215.
62 Esselbrügge 1980, 23.
63 Boussemart n. d.
64 Jean Baudrillard, after the Paris May of 1968, considered the streets to be "the alternative and subversive form of mass media", in that they are "free space for the symbolic exchange of ephemeral and fleeting words" (see Baudrillard 1978, 101. Translated from the German).
65 "That the common people, that formally weighed so little in scales of the French kingdom, and now weighs so much, requires educating as a matter of the greatest urgency, for which purpose the strenuous attempt is now being made to bring this about through people's books." *Minerva*, 1, January–March 1792. Quoted in Lüsebrink and Reichardt 1996, 98.
66 Lüsebrink and Reichardt 1996, 79.

67 Jacques-Marie Boyer-Brun. 1792. *Histoire des Caricatures de Révolte des Français*, 1: 9. Paris. Quoted in Lüsebrink and Reichardt 1996, 91.

68 Campe 1985, 23.

69 The quotation in the pamphlet reads: "c'est lui, c'est ce monstre, qui dernièrement avoit jeté l'alarme parmi vous, sur l'accident malheureux arrivé à nos Frères dans le beau jour de fête".

70 "Récemment encore, un nouveau nuage s'élève sur une des Maisons du Seigneur; ON ME L'A DIT l'apprend, & le monstre parcourt à l'instant toute la Ville", etc.

71 Oelsner 1985, 411.

72 Campe 1985, 40.

73 Campe 1985, 41.

74 Farge 1992. [Translated from the German: Farge 1993, 12]

75 Oelsner 1985, 412, and Delumeau 1978, 252.

76 See Delumeau 1978, 245.

77 Delumeau 1978, 240. [Translated from the German]

78 Farge, Revel, 108. Following: 103. [Translated from the German]

79 Delumeau 1978, 247.

80 John 20, 29.

81 Bloch 1993. [Translated from the German: Bloch 1974, 51]

82 See Szondi 1978, 274.

83 Virgil 1998, 96. Following: 94, 95, 96.

84 Virgil 1998, 96.

85 Goethe 1996, 63.

86 Goethe 1996, 64. [Revised by translator]

87 Cicero 1949, 333.

88 Goethe 1887, 179.

89 In the Aeneas *fama* also has the other meaning of renown and reputation; Fama with a capital can only mean rumour. See Kraft 1986, 23, also Ogle 1924.

90 Virgil 1998, 96–97 [Revised by translator]. Following: 97, 98.

91 Homer 1998a, 69.

92 Heinze reduces her to this (Heinze 1915, 305).

93 Fama is a child of sadness, despite what Ribbeck believes (see Ribbeck 1889, 75). "The figure of Fama has no equivalent in Greek poetry" (Pöschl 1977, 107). Some philologists accuse Virgil of a "lack of taste" and complain that Fama is described without any feel for proportion and does not fit the context of the work. (See Delande , 431, also Cartault 1926, 311).

94 Cicero 1929, 101.

95 To these other things belong "persons and wares, weapons and works of art, fine foods for the imperial kitchen or wild animals for the circus in Rome" (Fontius 1988, 268).

96 See Christ 1988, 57.

97 Laurence 1994, 64.

98 See Best 1974.

99 Laurence 1994, 65.

100 Laurence 1994, 69.

101   Ovid 1998. 275–276 [Revised by translator].

102   Homer – Odyssey, 150.

103   Ovid 1998, 203.

104   For a discussion of the influence of Ovid's personifications in later literature, see Miller 1916.

105   Quintilian 1921, 163.

106   Livius reports the same at an even earlier date, such as after the lost battle with Hannibal at Lake Trasemene. See Livius 1991, Book XX, 7, 1.

107   Christ 1988, 182.

108   Tacitus 1931, 443. Following: 443, 443, 444–445.

109   Tacitus 1937b, 275.

110   Lion Feuchtwanger's novel, *Der Falsche Nero* is a memorial to him. (Feuchtwanger 1949)

111   Tacitus 1970, 107. Tacitus takes his criticism of sources very seriously; he refutes the rumour about Nero's alleged murder of his son, Drusus, with poison. More than any other historian of his time, Tacitus had a refined sense of the significance of Fama, as has been shown with great care by Wolfgang Ries (Ries 1969). In around one hundred and fifty places Tacitus treats Fama's manifestations; only Livius had as developed a sense of the psychology of the masses.

112   Tacitus, 1937a, 21.

113   Heidegger 1986, 126.

114   Unlike content, material is that "with which artists actually work", Adorno 1973, 222.

115   Beaumarchais 1964, 62.

116   Smoltczyk, Klinggräff 1989, 126.

117   Including bill posters, prints, pictures, caricatures and tens of thousands of pamphlets. David alone produced over twenty thousand of these. See Lüsebrink and Reichardt 1996, 89.

118   Knigge 1792, 43.

119   Bosse 1981, 106.

120   Bosse 1981, 8.

121   Flaubert 1992, 73. Here Fama really has "degenerated into a tawdry figure". See Kraft 1986, 31.

122   Flaubert 1992, 73. Following: 73–74.

123   See Bernet 1998.

124   In Horace Fama shall bear up Proculeius, who divided his property between his brothers after they had lost theirs in the civil wars, "on wings / that refuse to droop" (Horace 1983, 106) ; since the early Roman Empire, Fama crops up in the work of the most varied writers. Many of them vary the structure and attributes of Virgil's and Ovid's goddess: Valerius Flaccus, Silius Italicus, Statius, Apuleius, Claudian and others have the goddess fly over land and ocean or, like Nike, ride in a chariot.

125   On the development of printed newspapers from the forms and methods of distribution of the newsletter, see Weber 1997, 138.

126   *Teutsche Chronik*, 633.

127   Blumauer n. d., 65.

128 Chaucer 1988, 349. On the rumour in the Middle Ages, see *Médiévales*.
129 Chaucer 1988, 352. Following: 354, 356.
130 Chaucer 1988, 357. Following: 357, 356, 357, 357.
131 Chaucer 1988, 360.
132 Chaucer 1988, 361.
133 Chaucer 1988, 364–365. Following: 366, 367, 368, 367, 368.
134 Chaucer 1988, 370.
135 Chaucer 1988, 369–370. Following: 371, 372, 372.
136 Chaucer 1988, 373. Following: 373, 373, 373. Similarly to ...
137 Pope 1993, 115.
138 Rabelais 1955, 678. Following: 678, 678.
139 Rabelais 1955, 679. Following: 679.
140 Rabelais 1955, 679.
141 Rabelais 1955, 679.
142 "How exactly should one differentiate between the possible and the impossible, according to what criteria?" asks Lucien Febvre about the century following Rabelais (Febvre 1990b, 204. Translated from the German).
143 Marperger, Paul Jacob. 1726. *Anleitung zum rechten Verstand und nutzbarer Lesung Allerhand ... Zeitungen oder Avisen ...* n. p. Quoted in Würgler's instructive essay (Würgler 1996, 27).
144 Febvre 1990b, 204 [translated from the German]. Febvre is here alluding to Rabelais' old man.
145 Rabelais 1995, 679. Following: 679, 679–680.
146 Herodotus 1920, 425.
147 Ripa 1669, 540. Image of Rumore: 541. That of Fama Chiara: 193.
148 This is his description on the title page of Ripa, *Della Novissima Iconologia* (Ripa 1625).
149 At the same time they form an accessible repertoire of classical mythology for the whole of educated Europe of the time – and in doing so represent the measure of worldly education. Like the books of emblems, the iconographies also contain pictures, commentaries and quotations from other texts, with the media all commenting upon and complementing one another, with the poetry becoming Horace's "ut pictura poiesis" – "speaking pictures", and the images becoming "muet poesie".
150 Würgler 1996, 20.
151 Campion 1909, 149.
152 For Jonson's own *Masque of Queens* in 1609, Inigo Jones created a "temple of Fame" on the stage, which took Chaucer's description as its model.
153 Campion 1909, 151. Following: 151, 151, 151.
154 Ben Jonson's *Time Vindicated*. Quoted in Chew 1962, 182.
155 See Doebler 1974, 17.
156 Campion 1909, 150. Following: 150.
157 Recent research has suggested that the two dramas should be thought of as being one, with time considerations forcing its dismantling into two parts. Thus is Rumour's appearance all the more important (see Iser 1988, 131).
158 Shakespeare 1977, 51.

159 Shakespeare 1977, 51. Following: 52.

160 Bacon 1994, 194.

161 Bacon n. d., 234.

162 See Briggs 1987, 117. On the life of Bacon, see Krohn.

163 Bacon 1853, 49.

164 Bacon 1853, 49.

165 Stendhal 1997, 49.

166 Raulff, 1990b.

167 Stendhal 1997, 80.

168 Benjamin 1980, 439. Already by the end of 1914 the collection of "war literature" at the German Library numbered 1836 publications; many of these were compilations of, in part, soldiers' letters which had already been published in newspapers. See Langenhove 1916, 186.

169 Dietzsch 1998, 110. Dietzsch goes on to write that the "decisive intellectual-historical disturbances" caused by the First World War "show up strikingly precisely in the development of a new acceptance of lying".

170 Cru 1930, 20. On the reception of this sensational work, see Raulff 1995, 211.

171 Cru 1930, 20.

172 Freud 1986, 39.

173 Bloch 1966b, 53.

174 Bloch 1966b, 53.

175 See Raulff 1990a and Raulff 1990b.

176 Raulff 1995, 210.

177 See Raulff 1995, 77.

178 Bloch 1966b, 41.

179 Baczko 1984, 18.

180 Raulff 1995, 92. See also 81.

181 Cru 1930, 35.

182 Cru 1930, 39.

183 Graux 1918, 1, 4. Lucien Graux's *Les fausses nouvelles de la Grande Guerre* consists of twenty heavy volumes, the first eight of which I could see in Paris' Bibliothèque Nationale. The work is presented, unlike the work of many of his colleagues, explicitly as a biased collection, which is why "neither the documentation nor the manner in which the problems were posed" were to Bloch's liking. (Bloch 1966b, 46. Translated from the German.)

184 Stern 1902, 315. See also Hartmann 1995. See also the final chapter of this book.

185 Duhr 1915.

186 Ponsonby 1928, 64.

187 Ponsonby 1928, 63.

188 See Ponsonby 1928, 67–70.

189 Bonaparte 1946, 106.

190 Bonaparte 1946, 84.

191 Ponsonby 1928, 102–113.

192 Ponsonby 1928, 113.

193 See the *Kölnische Volkszeitung*. 6.8.1914, 8.8.1914, 10.8.1914, 11.8.1914, and may other editions from this time.
194 See Shibutani 1966, 111.
195 See Langenhove 1916. See also Duhr 1915.
196 See Ponsonby 1928, 63.
197 Viktor Schklowski in his memoirs *Sentimentale Reise*. Quoted in Schröder 1994, 343.
198 "The news, which came from far away ..., had an authority that gave it validity, even when it could not be brought under control. Information, however, requires prompt verifiability."
199 Shibutani 1966, 89.
200 Bloch 1966b, 54. Following: 54.
201 Graux 1918, 2, 256.
202 Keller 1993, 433.
203 Bloch 1966b, 56.
204 Stuart 1920, 2. Following: 64, 64 (both from the leaflet reproduced here).
205 See Stuart, 92.
206 This was the name given to war rumours and similar forms of informal military communication in the Russian army. "With this the mood in the army is expressed very well" (Bysow 1928, 421); Bysow (420) gives further examples of this "news".
207 Graux 1918, 2, 247.
208 Graux 1918, 2, 255.
209 Bloch 1966b, 55.
210 Langenhove 1916, 192.
211 Bernheim 1905, 85.
212 Bloch, 1966a, 8.
213 Ponsonby (1928, 21, 27) sees the use of the radio as a propaganda instrument – and emphasises its lead on balloons and aeroplanes.
214 Morin 1969. The witness has made a mistake, since the date was actually 31 May.
215 Pius Alexander Wolff, for whom Goethe wrote his *Regeln für Schauspieler* ["Rules for Actors"] even made the figure of a lecherous Jewish slave-trader into an anti-Semitic theatrical figure. On this, and also on the broader context of such plays, see Neubauer 1994.
216 See Neubauer 1994, 10.
217 See Schmidt 1988.
218 Hosemann, Sigismund. 1699. *Das schwer zu bekennende Juden-Hertz* (1699) quoted in Rohrbacher and Schmidt 1991, 280.
219 Hsia 1997, 80.
220 Schmidt 1988, 48.
221 Delhoven 1966, 231. On the context of this case see Neubauer 1994, 10–34.
222 Delhoven 1988, 232.
223 Delhoven 1988, 21.
224 Blum, Herloßsohn and Marggraf 1842, 7, 36. See also Le Bon 1998.

225   Adorno 1987, 141. Compare also: "The destruction of graveyards is not an excess of anti-Semitism, it is anti-Semitism itself" (Horkheimer, Adorno, 1979, 164).

226   Jakobsen, Pomorska 1982, 21. [Translated from the German]

227   Kleist 1980, I, 1, 10.

228   Goffman 1990, 37. Following: 163–164, 161.

229   Gogol 1961, 17. Following: 20, 20–21.

230   Gogol 1961, 195. Following: 194, 195, 195, 190.

231   Gogol 1961, 195. Following: 195, 197.

232   See Colson, 1953.

233   Gogol 1961, 223.

234   Gogol 1961, 230. Following: 230.

235   Bulgakov 1972, 166. Following: 166–167.

236   See Gluckman 1963. For the functionalist Gluckman, (pseudo-)privacy, the central principle for the differentiation of gossip and rumour, played only a subordinate role (see Paine 1968). Bergmann presents an excellent critical overview of social-scientific research on gossip (Bergmann 1987).

237   Lessing 1954, 111. Adorno 1981, 331.

238   Raabe 1983, 34.

239   See Delacampagne 1982.

240   Raabe 1983, 21.

241   Raabe 1983, 84–85. Following: 3, 3.

242   See Schmidt 1992, 134.

243   Raabe 1983, 84. Following: 84.

244   Malinowski 1923.

245   Malinowski 1923, 478. Following: 478.

246   See Jakobson, 1979.

247   Modern evolutionary biology also confirms this. See Dunbar 1998.

248   Malinowski 1923, 478.

249   Raabe 1983, 85. Following: 85, 85, 84.

250   Heidegger 1986, 127. Following: 127.

251   Quoted by Preisendanz in Raabe 1980, 203.

252   Raabe 1983, 53. Following: 54. [Both revised by translator]

253   Raabe 1983, 85.

254   Keller 1993, 584.

255   Keller 1993, 611. Following: 621.

256   For example, Jane Austen, George Meredith and William Thackeray.

257   Malinowski 1923, 478.

258   Aristotle 1998, 94.

259   Becker 1992, 32. Following: 26.

260   See Simmel 1992, 413.

261   Becker 1992, 102.

262   Becker 1992, 83.

263   Becker 1992, 36. Following: 73.

264   Becker 1992, 164. Following: 169.

265   That truth finds a path through the ear rather than through the eye is a theme which Becker, with a subtle dialectic, also develops in other places

in the book. The narrator of his *Bronsteins Kinder* first learns the truth about his father and his father's friends through strained whispering (see Becker 1989, 223).

266   Geertz 1993b, 14.
267   See Greenblatt 1992b.
268   Gadamer 1990, 112.
269   See Huizinga 1991, 16. For a criticism of Huizinga's concept of game, see Caillois 1982.
270   *Sächsische Vaterlandsblätter* in Wander 1964, 1578.
271   Sälter 1996, 12.
272   Farge 1992 [translated from the German: Farge 1993, 39. Following: 36].
273   Würgler 1996, 24.
274   Entry for "Rumeur" in the 1st edition of the *Encyclopaedie* of 1751.
275   Leclerf and Parker 1987, VIII.
276   Musäus, Märchen 3, 116; quoted in Grimm 1987, 3758.
277   See Fleischer 1994.
278   Reproduced in Allport and Postman 1947, beside 16.
279   Fleischer 1994, 230.
280   Allport and Postman 1947, beside 16.
281   Knapp 1944, 22.
282   Rosnow and Fine 1976, 121.
283   See Caplow 1947, 298. For a report of an officer who worked with rumours in Asia, see MacDonald 1947.
284   "Standards for Agencies", 235.
285   Allport and Postman 1947, 19.
286   Allport and Postman 1947, 19. Following: 20, 21.
287   See Arndt 1967.
288   This was admitted by German functionaries of the German embassy in Washington after the war. See Strempel 1946, 231.
289   "Standards for Agencies", 238. *The War of the Worlds* was a wake-up call for empirical social psychology; Cantril offers a detailed description of the events. See Cantril 1966. On the dramaturgic method of the radio play, see Neubauer 1993, 68–71. Allport also investigated this media event as a prelude to his work on rumours.
290   Allport and Postman 1947, 21.
291   See Derrida 1982, 317.
292   Foucault 1998, 205.
293   See Allport and Lepkin 1945, 13, 7, 35.
294   Allport and Postman 1947, 219.
295   Knapp 1944, 35.
296   Knapp 1944, 36.
297   Klemperer 1990, 293.
298   See Dröge 1970, 214. See also Dördelmann 1997.
299   Dower 1993, 110.
300   See Comtesse 1942, 51. The public law specialist Comtesse questions the logic of penalising people for passing on rumours: "As soon as a person

knows for sure that what he is saying is true or untrue, then it is no longer a rumour" (Comtesse 1942, 51).

301 Ettinger 1946, 336.
302 Knapp 1944, 37.
303 See Smith 1956, 48, and also Festinger, Back et al., 1950.
304 Allport and Postman 1947, 2. Following: 2.
305 See Tapp 1953a and also 1953b.
306 Knopf 1975b, 33 and also Knopf 1975a.
307 National Advisory Commission 1968, 173. This report took a lead from a similar document belonging to the FBI, a handbook on the *Prevention and Control of Mobs and Riots* (Washington DC: General Printing Office. 1967, 26).
308 "Standards and Guidelines", 134.
309 See Knopf 1975b, 302.
310 Knopf 1975b, 307.
311 Knopf 1975b, 305. Following: 311.
312 "Standards and Guidelines", 137.
313 "If everybody thinks of their own circle as the centre, then there is no centre" Negt and Kluge 1981, 357.
314 Advertisement for the *Frankfurter Allgemeine*, February 1995.
315 Meyn 1998, 72.
316 Kornelius 1998.
317 Stevenson 1998.
318 Virgil 1998, 97. Following: 97.
319 Ovid 1998, 275. Following: 275, 275, 275, 275.
320 Münsterberg 1922, 141. Following: 141, 148, 148.
321 Durkheim 1982, 59.
322 Jaffa 1903, 79.
323 Stern 1902, 315.
324 See Bernheim 1905, 81.
325 Stern 1902, 325. Following: 327.
326 Jaffa 1903, 94.
327 Stern 1902, 362.
328 Stern 1902, 326.
329 See Schramm 1911.
330 Oppenheim 1911, 348. Oppenheim worked with women between the ages of 20 and 28: 1 sports teacher, 1 librarian, 1 book-keeper and 2 active members of the Breslauer Gruppe für Soziale Hilfsarbeit.
331 Oppenheim 1911, 353.
332 Gennep 1920, 158. Here he describes the scene with the clown and the Moors which took place in Göttingen.
333 Every theory concerned with the phenomena of public opinion has metaphorical elements. See Back 1988, 280.
334 Bysow 1928, 421.
335 Bysow 1928, 421.
336 Neubauer 1998.
337 Winkle 1997, XXII.

338   Bysow 1928, 304/305.

339   Günzel in Neubauer 1998.

340   Günzel in Neubauer 1998.

341   Dunstan 1982, 764. For an opposing view see Heuser 1989, 26. An attempt has even been made to determine the percentage of the population which never hears a rumour, even when it has spread throughout the whole population. See Sudbury 1985.

342   Günzel in Neubauer 1998.

343   Winkle 1997, XXII.

344   Allport and Postman 1947, 43.

345   Later experiments confirmed Allport and Postman's results. See Schachter 1955, 371. But Ralph Rosnow raises doubts. See Rosnow 1988, 18.

346   Lauf 1990, 135.

347   See Chorus 1953, 313.

348   Lienhardt 1975, 130. Following: 128, 128.

349   Jung 1969, 43.

350   Starobinski 1971, 13.

351   Brednich in Neubauer 1998. Brednich takes the opposing view to Jules Gritti: "A rumour does not appraise itself; it does not catch sight of itself and indeed cannot catch sight of itself" (Gritti 1978, 105).

352   More than one example in this book would tend to confirm this.

353   Definition in *The New Shorter Oxford English Dictionary*.

354   Jung, in a later phase of his work, again attempts a psychoanalytical interpretation of the rumour, turning to the sightings of UFOs as "collective visions". See Jung 1969, and also Dégh 1977.

355   Bacon 1853, 50.

356   Ovid 1998, 275.

Bibliography

Adorno, Theodor W. 1973. *Aesthetische Theorie*, edited by Gretel Adorno and Rolf Tiedemann. Frankfurt am Main.

Adorno, Theodor W. 1980. "Titel. Paraphrasen zu Lessing" in *Noten zur Literatur*. Frankfurt am Main.

Adorno, Theodor W. 1987. *Minima Moralia. Reflexionen aus dem beschädigten Leben*. Frankfurt am Main.

Aeschines. 1919. *The Speeches of Aeschines*, translated by Charles Adams. Cambridge, Massachusetts.

Aeschylus. 1956. *The Oresteian Trilogy*, translated by Philip Vellacott. London.

Allport, Floyd and Lepkin, Milton. 1945. "Wartime Rumours of Waste and Special Privelege: Why some people belive them" in *The Journal of Abnormal and Social Psychology* 40, 1: 3–36.

Allport, Gordon and Postman, Leo. 1947. *The Psychology of Rumour*. New York.

Aristotle. 1925. *The Nicomachean Ethics*. Oxford.

Arndt, Johan. 1967. *Word of Mouth Advertising*. New York.

Bachtin, Michail. 1971. *Probleme der Poetik Dostojevskis*. Munich.

Back, Kurt W. 1988. "Metaphors for Public Opinion in Literature" in *Public Opinion Quarterly* 52, 3: 278–288.

Bacon, Francis. 1853. "A Fragment on Fame" in *Essays Civil and Moral*: 49–50. London.

Bacon, Francis. 1994. *Novum Organum*, translated and edited by Peter Urbach and John Gibbon. Chicago and La Salle.

Bacon, Francis. n. d. "The Wisdom of the Ancients" in *The Essays of Francis Bacon*. London.

Baczko, Bronsilaw. 1984. *Les Imaginaires Sociaux*. Paris.

Banfield, Ann. 1982. *Unspeakable Sentences. Narration and Representation in the Language of Fiction*. London.

Barron, John. 1991. "Dezinformatsiya" in *The Penguin Book of Lies* edited by Philip Kerr: 420–423. London.

Barthes, Roland. 1993. *Mythologies*, translated by Annette Lavers. London.

Baudrillard, Jean. 1978. *Kool Killer ou l'Insurrection par les Signes*. Paris.

Beaumarchais, Caron de. 1964. *The Barber of Seville / The Marriage of Figaro*, translated by John Wood. London.

Becker, Jurek. 1989. *Bronsteins Kinder*. Frankfurt am Main.

Becker, Jurek. 1992. *Jakob der Lügner*. Frankfurt am Main.

Benjamin, Walter. 1980. "Der Erzähler. Betrachtungen zum Werk Nikolai Lesskows" in *Gesammelte Schriften*, II, 2, edited by Rolf Tiedemann and Hermann Schweppenhäuser. Frankfurt am Main.

Bergmann, Jörg R. 1987. *Klatsch. Zur Sozialform der diskreten Indiskretion*. Berlin and New York.

Bergson, Henri. 1993. *Le Rire: Essai sur la Signification du Comique*. Paris.

Bernet, David. 1998. "Ein Grab und zwei Pharonen. Vor 75 Jahren enststand die Legende vom Fluch des Pharaos Tut-ench-Amun" in *Berliner Zeitung*, 28.2/1.3.1998.

Bernheim, Ernst. 1905. *Einleitung in die Geschichtswissenschaft*. Leipzig.

Best, Edward E. 1974. "Literacy and Roman Voting" in *Historia. Zeitschrift für Alte Geschichte*, 23: 428–438.

Bloch, Marc. 1954. *The Historian's Craft*, translated by Peter Putnam. London.

Bloch, Marc. 1966a. "Que Démander à l'Histoire?" in *Mélanges Historiques*, I: 3–15. Paris.

Bloch, Marc. 1966b. "Réflexions d'un Historien sur les Fausses Nouvelles de la Guerre" in *Mélanges Historiques*, I: 41–57. Paris.

Bloch, Marc. 1974. *Apologie der Geschichte oder der Beruf des Historikers*. Stuttgart.

Bloch, Marc. 1993. *Apologie pour l'Histoire, ou Métier d'Historien*. Paris.

Blum, R., Herloßsohn, K. and Marggraf, H. (editors). 1842. *Allgemeines Theater-Lexicon*, 7. Altenburg and Leipzig.

Blumauer, Aloys. n. d. *Virgil's Aeneis. Travestiert von Aloys Blumauer*. Leipzig.

Böhm, Andrea. 1993. "Jubel nach dem Urteil in Los Angeles" in *die tageszeitung*, 19.4.1993.

Böhme, Hartmut. 1998. "Mediale Projektionen. Von der Vernetzung zur Virtualisierung der Städte" in *Neue Rundschau*, 109, 2: 64–76.

Bonaparte, Marie. 1949. *Mythes de Guerre*. London.

Bosse, Heinrich. 1981. *Autorschaft ist Werkherrschaft. Über die Entstehung des Urheberrechts aus dem Geist der Goethezeit*. Paderborn, Munich, Vienna and Zurich.

Böttinger, C. A. 1850. *Kleine Schriften Archäologischen und Antiquarischen Inhalts*, II, edited by Julius Sillig. Leipzig.

Boussemart, M. L. R. n. d. ON ME L'A DIT. Paris.

Braudel, Fernand. 1958. "La Longue Durée" in *Annales. Économies, Sociétés, Civilisations*. 13: 725–753.

Brednich, Rolf Wilhelm. 1994. *Sagenhafte Geschichten von Heute*. Munich.

Briggs, Asa. 1987. *A Social History of England*. London.

Brockhaus, Hermann (editor). 1856. *Allgemein Encyclopädie der Wissenschaften und Künste in alphabetischer Folge von genannten Schriftstellern bearbeitet*, 1, 62. Leipzig.

Der Neue Brockhaus. Lexicon und Wörterbuch in fünf Bänden und einem Atlas. 1975. Wiesbaden.

Bulgakov, Mikhail. 1972. *Diaboliad and Other Stories*, translated by Carl R. Proffer, edited by Ellendea Proffer and Carl R. Proffer. Bloomington and London.

Bysow, L. A. 1928. "Gerüchte" in *Kölner Vierteljahreshefte für Soziologie*, 7: 301–308, 416–426.

Canetti, Elias. 1980. *Masse und Macht*. Frankfurt am Main.

Caillois, Roger. 1958. *Les Jeux et Les Hommes (Le Masque et le Vertige)*. Paris.

Campe, Johann Heinrich. 1985. "Briefe aus der Zeit der Revolution geschrieben", second letter of 9 August 1789 in *Die Französische Revolution. Berichte und Deutungen deutscher Schriftsteller und Historiker*. Frankfurt am Main.

Campion, Thomas. 1909. "The Description of a Masque, Presented in the Banqueting Roome at Whitehall ..." in *Campion's Works*, edited by Percival Vivian. Oxford.

Cantril, Hadley. 1966. *The Invasion from Mars. A Study in the Psychology of Panic. With the complete script of the Orson Welles broadcast*. New York.

Caplow, Theodore. 1947. "Rumours in War" in *Social Forces*, 25: 298–302.

Cartault, A. 1926. *L'art de Virgile dans L'Enéide*. Paris.

Cassirer, Ernst. 1988. *Philosophie der Symbolischen Formen*, 1: *Die Sprache*. Darmstadt.

Chaucer, Geoffrey. 1988. "The House of Fame" in *The Riverside Chaucer*. Oxford.

Chew, Samuel C. 1962. *The Pilgrimmage of Life*. London.

Chorus, A. 1953. "The Basic Law of Rumor" in *The Journal of Abnormal and Social Psychology*, 48.

Christ, Karl. 1988. *Geschichte der römischen Kaiserzeit*. Munich.

Cicero. 1929. *The Letters to his Friends*, 2. London and New York.

Cicero. 1949. *De Inventione. De Optimo Genere Oratorum. Topica*. Cambridge, Massachusetts.

Colson, Elizabeth. 1953. *The Makah Indians*. Manchester.

Comtesse, Frédéric. 1942. *Der strafrechtliche Staatsschutz gegen hochverräterische Umtrieb im schweizerischen Bundesrecht*. Zurich.

Cru, Jean Norton. 1930. *Du Témoignage*. Paris.

Dégh, Linda. 1977. "UFO's and How Folklorists Should Look at Them" in *Fabula. Zeitschrift für Erzählforschung*, 18: 242–248.

Delacampagne, Christian. 1982. "A propos des cagots et de quelques autres peuplades non moins énigmatiques" in *Le Genre Humain*, 5: *La Rumeur*. Paris.

Delande, Jacques. "Deux Allégories d'Ovide. L'Envie; La Renommé" in *Les Études Classiques. Revue Trimestrielle d'Enseignement et de Pédagogie*, 4: 277–285 and 428–435.

Delhoven, Joan Peter. 1966. *Die rheinische Dorfchronik des Joan Peter Delhoven aus Dormagen (1783–1823)*, edited by Hermann Cardauns and Reiner Müller. Dormagen.

Delumeau, Jean. 1978. *La peur en Occident (XIVe-XVIIIe Siècles)*. Paris.

Derrida, Jacques. 1982. "Signature Event Context" in *The Margins of Philosophy*, translated by Alan Bass: 307–330. Brighton.

Detienne, Marcel. 1982. "La Rumeur, elle aussi, est une déesse" in *Le Genre Humain*, 5: *La Rumeur*. Paris.

Detienne, Marcel. 1984. "Mythologie ohne Illusion" in *Mythos ohne Illusion*: 12–46. Frankfurt am Main.

Dieck, Alfred. 1950 "Der Weltuntergang am 17. März 1949 in Südhannover. Ein Beitrag zur Erforschung von Gerüchten" in *Archiv für Landes – und Volkskunde von Niedersachsen*, 20: 704–720.

Dietzsch, Steffen. 1998. *Kleine Kulturgeschichte der Lüge*. Leipzig.

Doebler, John. 1974. *Shakespeare's Speaking Pictures. Studies in Iconic Imagery*. Albuquerque.

Dördelmann, Katrin. 1997. *Die Macht der Worte. Denunziation im nationalsozialistischen Köln*. Cologne.

Dower. John W. 1993. *Japan in War and Peace. Selected Essays*. New York.

Dröge, Franz. 1970. *Der zerredete Widerstand. Zur Soziologie und Publizistik des Gerüchts im 2. Weltkrieg*. Düsseldorf.

Duhr, Bernhard. 1915. *Der Lügengeist im Völkerkrieg. Kriegsmärchen*. Munich, Regensburg.

Dunbar, Robin. 1996. *Grooming, Gossip and the Evolution of Language*. London.

Dunstan, Ross. 1982. "The Rumour Process" in *The Journal of Applied Probability*, 19: 759–766.

Durkheim, Emile. 1982. *The Rules of Sociological Method*, translated by W. D. Halls, edited by Steven Lukes.

Eisenfeld, Bernd. 1996. "Gerüchteküche DDR – Die Desinformationspolitik des Ministeriums für Staatssicherheit" in *Werkstatt Geschichte*, 15, 5: *Politik des Gerüchts*: 41–53.

Encyclopaedie, 1ère Édition. 1751. Paris.

Ejchenbaum, Boris. 1988. "Die Illusion des *skaz*" in *Russischer Formalismus. Texte zur allgemeinen Literaturtheorie und zur Theorie der Prosa*, edited by Jurij Striedter: 161–167. Munich.

Esselbrügge, Kurt. 1980. "Begegnung mit A. Paul Weber. Tagebuchnotizen 1949–1952" in *A. Paul Weber, Das Graphische Werk 1930–1978. Hand zeichnungen und Lithographien*, edited by Georg Reinhardt. Munich.

Ettinger, Karl. 1946. "Foreign Propaganda in America" in *Public Opinion Quarterly*, 10: 329–342.

Evard, Jean-Luc. 1989. "Die alltägliche Ökonomie des Gerüchts, oder: Das Rauschen des Sozialen" in *Mediendämerung. Zur Archäologie der Medien*, edited by Peter Klier and Jean-Luc Evard: 90–104. Berlin.

Falkenberg, Gabriel. 1982. *Lügen. Grundzüge einer Theorie sprachlicher Täuschungen*. Tübingen.

Farge, Arlette. 1992. *Dire et Mal Dire: L'Opinion Publique au XVIIIᵉ Siècle*. Paris.

Farge, Arlette. 1993. *Lauffeur in Paris. Die Stimme des Volkes im 18. Jahrhundert*. Stuttgart.

Farge, Arlette and Revel, Jacques. 1989. *Die Logik des Aufruhrs*. Frankfurt am Main.

Febvre, Lucien. 1990a. "Ein Historiker prüft sein Gewissen. Antrittsvorlesung am Collège de France 1933" in *Das Gewissen des Historikers* translated and edited by Ulrich Raulff: 9–22. Berlin.

Febvre, Lucien. 1990b. "Zwischen dem Ungefähr und dem strengen Wissen liegt das Hören-Sagen" in *Das Gewissen des Historikers*, translated and edited by Ulrich Raulff: 199–205. Berlin.

Festinger, Leon and Back, Kurt et al. 1950. *Theory and Experiment in Social Communications*. Ann Arbor.

Feuchtwanger, Lion. 1949. *Der Falsche Nero*. Berlin.

Fine, Gary Alan and Severance, Janet S. 1987. "Gerücht" in *Enzyklopädie des Märchens. Handwörterbuch zur historischen und vergleichenden Erzählforschung*, edited by Rolf Wilhelm Brednich, 5: 1102–1109. Berlin and New York.

Flacelière, Robert. 1959. *La Vie Quotidienne en Grèce au Siècle de Périclès*. Paris.

Flaubert, Gustave. 1992. *Madame Bovary*, translated by Geoffrey Wall. London.

Fleischer, Andreas. 1994. *"Feind hört mit!" Propagandakampagnen des Zweiten Weltkriegs im Vergleich*. Münster and Hamburg.

Fontius, Martin. 1988. "Post und Brief" in *Materialität der Kommunikation*, edited by Hans Ulrich Gumbrecht and Karl Ludwig Pfeiffer. Frankfurt am Main.

Foucault, Michel.1998. "What is an Author?" In *Aesthetics, Method and Epistemology. The Essential Works 2*, translated by Robert Hurley et al., edited by James D. Faubon: 205–222. London.

Franck, Sebastian. 1876. *Sebastian Franck's erste namenlose Sprichwörtersammlung vom Jahre 1532 in getreuem Abdruck ...*, edited by Friedrich Latendorf. Poesneck.

Freud, Sigmund. 1986. "Zeitgemäßes über Krieg und Tod" in *Kulturtheoretische Schriften*. Frankfurt am Main.

Gadamer, Hans-Georg. 1990. *Wahrheit und Methode. Grundzüge einer Philosophischen Hermeneutik. Gesammelte Werke*, I: *Hermeneutik 1*. Tübingen.

Gallagher, Carole. 1995. *American Ground Zero. Secret Nuclear War*. Cambridge, Massachusetts.

Geertz. 1993a. *The Interpretation of Cultures. Selected Essays*. London.

Geertz. 1993b. "Thick Description: Toward an Interpretative Theory of Culture" in Geertz 1993a: 3–30.

Gennep, Arnold van. 1920. *La Formation de Légendes*. Paris.

Giese, Bettina. 1992. *Untersuchung zur Sprachlichen Täuschung*. Tübingen.

Gill, Christopher. 1993. "Plato on Falsehood – not Fiction" in *Lies and Fiction in the Ancient World*, edited by Christopher Gill and T. P. Wiseman. Exeter.

Glockhamer, Heidi. 1985. "Fama and Amor. The Function of Eroticism in Goethe's *Römische Elegien*" in *Eighteenth-Century Studies*, 19, 2: 235–253.

Goethe, Johann Wolfgang von. 1887. *Goethes Werke*. Weimar.

Goethe, Johann Wolfgang von. 1996. *Roman Elegies*, translated by Michael Hamburger. London.

Goffmann, Erving. 1990. *Stigma. Notes on the Management of Spoiled Identity*. London.

Gogol, Nikolai. 1961. *Dead Souls*, translated by David Magarshack. London.

Graux, Lucien. 1918. *Les fausses nouvelles de la Grande Guerre*, 20 vols. Paris.

Greenblatt, Stephen. 1990a. *Learning to Curse. Essays in Early Modern Culture*. New York and London.

Greenblatt, Stephen. 1990b. "Towards a Poetics of Culture" in Greenblatt 1990a: 146–160.

Grimm, Jakob and Grimm, Wilhelm. 1897. *Deutsches Wörterbuch*, IV, I, 2.

Gritti, Jules. 1978. *Elle Court, Elle Court, La Rumeur*. Montreal.

Hadeln, Detlev von. 1978. *Paolo Veronese*, edited by Gunter Schweikhart. Florence.

Hartmann, Andreas. 1995. "Eine Volkskundliche Erinnerung an William Stern und seinen Kreis" in *Zeitschrift für Volkskunde*, 91: 65–79.

Heidegger, Martin. 1986. *Sein und Zeit*. Tübingen.

Heinze, Richard. 1915. *Virgils epische Technik*. Leipzig and Berlin.

Herodotus. 1920. *The Persian Wars, Books I-II*, translated by A. D. Godley. Cambridge, Massachussets.

Hesiod. 1936. *Homeric Hymns. Epic Cycle. Homerica*, translated by Hugh G. Evelyn-White. Cambridge, Massachusetts.

Heuser, Harro. 1989. *Gewöhnliche Differentialgleichungen. Einführung in Lehre und Gebrauch*. Stuttgart.

Holy Bible. Revised Standard Version. 1971. Oxford.

Homer. 1998a. *The Iliad*, translated by Robert Fitzgerald. Oxford.

Homer. 1998b. *The Odyssey*, translated by Walther Shewring. Oxford.

Horace. 1983. *The Complete Odes and Epodes*, translated by W. G. Shepherd. London.

Horkheimer, Max and Adorno, Theodore W. 1979. *Dialektik der Aufklärung. Philosophische Fragmente*. Frankfurt am Main.

Hsia, R. Po-Chia. 1997. *Trient 1475. Geschichte eines Ritualmordprozesses*. Frankfurt am Main.

Huizinga, Johan. 1991. *Homo Ludens. Vom Ursprung der Kultur im Spiel*. Reinbeck bei Hamburg.

Hunter, Virginia. 1990. "Gossip and the Politics of Reputation in Classical Athens" in *Phoenix. The Journal of the Classical Association of Canada*, 44, 4: 299–325.

Iser, Wolfgang. 1988. *Shakespeares Historien. Genesis und Geltung*. Konstanz.

Jaffa, Sally. 1903. "Ein psychologisches Experiment im kriminalistischen Seminar der Universität Berlin. Zugleich ein Beitrag zur Methode der Untersuchung" in *Beiträge zur Psychologie der Aussage. Mit besonderer Berücksichtigung von Problemen der Rechtspflege, Pädagogik, Psychiatrie und Geschichtsforschung*, I: 79–99.

Jakobson, Roman. 1979. "Liguistik und Poetik" in *Poetik. Ausgewählte Aufsätze 1921–1971*, edited by E. Holenstein and T. Schelbert: 83–121. Frankfurt am Main.

Jakobson, Roman and Pomorska, Krystina. 1982. *Poesie und Grammatik. Dialoge*. Frankfurt am Main.

Jung, Carl Gustav. 1969. "Ein Beitrag zur Psychologie des Gerüchts" in *Freud und die Psychoanalyse. Gesammelte Werke*, 4. Zurich and Stuttgart.

Jung, Carl Gustav. 1974. "Ein moderner Mythus. Von Dingen die am Himmel gesehen werden" in *Zivilisation im Übergang. Gesammelte Werke*, 10. Olten and Freiburg.

Kapferer, Jean-Noël. 1987. *Rumeurs. Le plus vieux média du Monde*. Paris.

Keller, Gottfried. 1993. "Das verlorene Lachen" in *Die Leute von Seldwyla. Erzählungen*. Munich.

Kleist, Heinrich von. 1980. *Die Familie Schroffenstein, Ein Trauerspiel in fünf Aufzügen*. Stuttgart.

Klemperer, Victor. 1990. *LTI. Notizbuch eines Philologen*. Leipzig.

Knapp, Robert H. 1944. "A Psychology of Rumour" in *The Public Opinion Quarterly*, 8: 22–37.

Knigge, Adolph Freiherr. 1792. *Ueber den Bücher-Nachdruck. An den Herrn Johann Gottwerth Müller*. Hamburg.

Knopf, Terry Ann. 1975a. "Rumour Controls: A Reappraisal" in *Phylon. The Atlanta Univeristy Review of Race and Culture*: 23–31.

Knopf, Terry Ann. 1975b. *Rumors, Race and Riots*. New Brunswick and New Jersey.

Kölnische Volkszeitung. 6.8.1914, 8.8.1914, 10.8.1914, 11.8.1914.

Kornelius, Stefan. 1998. "Das dreiste Geschäft mit dem Klatsch. Gefährden die modernen Massenmedien die Demokratie? Die Affäre um Bill Clinton als Menetekel" in *Süddeutsche Zeitung*, 14/15.2.1998.

Kraft, Margarete. 1986. "Die Gestalt der Fama: bei Vergil – bei Ovid – in der europäischen Literatur" in *Der Altsprachliche Unterricht*, 29, 3: 22–39.

Krohn, Wolfgang. 1987. *Francis Bacon*. Munich.

Lauf, Edmund. 1990. *Gerücht und Klatsch. Die Diffusion der "abgerissenen Hand"*. Berlin.

Langenhove, Fernand van. 1916. *Comment naît un Cycle de Légendes. Franc-Tireurs et Atrocités en Belgique*. Lausanne and Paris.

Laurence, Ray. 1994. "Rumour and Communication in Roman Politics" in *Greece & Rome*, 41, 1: 62–74.

Le Bon, Gustav. 1998. *Psychologie des Foules*. Paris.

Leclerf, Yves and Parker, Édouard. 1987. *L'Affaire Tchernobyl. La Guerre des Rumeurs*. Paris.

Lessing, Gotthold Ephraim, 1954. "Hamburgische Dramaturgie" in *Gesammelte Werke*, 6, edited by Paul Rilla. Berlin.

Lienhardt, Peter. 1975. "The Interpretation Of Rumour" in *Studies in Social Anthropology. Essay in Memory of E. E. Evans-Pritchard by his former Oxford Colleagues*, edited by J. H. M. Beattie and R. G. Lienhardt: 105–131. Oxford.

Livius, T. 1991. *Römische Geschichte*, edited by Josef Feix. Munich and Zurich.

Luhmann, Niklas. 1996. *Die Realität der Massenmedien*. Opladen.

Lurker, Manfred. 1988. *Wörterbuch der Symbolik*. Stuttgart.

Lüsebrink, Rolf Reichardt. 1996. "Colporteur la révolution. Médias et prises de parole populaires" in: *Colportage et lecture populaire, Imprimés de large circulation en Europe XVIe – XIXe siècles*. Actes du colloque des 21–24 avril 1991 à Wolfenbüttel sous la direction de Roger Chartier et Hans-Jürgen Lüsebrink: 71–107. Paris.

MacDonald, Elizabeth P. 1947. *Undercover Girl*. New York.

Malinowski, Bronislaw. 1923. "The Problem of Meaning in Primitive Languages" in Ogden, C. K. and Richards, I. A., *The Meaning of Meaning: A Study of the Influence of Language upon Thought and the Science of Symbolism*: 451–510. London.

Mandelstam, Ossip. 1994. *Gespräch über Dante. Gesammelte Essays*, 2, 1925–1935. Frankfurt am Main.

Max, Hubert. 1943. "Immun durch Vertrauen" in *Die Innere Front. NSK. Pressedienst der NSDAP*, 194 / 20.8.43: 1–3.

Médiévales, 1993, 24: *La Renommée*.

Meyn, Hermann. 1998. "Clinton ein Opfer des Internet?" [Interview], in *com!*, 3/98: 72.

Miller, Frank J. 1916. "Some Features of Ovid's Style: I. Personification of Abstractions" in *The Classical Journal*, 11, 9: 516–534.

Morin, Edgar et al. 1969. *La Rumeur d'Orléans*. Paris.

Müller, Achatz Freiherr von. 1977. *Gloria Bona Fama Bonorum. Studien zur sittlichen Bedeutung des Ruhmes in der frühchristlichen und mittlealterlichen Welt*. Husum.

Münsterberg, Margaret. 1922. *Hugo Münsterberg: His Life and Work*. New York.

National Advisory Commission on Civil Disorders. 1968. *Report of the National Advisory Commission on Civil Disorders*. Washington D. C., General Printing Office.

Negt, Oskar and Kluge, Alexander. 1981. *Geschichte und Eigensinn*. Frankfurt am Main.

Neubauer, Hans-Joachim. 1993. "'frei von Harmonie'. Hörspiele von Dieter Schnebel, Mauricio Kagel and John Cage" in *Musik-Konzepte 81: Autoren-*

musik edited by Heinz-Klaus Metzger, Rainer Riehn and Günter Peters: 66–89. Munich.

Neubauer, Hans-Joachim. 1994. *Judenfiguren. Drama und Theater im frühen 19. Jahrhundert.* Frankfurt am Main.

Neubauer, Hans-Joachim. 1996a. "In der 'Zone der Legendenbildung'. Zu einigen Kontexten der amerikanischen *rumor clinics* im Zweiten Weltkrieg" in *Werkstatt Geschichte*, 15, 5: *Politik des Gerüchts*: 33–40.

Neubauer, Hans-Joachim. 1996b. "Wildes Erzählen. Von der Magie der Gerüchte" in *Neue Rundschau*, 2: 64–76.

Neubauer, Hans-Joachim. 1998. *Das unsichtbare Wild. Die Jagd der Wissenschaft auf das Gerücht* (Radiosendung), Radio Bremen, produced by Christiane Ohaus, edited by Jörg Dieter Kogel. First broadcast on 5.3.98.

Oelsner, Konrad Engelbert. 1985. "Historische Briefe über die neuesten Begebenheiten Frankreichs (1792/1793)" in *Die Französische Revolution. Berichte und Deutungen deutscher Schriftsteller und Historiker*, edited by Horst Günther: 385–472. Frankfurt am Main.

Ogle, Marbury B. 1924. "Dame Gossip's Rôle in Epic and Drama" in *Transactions and Proceedings of the American Philological Association*, 55: 90–119.

Ong, Walter J. 1985. *Orality and Literacy: The Technologizing of the Word.* London.

Oppenheim, Rosa. 1911. "Zur Psychologie des Gerüchts" in *Zeitschrift für angewandte Psychologie und psychologische Sammelforschung (Instituts der Gesellschaft für experimentelle Psychologie)*, edited by William Stern and Otto Lipmann, 5: 344–355.

Ovid. 1998. *Metamorphoses*, translated by A. D. Melville. Oxford.

Paine, Robert. 1968. "Gossip and Transaction" in *Man*, 3: 305–308.

Pausanius. 1918. *Description of Greece. Books I-II*, translated by W. H. S. Jones. Cambridge, Massachusetts.

Perger, H. A. (editor). 1841. *Universal Lexicon der Gegenwart und Vergangenheit oder neuestes encyclopädisches Wörterbuch der Wissenschaften, Künste und Gewerbe ...*, 7. Altenburg.

Pignatti, Terisio, 1976. *Veronese*, I: *Test e Cataloghi*. Venice.

Pindar. 1997. *Nemean Odes. Isthmian Odes. Fragments*, edited and translated by William H. Race. Cambridge, Massachusetts.

Plato. 1926a. *Laws, Books I-VI*, translated by R. G. Bury. Cambridge, Massachusetts.

Plato. 1926b. *Law, Books VII-XII*, translated by R. G. Bury. Cambridge, Massachusetts.

Plutarch. 1939. *Moralia, Volume VI*, translated by W. C. Helmbold. Cambridge, Massachusetts.

Polanyi, Michael. 1983. *Tacit Dimension.* Gloucester, Massachusetts.

Ponsonby. Arthur. 1928. *Falsehood in War-Time. Containing an Assortment of Lies Circulating throughout the Nation during the Great War.* London.

Pope, Alexander. 1993. *Alexander Pope*, edited by Pat Rogers. Oxford.

Popow, Jewgeni. 1995. "Wie sie den Hahn gegessen haben" in *Tigerliebe, Russische Erzähler am Ende des 20. Jahrhunderts. Eine Anthologie*, edited by Viktor Jerofejew. Berlin.

Pöschl, Viktor. 1977. *Die Dichtkunst Virgils. Bild und Symbol in der Äneis.* Berlin.

Preisendanz, Wolfgang. 1980. "Nachwort" in Raabe 1980.

Prevention and Control of Mobs and Riots. 1967. Washington D. C., General Printing Office.

Qualter, Terence H. 1962. *Propaganda and Psychological Warfare*. New York.

Quintilian. 1921. *The Institutio Oratoria of Quintilian*. Cambridge, Massachusetts.

Raabe, Wilhelm. 1980. *Horacker*. Stuttgart.

Raabe, Wilhelm. 1983. *Horacker*, translated by John E. Woods. New York.

Rabelais, François. 1955. *Gargantua and Pantagruel*. London.

Rambeau. A. 1880. "Chaucer's 'House of Fame' in seinem Verhältnis zu Dante's 'Divina Commedia' in *Englische Studien. Organ für englische philologie uner mitberücksichtigung des englischen unterrichts aud höheren schulen* ..., 3. Heilbronn.

Raulff, Ulrich. 1985. "Münsterbergs Erfindung oder der elektrische Zeuge" in *Freibeuter*, 24: 33–42.

Raulff, Ulrich. 1990a. "Clio in Dünsten. Über Geschichte und Gerüchte" in *Merkur*, 44, 6: 461–472.

Raulff, Ulrich. 1990b. "Der Zeuge der Schlacht. Marc Bloch" in *Geschichte als Literatur. Formen und Grenzen der Repräsentation von Vergangenheit*, edited by H. Eggert, U. Proflich and K. R. Scherpe: 196–206. Stuttgart.

Raulff, Ulrich. 1995. *Ein Historiker im 20. Jahrhundert. Marc Bloch*. Frankfurt am Main.

Ribbeck, Otto. 1889. *Geschichte der Römischen Dichtung, 2: Augusteisches Zeitalter*. Stuttgart.

Ries, Wolfgang. 1969. *Gerücht, Gerede, öffentliche Meinung. Interpretation zur Psychologie und Darstellungskunst des Tacitus*. Diss. Phil. Mannheim.

Ripa, Cesare. 1625. *Della Novissima Iconologia di Cesare Ripa Perugino*. Padua.

Ripa, Cesare. 1669. *Iconologia*. Venice.

Roberts, John M. 1964. "The Self-Management of Cultures" in *Explorations in Cultural Anthropology. Essay in Honor of George Peter Murdock*, edited by Ward H. Goodman: 433–454. New York.

Rohrbacher, Stefan and Schmidt, Michael. 1991. *Judenbilder. Kulturgeschichte antijüdischer Mythen und antisemitischer Vorurteile*. Reinbeck bei Hamburg.

Rosnow, Ralph L. 1988. "Rumor as Communication: A Contextualist Approach" in *Journal of Communication*, 38 (1): 12–28.

Rosnow, Ralph L. and Fine, Gary Alan. 1976. *Rumor and Gossip. The Social Psychology of Hearsay*. New York, Oxford and Amsterdam.

Sahlins, Marshall. 1985. *Islands of History*. Chicago.

Sälter, Gerhard. 1996. "Gerüchte als subversives Medium. Das Gespenst der öffentlichen Meinung und die Pariser Polizei zu Beginn des 18. Jahrhunderts" in *Werkstatt Geschichte* 15, 5: *Politik des Gerüchts*: 11–19.

Schachter, Stanley and Burdick, Harvey. 1955. "A Field Experiment on Rumor Transmission and Distortion" in *The Journal of Abnormal and Social Psychology*, 50, 3: 363–371.

Schmidt, Arno. 1997. "Schwarze Spiegel" in *Leviathan und Schwarze Spiegel*. Frankfurt am Main.

Schmidt, Michael. 1988. "Ritualmordbeschuldigungen und exemplarisches Wissen" in *Stereotypvorstellungen im Alltagsleben. Beiträge zum Themenkreis*

Fremdbilder – Selbstbilder – Identität. Festschrift für Georg R. Schroubek: 44–56. Munich.

Schmidt, Michael. 1992. "Nichts als Vettern? Anspielungsstrukturen in Wilhelm Raabe's Erzählung 'Zum wilden Mann'" in *Jahrbuch der Raabe-Gesellschaft*: 109–138.

Schramm, Fritz. 1911. "Zur Aussagetreue der Geschlechter" in *Zeitschrift für angewandte Psychologie und psychologische Sammelforschung (Instituts der Gesellschaft für experimentelle Psychologie)*, edited by William Stern and Otto Lipmann, 5: 355.

Shakespeare, William. 1977. *Henry IV: Part Two*, edited by P. H. Davison. London.

Shibutani, Tamotsu. 1966. *Improvised News. A Sociological Study of Rumor*. Indianapolis and New York.

Shorter Oxford English Dictionary, The New. 1993. Oxford.

Simmel, Georg. 1992. "Zur Psychologie und Soziologie der Lüge" in *Aufsätze und Anhandlungen 1894 bis 1900. Gesammtausgabe*, 5, edited by Heinz-Jürgen Dahme and David P. Frisby. Frankfurt am Main.

Smith, Bruce Lannes and Smith, Chitra M. 1956. *International Communication and Political Opinion. A Guide to the Literature*. Princeton and New Jersey.

Smoltczyk, Alexander and Klinggräff, Fritz von. 1989. *Auf der Suche nach der verlorenen Revolution. Pariser Spaziergänge mit Mogniss Abdullah u. a.*, with an essay by Jean-Pierre Faye. Berlin.

Sophocles. 1994. *Ajax. Electra. Oedipus Tyrannus*, edited and translated by Hugh Lloyd-Jones. Cambridge, Massachusetts.

Stahl, Sandra K. D. 1977. "The Oral Personal Narrative in its Generic Context" in *Fabula. Zeitschrift für Erzählforschung*, 18: 18–39.

"Standards and Guidelines for Rumor Control Centers", appendix to Rosnow and Fine, 1976.

"Standards for Agencies Working on the Prevention and Control of Wartime Rumor" , appendix to Allport and Postman, 1947.

Starobinski, Jean. 1971. *Les mots sous les mots*. Paris.

Stendhal. 1997. *The Charterhouse of Parma*, translated by Margaret Mauldon. Oxford.

Stern, William. 1902. "Zur Psychologie der Aussage. Experimentelle Untersuchungen über Erinnerungstreue" in *Zeitschrift für die gesamte Strafrechtswissenschaft*, 22: 315.

Stevenson, Seth. 1998. "Invisible Ink. How the story everyone's talking about stayed out of the papers" in *Slate*, 22.1.98: http://www.slate.com/TangledWeb/98-01-22/TangledWeb.asp

Streck, Berhard. 1997. "Ethnologie as differentielle Soziologie. Perspektiven und Refraktionen" in *Zeitschrift für Ethnologie*, 122, 1: 111–120.

Strempel, Heribert von. 1946. "Confessions of a German Propagandist. Testimony by Dr. Heribert von Strempel" in *Public Opinion Quarterly*, 10: 216–233.

Stuart, Campbell. 1920. *Secrets of Crewe House. The Story of a famous Campaign*. London, New York, Toronto.

Sudbury, Aidan. 1985. "The Proportion of the population never hearing a rumour" in *Journal of Applied Probablity*, 22: 443–446.

Szondi, Peter. 1978. "Über philologische Erkenntnis" in *Schriften I*. Frankfurt.

Tacitus. 1931. *Histories, Books IV-V. Annals, Books I-III*, translated by Clifford H. Moore and John Jackson. Cambridge, Massachusetts.

Tacitus. 1937a. *Annals, Books IV-VI and XI-XII*, translated by John Jackson. Cambridge, Massachusetts.

Tacitus. 1937b. *Annals, Books XIII-XVI*, translated by John Jackson. Cambridge, Massachusetts.

Tacitus. 1970. *Agricola. Germania. Dialogus*, translated by M. Hutton and W. Peterson. Cambridge, Massachusetts.

Tapp, June L. 1953a. "Children can understand rumor" in *Social Education*, 18: 163–165.

Tapp, June L. 1953b. "Pictures can help children conduct a 'rumor clinic'" in *Educational Screen*, 32: 20.

Teutsche Chronik, 4, 80, 9.10.1777. Reprint 1975. Heidelberg.

Theophrastus. 1993. *Characters*, edited and translated by Jeffrey Rusten. Cambridge, Massachusetts.

Thucydides. 1919. *History of the Peloponnesian War, Books I and II*, translated by C. F. Smith. Cambridge, Massachusetts.

Thucydides. 1923. *History of the Peloponnesian War, Books VII-VIII*, translated by C. F. Smith. Cambridge, Massachusetts.

Vernant, Jean-Pierre. 1974. Mythe et Société en Grèce Ancienne. Paris.

Vernant, Jean-Pierre. 1984. "Der reflektierte Mythos" in *Mythos ohne Illusion*, with contributions from Jean-Pierre Vernant et. al.: 7–11. Frankfurt am Main.

Vernant, Jean-Pierre. 1987. *Mythos und Gesellschaft im alten Griechenland*. Frankfurt am Main.

Veyne, Paul. 1988. "Ein Inventar der Differenzen. Antrittsvorlesung am Collège de France" in *Die Originalität des Unbekannten*: 7–42. Frankfurt am Main.

Vinogradov, Viktor. 1988. "The Problem of *skaz* in der Stilistik" in *Russischer Formalismus. Texte zur allgemeinen Literaturtheorie und zur Theorie der Prosa*, edited by Jurij Striedter: 169–207. Munich.

Virgil. 1998. *The Aeneid*, translated by C. Day Lewis. Oxford.

Wander, Karl Friedrich Wilhelm. 1964. *Deutsches Sprichwörter-Lexicon. Ein Hausschatz für das deutsche Volk*, 1. Darmstadt.

Wassermann, Felix. 1920. *Fama. Geschichte eines Motivs der antiken Dichtung*. Diss. Phil. Freiburg.

Weber, Johannes. 1997. "Deutsche Presse im Zeitalter des Barock. Zur Vorgeschichte öffentlichen politischen Räsonnements" in *"Öffentlichkeit" im 18. Jahrhundert*, edited by Hans-Wolf Jäger: 137–149. Göttingen.

Weinrich, Harald. 1966. *Linguistic der Lüge. Antwort auf die Preisfrage der Deutschen Akademie für Sprache und Dichtung im Jahre 1964*. Heidelberg.

Wilamowitz-Moellendorf, Ulrich von. 1955. *Der Glaube der Hellenen*, I. Darmstadt.

Winkle, Stefan. 1997. *Geißeln der Menschheit. Kulturgeschichte der Seuchen*. Düsseldorf.

Wolff, Pius Alexander. 1823. "Pflicht um Pflicht" in *Dramatische Spiele von Pius Alexander Wolff*: 1–58. Berlin.

Wörterbuch der Religionen. 1985. Stuttgart.

Würgler, Andreas. 1996. "Fama und Rumor. Gerücht, Aufruhr und Presse im Ancien Régime" in *Werkstatt Geschichte*, 15, 5: *Politik des Gerüchts*: 20–32.

Zedler, Johann Heinrich. 1735. *Grosses Universal Lexicon Aller Wissenschaften und Künste ...*, 10. Halle and Leipzig.

Index